Conservative Catholicism and the Carmelites

VOLUME 30 IN THE SERIES

Religion in North America

Catherine L. Albanese and
Stephen J. Stein, editors

Conservative Catholicism and the Carmelites

IDENTITY, ETHNICITY, AND TRADITION IN THE MODERN CHURCH

DARRYL V. CATERINE

Indiana University Press *Bloomington & Indianapolis*

This book is a publication of

Indiana University Press

601 North Morton Street
Bloomington, IN 47404-3797 USA

http://iupress.indiana.edu

Telephone orders 800-842-6796
Fax orders 812-855-7931
Orders by e-mail iuporder@indiana.edu

© 2001 by Darryl V. Caterine

MANUFACTURED IN THE UNITED STATES OF AMERICA

Library of Congress Cataloging-in-Publication Data

Caterine, Darryl V.
Conservative Catholicism and the Carmelites :
identity, ethnicity, and tradition in the modern church /
Darryl V. Caterine.
p.   cm. — (Religion in North America)
Includes bibliographical references (p.   ) and index.
ISBN 0-253-34011-X
1. Carmelite Sisters of the Most Sacred Heart of Los
Angeles—History—20th century.   2. Conservatism—
Religious aspects—Catholic Church—History—20th century.
3. Hispanic American Catholics—Religious life—History—
20th century.   I. Title.   II. Series.

BX4318 .C38   2001
271'.971073—dc21
2001001678

1 2 3 4 5   06 05 04 03 02 01

FOR

Clara May Currier
and Louis Caterine

CONTENTS

FOREWORD

When Darryl Caterine wandered into Our Lady of Sorrows Roman Catholic Church in Santa Barbara in search of a saint to study, he discovered Mother Luisa Josefa (1866–1937), the Mexican founder of a religious order now known as the Carmelite Sisters of the Most Sacred Heart of Los Angeles. According to his own report, he was excited and intrigued, but he little knew that Mother Luisa—who had been declared by the Vatican a "Servant of God" and was posthumously progressing through the saint-making bureaucracy of the church—had become especially important, through the religious community she founded, for the conservative wing of American Catholicism. His encounter with the Carmelite Sisters of Los Angeles and the communities they serve led him from disclosure to disclosure so that, in the end, Caterine's study evolved in ways he neither anticipated nor originally intended to explore. His willingness to follow the nuns and their lay devotees and his readiness to be taught by them are testimonies to the best sort of scholarship—in which freshness and discovery emerge from a meeting with one's subjects in ways that change the scholar and shape that scholar's knowledge.

Briefly, much of what shapes Caterine's work is his discovery of the relationship between the Los Angeles Carmelites and the Council of Major Superiors of Women Religious, begun as a counter-organization to the liberal-leaning Leadership Conference of Women Religious. Founded as the Consortium Perfectae Caritatis in 1971 by the Catholic priest James Viall, the council is no longer led by Father Viall, but instead by Mother Vincent Marie Finnegan, who is also Mother Superior of Mother Luisa's American order. The Council has had canonical approval from the Vatican since 1992 and counts as members roughly 10 percent of Catholic nuns in the United States. Moreover, it was the same Father Viall who invited the Los Angeles Carmelites, who had been members of the Consortium from its beginning, to St. Rose of Lima Church in Cleveland, Ohio (one of the major sites that Caterine studies). Therein, one might say, hangs a tale.

Against this backdrop, Caterine's new book is a careful, perceptive, and, likewise, original critique of notions of conservatism and liberalism as applied to the contemporary American Catholic church. Caterine, in fact, identifies three "churches" within the framework of the larger ecclesia, with only one of the three liberal. The other two are formed, he argues, first, from shifting currents of an invented tradition called "neotraditionalism," and second, from various ethnic self-understandings. Caterine comes to these conclusions through a microstudy that leads him to larger and larger Catholic worlds. He uses one rather small religious order—which is, as we have seen, at the forefront of the conservative cause among today's Roman Catholic religious—as a way to explore the intricacies of the neotraditionalist designation. In each site in which the Carmelite sisters find themselves, Caterine probes their own and their parishioners' stories about who they are as Catholics and as representatives of various national groups. He reveals a conservative—or, as he says, "neotraditionalist"—world that intersects with various forms of Latino consciousness and with a very non-Latino white world. In a study that is lush with context, we learn how the nuns stand as symbols for a variety of tangled ideals and motives in disparate settings across the nation—in Los Angeles, California; the Arizona borderland at Douglas; Miami, Florida; and Cleveland, Ohio.

Throughout, Caterine writes with ease and facility. There is an almost journalistic quality about his study, a quality of address to topic and theme that leads and draws readers along by a prose that is, in its own way, seductive. Indeed, Caterine possesses a sensitivity to place and style that conveys the texture of Catholic lives in various and distinctively different settings. In his work, ethnography blends easily with history and with critical analysis; archival work stands beside interviews; and conservative Catholicism achieves a cultural context that is densely and richly drawn.

The editors predict that this book will make a large contribution to the discussion of conservative Catholicism, representing a major advance in the understanding of the phenomenon. Caterine's work plainly gets us out of the boxes and sterile round robins in which liberal-conservative polarities are characteristically cast, and it puts us in a place in which we can look at conservative and ethnic identities in the Catholic church together and anew. By triangulating the categories that are now current for understanding Catholicism—by viewing ethnic identity as at once the ally of neotraditionalism and its own independent world with separate if overlapping concerns, and by placing liberalism alongside both—Caterine complicates the picture of American Catholicism in productive and evocative ways. Liberals may be left of center, but that is hardly the only news to report, and Caterine, with nuance and subtlety, give us a compelling narrative to tell us more.

Beyond that, from the point of view of the Religion in North America series, Caterine's book is especially important because it is the first volume in the series dealing fully and specifically with some aspect of the Roman Catholic tradition. It is time past time for a book about Catholics to appear in the series, and we are especially pleased that our first "Catholic" book addresses themes of contemporary (especially Latino) ethnicity and identity; of saints and social bodies; and of political currents and trends in a remarkably complex American Catholic church.

Catherine L. Albanese

Stephen J. Stein

SERIES EDITORS

INTRODUCTION

The year was 1961 when John F. Kennedy, a Roman Catholic descendant of Irish immigrants to America, became the thirty-fifth president of the United States. For American Catholics, Kennedy's election signaled not only a political triumph, but also their symbolic inclusion into a country that had defined itself since Puritan times in righteous opposition to a demonized Catholic past. Pilgrims sailing to the New World on the *Mayflower* had cast their European Catholic contemporaries as minions of the papal Antichrist, while architects of the American nation in the eighteenth century, though tolerant of religious expression, shared with their Puritan ancestors a suspicion that Roman Catholicism was fundamentally antithetical to Enlightenment ideals of personal freedom and rational inquiry. In an inversion of America's traditional religious nationalism, the Roman Catholic president aligned himself with the Anglo-Protestant, Enlightenment tradition in his January 20 inaugural address. "We dare not forget today that we are heirs of that first revolution," Kennedy spoke on behalf of his country; "Let the word go forth from this time and place, to friend and foe alike, that the torch has been passed to a new generation of Americans."[1]

It was indeed a new generation of Americans that Kennedy addressed. Not only was the country witnessing in his election the erasure of old lines defining its ethnic, economic, and religious landscapes, but also—unforeseeable to anyone at the time—it stood poised on the brink of what would come to be a watershed decade for the nation. Beginning with the assassination of the president himself, the subsequent years saw the rise of the civil rights movement, the escalation of the Vietnam War and virulent protests against it, and the rise of the hippie counterculture that replaced the Old Left in its critique of the American bourgeoisie. Inaugurating the decade with an invocation of revolution, Kennedy had unwittingly prophesied the course of its immediate future. No sooner had a leader arisen from the former margins of American society than the meaning of America itself lost its clarity.

This book is a study of one American Catholic religious community that has risen to a place of national prominence in the Roman Catholic church since the aftermath of the 1960s. The Carmelite Sisters of the Most Sacred Heart of Los Angeles, founded in 1927 by the Mexican sister Maria Luisa Josefa, existed until the 1960s as a semi-cloistered teaching order quietly serving Mexican-American families in the Los Angeles diocese. Since that time, the order has led a movement among American Catholic women religious that seeks to redress the "liberal" trend merging American civic with Roman Catholic religious identity. In the last two decades, the neotraditionalist order has extended its apostolic teaching mission far beyond the Los Angeles diocese in response to invitations by bishops sharing their theological and political vision of the American church. Today the Carmelites run and staff schools in four neighborhoods throughout the greater Los Angeles metropolitan area; a borderlands town straddling Arizona and Sonora, Mexico; an affluent Cuban-American suburb outside Miami; and an inner-city parish in Cleveland, Ohio.

The appeal of the Carmelite order among American Catholics almost four decades after the Second Vatican Council (1962–1965) carries important implications for an understanding of both contemporary Catholicism and twenty-first-century American religion more generally. For the Carmelite order, and the neotraditionalist Catholicism they espouse, is part of a unprecedented reconfiguration of American religions noted by James Davidson Hunter in his work *Culture Wars*. In Hunter's analysis, previous denominational distinctions among Protestants, Catholics, and Jews no longer constitute an accurate analysis of American religions since the 1960s. New denominational alliances have emerged that center on common political and/or cultural concerns, pitting denominations against themselves. The essential difference between what Hunter calls orthodox and progressive religious groups lies in their respective teachings on the ultimate source of moral authority. Orthodox groups reject "the spirit of the modern age, a spirit of rationalism and subjectivism . . . [in which moral] truth tends to be viewed as a process, as a reality that is ever unfolding." Orthodox religious groups situate moral authority in their respective inherited traditions, which define "at least in the abstract, a consistent, unchangeable measure of value, purpose, goodness, and identity, both personal and collective." Progressive groups, in contrast, defend the individual conscience as the final locus of moral authority.[2] This shift in emphasis away from the inviolability of tradition and toward that of the individual allows progressive communities to reconceptualize their inherited creeds, rituals, and mores to address contemporary issues and challenges facing their members.

In the American Catholic church, the political reconfigurations discussed by Hunter emerged in the wake of the Second Vatican Council. Between 1962 and 1965, Pope John XXIII brought together the world's bishops in a reconceptualization of Catholicism that had not been seen since the Council of Trent in the sixteenth century. The pontiff called for an *aggiornamento,* or "updating" of the Roman tradition, a thoroughgoing revision or reinterpretation of Catholic teachings in light of modern humanistic and social scientific knowledge. The theological, liturgical, ecclesiastical, and ecumenical changes effected by the council were appropriated differently from one country to the next, but within the United States, the initial reception of Vatican II was shaped by the patriotic optimism of Euro-Americans leading up to and culminating in the Kennedy election. It was, in effect, a twentieth-century Catholic re-enactment of the American Revolution, a celebration of the most cherished Anglo-Protestant mores and beliefs and a break from inherited European traditions. Theologically, the church's historic emphasis on the salvific power of the sacraments was dwarfed by a newfound emphasis on the individual's relationship with a salvific God—the central characteristic of what Harold Bloom has termed simply "the American religion."[3]

Changes in liturgy followed logically as rituals were simplified or in some cases eliminated, the rites of Mass translated from Latin into vernacular tongues, and church interiors redesigned to reflect an austerity and simplicity reminiscent of colonial Puritan meeting houses. Ecclesiastically, the council triggered profound critiques of hierarchical structures in the name of that most hallowed of all American institutions, democracy, while ecumenically the church's claim as defender of the exclusive faith gave way to dialogue with other churches as well as with traditions outside the Christian and even Judeo-Christian faith. In short, American Catholicism came in an extremely short period of time to resemble liberal Protestantism, just as the first Catholic president had won the highest office of the land in minimizing differences between Roman Catholic and Protestant American identity.

With a near-Hegelian finality, such prominent scholars as Harvey Cox of Harvard Divinity School—in his widely read book *The Secular City*—predicted prematurely the inevitable and unilinear demise of traditional religions like preconciliar Catholicism. "Secularization rolls on, and if we are to understand and communicate with our present age we must learn to love it in its unremitting secularity," he wrote. "We must learn, as [Dietrich] Bonhoeffer said, to speak of God in a secular fashion and find a nonreligious interpretation of biblical concepts."[4] Closer to the Catholic developments, prolific writer and priest Andrew Greeley conducted numerous sociological surveys that seemed to ensure the total Protestantization of the church together with other American denominations. In one of his works, *Religion in the Year 2000,* Greeley wrote:

> I am . . . predicting that in the years to come the churches will become more democratic in this broad sense of the word—*not so much out of conviction as out of necessity.* The implicit voluntarism contained in the Reformation and in the American democratic style (and vigorously defended by the American Catholic theorists of the nineteenth century) will come pretty close to having its final organizational effect on the religious denominations. This may very well be the most important historical development in religious organizations since the Reformation. [italics added][5]

Even a new newspaper, the *National Catholic Reporter,* was founded to give voice to what one scholar has characterized as "a new Catholic emphasis on self-criticism [of inherited tradition that] appealed especially to upper-class and upper-middle-class parishioners in the Middle West and Middle Atlantic states."[6] Judging from the plethora of articles in this one paper, journalism seemed to confirm the predictions of sociologists: the history of American Catholicism had reached its teleological end in the Protestantization and democratization of the church.

What neither the *Reporter* nor many contemporary analysts took seriously amidst the flurry of ecclesiastical changes were the dissident voices of Catholics deeply critical of them. In American Catholic parlance, the labels "liberal" and "conservative" were coined early on—by liberals—to describe those who supported or resisted the changes, respectively. While such classifications intended at face value to designate theological positions, they implicitly advanced presuppositions about the meaning and contours of American identity. In terms of the various secularization and Americanization hypotheses, traditionalists resisting religious changes in light of the council's guidelines were implicitly portrayed as trying to stop the course of American history. As one scholar has observed:

> Whatever the historical antecedents, the use of the cribbed political terms *liberal* and *conservative* as all-purpose ecclesiastical identifiers in American Catholicism vastly accelerated under the impact of the "Xavier Rynne" [a.k.a. Francis X. Murphy, C.SS.R.] articles and books on the Second Vatican Council [*Letters from Vatican City—Vatican Council II,* published in four parts from 1963 to 1966]. Here, the deliberations of some two thousand bishops, who conducted their business in an arcane ancient language absent the real-time scrutiny of CNN, were rendered intelligible, or at least explicable, to American readers . . . by a brilliantly simple interpretive device: good guys and bad guys, "liberals" and "conservatives," were con-

testing the future of the world's oldest institution, the Roman Catholic Church. . . .

But "Rynne's" plot line also contained a prescriptive subtext: all right-thinking people were, or ought to be, on the side of the "liberal" good guys—especially right-thinking Americans, citizens of the nation which believed itself to embody (at least in the early 1960s) the inevitability of progress and the benignity of "change." To sympathize with even some of the concerns of the "conservatives" was to confess to a psychological, and perhaps even moral, aberration.[7]

And to the best of contemporary historical knowledge, this caricature did not seem like such an unreasonable position. Since the arrival of Anglo Europeans on the eastern seaboard in the seventeenth century, the expansion of Protestant American culture at home and eventually throughout the world seemed indomitable, almost mystical in its power. More effectively than any sociological or historical concept, the mythic ideal of "progress"—popularized in the nineteenth century during the expansion of industrial capitalism—fittingly encapsulated the belief in their country's triumphalist and cosmically directed destiny, which had finally come to sweep the Catholics up into its course.

Intimated in liberal assumptions about American history were a complex of social myths and mores ultimately rooted in Puritan discourse, which will be referred to in this study as "Anglo-Protestant" culture. Architects of the United States had translated Calvinist and Reformation themes into the language of "self-evident truths" and "universal tenets of human nature." The sovereignty of a Calvinist God working through the inner stirrings of the sinner's heart was bequeathed to American culture as the inviolable authority of the conscience and disdain for any worldly, moral authority. The Reformation church—a "priesthood of all believers" united individually to God—became the template for a nation of self-reliant individuals. The drama of a final battle between good and evil in the New Testament Book of Revelation—once understood by Puritans to be enacted in the Protestant Reformation and the founding of New England—was secularized during and after the American Enlightenment as the myth of a divinely inspired, national history. It was in the nineteenth and twentieth centuries that the notion of "progress" came to stand for a movement of the democratic and scientific Anglo-Protestant culture ever closer to an age in which misery and suffering would be lessened if not banished from the world.[8]

Caught up in the power of these mythic themes, liberal Catholics seemed to speak the last word on their church's history for many Catholics and non-Catholic observers. As the scholarship of Catherine L. Albanese has effectively demonstrated, however, the history of religions in America has never been as clear-cut as liberal observers of Vatican II presupposed. Since their arrival in the New World, European and non-European religions alike have undergone complex transformations, both in their contact with each other and in their development within the dominant Anglo-Protestant and modern milieu. Albanese has suggested that religions reflect patterns of both "expansion" and "contraction" in the American context, both embracing and rejecting aspects of the world around them.[9] James Hunter has similarly emphasized in his own work the precedents of the present-day religious realignment in his overview of eighteenth- and nineteenth-century American history. The Fundamentalist Protestant, Conservative and Orthodox Jewish, and sectarian groups that he cites as precursors to modern orthodoxy exemplify "contractive" religions in Albanese's analysis. Liberal Protestants, Reform Jews, and the majority of Euro-American Catholics during the 1940s and 1950s were the expansive forerunners of modern progressivists.[10]

I have chosen the designation "neotraditionalist" in characterizing the Carmelites' theological and political worldview to emphasize an important discontinuity in conservative American Catholicism before and after the 1960s. Even though the sisters present themselves as simply continuing the preconciliar faith, redressing what they see as the excesses of the American reforms, their relationship to the surrounding society departs markedly from the patriotic faith of second- and third-generation Euro-American Catholics following the Second World War. While it is true that pre–Vatican II ecclesiological beliefs and liturgical practices are preserved through the sisters' lifestyle and observances, they are couched in a cosmology and theology tinged with apocalyptic themes of America's spiritual peril. Their America is no longer the righteous empire that once waged a cold war against godless communists, but a country that has lost its way in what they characterize as the excessive materialism, violence, and immorality of the culture. For them the power and presence of Satan and divine retribution for sins loom large in the contemporary national landscape, and the future of the country is uncertain. It is from this perspective that the sisters' radical separation from the contemporary world through a medievally styled monastic life is given rationale and meaning.

Pre–Vatican II models of American Catholic history focusing on tensions between a hegemonic Protestant society and marginalized Catholic immigrants no longer suffice to define the issues of an order like the Carmelite sisters. Neither do the models discussed extensively by Jay P. Dolan of a church hierarchy dominated by the Irish prelate attempting to socialize other European immigrants into their version of American Catholicism.[11]

Scholars striving to explain the rise of new religious landscapes since the 1960s would do well to begin with the abrupt "rise and fall" of Anglo-Protestant American identity leading up to and immediately following the Kennedy era. On the one hand, the 1960s represented for many European Americans the fulfillment of what James Truslow Adams memorialized as "the American Dream."[12] For Irish Catholics in particular, Kennedy's rise to the presidency was the culmination of decades of sacrifice and aspirations to realize their full inclusion in Anglo-Protestant society. This struggle began for Irish Catholics in the 1840s, the first decade of their mass migration to the United States, and was accelerated after the Second World War with the absorption of second- and third-generation Euro-American Catholics into the American middle class. The wave of enthusiastic patriotism as well as a dramatic increase in material affluence following America's victory in World War II helped erode traditional antipathies among Euro-American immigrants and their descendants. Not only had the shared hardship of war galvanized a new sense of American solidarity, but a booming postwar economy helped facilitate veterans' matriculation from postsecondary schools and their upward ascent into new socioeconomic classes.

On the other hand, the 1960s introduced new issues that would come to challenge the underlying myths and mores of the so-called American Dream. The Immigration Act of 1965 marked the beginning of new trends in immigration reflecting the histories and hopes of non-Europeans. The goal of eventual assimilation into Anglo-Protestant culture, particularly among many immigrants from Latin America, no longer defined the purpose of immigration. Longstanding and relatively unaddressed issues of racial oppression in American history exploded after Kennedy's and, the following year, Dr. Martin Luther King Jr.'s assassinations, exposing new social fault lines in the culture. The social role of women in American culture similarly emerged by the end of the decade as a new arena of cultural critique, extending political analysis into what were once considered the "private" domains of family and sexual life. Finally, the role and meaning of the United States government itself, once extolled by Euro-Americans as the defender of liberty, fell under fierce attack, beginning with protests during the Vietnam War, and suffered further throughout the scandalous years of Watergate. New historians cast the shadow of their nation in sharp relief, exposing America's longstanding role as an agent of imperialism and colonization.

In retrospect, early portrayals depicting the end of American Catholic history in the democratization of the church after Vatican II were unwittingly partial to the first set of American cultural forces championing former models of a triumphant Anglo-American society. If an American Catholic president had aligned himself with the political forebears of the Protestant nation, then why should not the ecclesiastical hierarchy model itself after the country's Protestant churches? This was indeed a compelling vision, but one that reflected a largely Euro-American and middle-class Catholic constituency, as the readership audience of the *National Catholic Reporter* suggests. While Pope John XXIII's expansive embrace of modernity sanctified white middle-class America's immersion in modern society, it did not necessarily speak to those still on its margins. It would take more than a decade before a new pope, John Paul II, would rise to power and espouse a vision of Catholicism and the modern world that spoke meaningfully to those groups still politically and/or economically disenfranchised through the Kennedy and Vatican II years.

With his election to the papacy in 1978, Karol Wojtyla resuscitated a decidedly contractive vision of Catholicism rooted in his own life and priestly formation in Poland. Born in 1920 in Wadowice, Wojtyla came of age during the German *Blitzkrieg* of his country in 1939, with the subsequent reduction of the Polish people to forced laborers for the Nazi regime and the mass extermination of Jews and other enemies of the Third Reich in the death camp of Auschwitz, seventeen miles from Wojtyla's home. Like their European neighbors, the Poles understood the emergence and temporary victory of Hitler's world order as the death knell for any hopes of a modern utopia promised by intellectual champions of the Enlightenment, once centered in Germany. As modern technology and statecraft alike were used to facilitate the mass dehumanization of peoples in European lands, the "progress" and "civilization" heralded since the beginning of the Scientific Revolution and the rise of modern states suddenly took an unexpected and fatal turn. As Pope John Paul II, Wojtyla would choose Auschwitz as his most potent symbol of modernity's decrepitude, referring to the death camp as "the Golgotha of the modern world."[13]

If Nazi occupation vilified modernity for Wojtyla, the subsequent political and cultural domination of Poland by the Soviet Union from 1944 to 1989 clarified for him the role of the church in the modern world. Catholic myth and ritual—epitomized in the devotion to Our Lady of Czestochowa, the Black Madonna and patron of Poland—fashioned Catholic Poles into a unified people in their struggles against Soviet state oppression through a fusion of Catholic and national identity. Less than a year after he was elected pope, John Paul returned to Poland, where he continued his earlier struggles with the government, speaking of a continuous, one-thousand-year-old Polish nation in blatant disregard of party history, which dated the birth of modern Poland to 1944. In a historically triumphant moment, the visiting pontiff lambasted the officially atheistic education of the Soviets in Warsaw's Victory Square on June 2, 1979. "Christ cannot be kept out of the history of man in any part of the globe," he declared," at any latitude or longitude of geography. The exclusion of Christ from the history of man is an act against man." In response, the crowd who heard him broke into cheers, song, and chants for an uninterrupted ten minutes, crying in unison, "We want God! We want God!" A Communist party leader was afterwards reported as saying, "This visit has undermined all our work in the last twenty-five years."[14]

Even before he became Pope John II, Wojtyla had articulated a religiopolitical vision that understood the events of the twentieth century as nothing less than an apocalyptic battle between good and evil on a global scale, a vision that has continued to shape his leadership through more than two decades. In a 1981 essay for the *National Catholic Reporter*, journalist Peter Hebblethwaite reported, "As Pope John Paul peers into the future, he sees not the next decade but the next 20 years. The year 2000 fascinates him like the eye of the basilisk. What is going to happen in this period is an intensification of the age-old struggle between good and evil. Two women stand guard over the whole sweep of history: the woman in the Book of Genesis who will 'crush the head of the serpent' and the woman of the Apocalypse."[15] It is within such a cosmological context that the pontiff's understanding of priesthood as a kind of heroism emerged. "The priest is on the front line of the battle," Hebblethwaite wrote. "He is a spiritual athlete, the hero of God, the champion who struggles single-handedly with the evil one."[16]

Not surprisingly, John Paul's ecclesiology has been characterized by its oppositional relationship between church and world. In a last-minute synod in 1985, the pope called the world's bishops together at the Vatican in the hopes of articulating a unified statement of the church's identity and mission in the late twentieth century. The synod's final report yielded not one but three distinct conceptualizations of the church, with the curial vision by far the most otherworldly. Bishops from Latin America, Asia, and Africa exhorted the church to champion the rights and dignity of economically and politically oppressed people. Recalling the ecclesiology of Vatican II, American, British, and Canadian bishops called for the church to be a sacrament, a visible sign of invisible grace, but did not hesitate to acknowledge the work of the Holy Spirit outside of the church in the world. Finally, curial bishops closest to the pope articulated an ecclesiology that one observer characterized as "neo-Augustinian" in its designation of the church as the only sign of God's kingdom on earth. Vatican bishops criticized John XXIII's optimism about the modern world as naive, focusing instead on the calamities befalling humanity before and since the council. In this scenario, the church emerged as a refuge in a storm, whose primary goal was to offer souls a means of eternal salvation.[17]

The leadership of Pope John Paul II came at a critical time in American history. The countercultural critiques of American history launched in the

1960s, particularly by leaders in the civil rights movement, had spawned divergent political strategies for seeking to reform the country. If Martin Luther King Jr. had expressed hope for America's redemption, there were other leaders for whom the words of black writer James Baldwin rang as more authentic: "Do I really *want* to be integrated into a burning house?"[18] Nor was this cry of protest limited to Americans struggling against racism. From the 1960s onward, the metaphor of America as a burning house could be applied by a variety of circles, from feminists to ecologists, who insisted that only the deepest structural changes in American society could stave off impending political and environmental calamity. It was in this context that the religious realignment noted by Hunter began to take shape, at first quietly, but quickly gathering a political momentum first noticed nationally in the 1980s with the rise of the so-called Christian Right.

For the Carmelite Sisters of the Most Sacred Heart of Los Angeles, John Paul II's papacy has transformed both their order's identity and its mission. The marked disjunction between their preconciliar status as a normative Catholic order and their postconciliar status as a religiously "contractive" community characterizes the Carmelites as an example of what Eric Hobsbawm has called an "invented tradition":

> "Invented tradition" is taken to mean a set of practices, normally governed by overtly or tacitly accepted rules and of a ritual or symbolic nature, which seek to inculcate certain values and norms of behavior by repetition, which automatically implies continuity with the past. . . . However, insofar as there is such reference to a historic past, the peculiarity of invented traditions is that the continuity with it is largely factitious. In short, they are responses to novel situations which take the form of reference to old situations, or which establish their own past by quasi-obligatory repetition. It is the contrast between constant change and innovation of the modern world and the attempt to structure at least some parts of social life within it as unchanging and invariant that makes the "invention of tradition" so interesting for historians of the past two centuries.[19]

Preconciliar Catholics had been warned since the turn of the twentieth century of the heresy of "Americanism": the potential adoption by the church of purportedly anti-Catholic ideals of pluralism, voluntarism, and individualism embodied in Anglo-Protestant U.S. culture. It was not until after the council, however, that groups like Mother Luisa's Carmelites began to define themselves primarily in opposition to an allegedly Americanist church. Muted by the patriotism of the postwar decades prior to Vatican II, fears of Americanism had lain dormant in the American church. Consistent with Hobsbawm's analysis, the tumultuous social and cultural changes of the 1960s—together with ecclesial reforms—triggered an equal and opposite reaction within the church. Turning to their religious tradition as a bastion, some Catholics insisted that their doctrines were inviolable to transformations of any kind.

The present study of the Carmelite Sisters of the Most Sacred Heart of Los Angeles is divided into two parts: a historical overview of their emerging identity since the 1960s and an ethnographic analysis of their reception by and meaning to the seven American parishes that they serve. On the one hand, Hunter's thesis of a "culture war" in the American church is certainly supported by the official theological statements of the Carmelite sisters themselves, whose life work is committed to defending what Vatican II called the unchanging "essentials" of monastic poverty, chastity, and obedience. On the other hand, the appeal of the order to many lay Catholics points to the mutual interdependence of conservative religious affiliation and ethnic identity politics not suggested by ecclesial developments alone. Outside of the order, neotraditionalism appeals most to ethnically homogenous communities who have arrived in the United States from Spanish Catholic countries.[20] The five American parishes who welcome the Carmelite sisters are either predominantly Filipino or predominantly Latino communities. Unlike the Euro-American immigrants to the nineteenth-century church, the Filipino and Latino laity supportive of the Carmelites deliberately define themselves at a critical distance from Anglo-Protestant culture. Like the neotraditionalist sisters themselves, these Catholics see in Anglo-Protestant society mores that threaten the cultures they wish to perpetuate, and they fail to see in an Anglo-Protestantized American church religiocultural symbols instrumental in the construction of community. The two parishes that reject the sisters as vestiges of an antiquated, preconciliar faith are either Anglo-American or multi-ethnic, groups who turn to the symbols and mores of Anglo-Protestant culture to define their religiocultural identity.

As heirs to Carmelite monasticism, the sisters have long had at their disposal a clear blueprint and plan for withdrawing from what they would see as the burning house of America. Since their inception as an American order in 1927, the Carmelites have identified themselves primarily as Catholic contemplatives who have symbolically died to whatever social identity they may have assumed before taking vows. Today, a woman seeking to join the Carmelites first becomes a "postulant" for a period of six to nine months, during which time she seeks to discern whether the particular rule and lifestyle are suited to her personal and spiritual needs. If she decides that the Carmelite order is indeed the community suited to her, she becomes a "novice" for a two-year period. During this time the potential sister no longer dresses in her former clothes but dons a blue and white habit worn by her fellow novices. She also assumes a new, spiritual name, and is exposed to more of the Carmelites' contemplative teachings and apostolic works. Finally, a sister becomes "professed" when she takes the public vows of poverty, chastity, and obedience to superiors within both the order and the church universal, leaving behind the lifestyles of her contemporary society.[21]

With the profession of public vows, Mother Luisa's Carmelite sisters don the traditional habit, the full-length religious dress worn by American sisters prior to the Second Vatican Council. Notwithstanding a few changes to their dress made in the 1970s, including a change of material from wool to a lighter cotton blend, the long, brown habits worn by the sisters today—complete with a white collar and a scapular worn beneath the clothing—differ little from the clothes of their Mexican foundress earlier in the century. Their typical attire includes a large crucifix worn around the neck and a long rosary dangling visibly from the waist—its beads made from the seeds of a tree indigenous to Mexico—on which are fastened metal medallions. With a raised engraving of Saint John of the Cross kneeling in prayer on one side and Mary with Saints Teresa of Avila and Thérèse of Lisieux on the other, the medals brush gently against the rosary beads to make a light jingling noise as the sisters move about. Once initiated, these American women become a symbolic link to their European Carmelite predecessors as well as to the sacred origins of the order, the mystical societies of Mount Carmel in Israel.[22]

As the Carmelite sisters receive their tradition, however, renditions of infused contemplation by Spanish mystics constitute but one part of their initiatory education. The Carmelite sisters of the Most Sacred Heart of Los Angeles are heirs not only to the Carmelite tradition, but more particularly to Carmelite spirituality as mediated by and understood through the life and example of their foundress, Mother Luisa. In response to Vatican II's call for religious communities to renew their vows in light of their founder's or foundress's charism, the sisters have discovered in Maria Luisa Josefa a model for world renunciation in the modern political context. Born Maria Luisa de la Peña in Atotonilco, Jalisco, in 1866, Mother Luisa came to Los Angeles in temporary exile from the Cristero Revolt in 1927. She and two other sisters literally fled the fighting between federal troops and Cristero rebels in the state of Jalisco, primary site of the battle between the Catholic church and the newly emerged Mexican nation state. Having already founded a Mexican congregation in 1920, which was later joined to the Order of Discalced Carmelites, Mother Luisa would come to inaugurate the establishment of an American chapter of her order during her two-year stay in Los Angeles. After the fighting in Jalisco subsided and some rapprochement between state and church was reached, Mother Luisa returned to her homeland. After her death in 1937, the Mexican and American chapters together were approved as an autonomous order in 1949 as the Carmelite Sisters of the Third Order, renamed the Carmelites of the Sacred Heart in 1968. In 1983, the American sisters were granted their own congregational autonomy as the Carmelite Sisters of the Most Sacred Heart of Los Angeles while retaining Mother Luisa as their foundress.

Like most Mexican Catholics of the Revolutionary period, Mother Luisa was less of an outspoken critic of nationalism than a bystander inescapably caught in an ideological battle in which each institution vilified the other. Nevertheless, the reconstruction of her life, written by Pope John Paul II's official biographers for her canonization process, highlights the oppositional relationship between the Catholic sister and the modern world. American Carmelites can thus assume their decidedly oppositional relationship to the secular political society around them as a religious act of imitating their foundress. With their superior, Mother Vincent Marie Finnegan, as the chairperson of the national organization of neotraditionalist sisters, the Conference of Major Superiors of Women Religious, the Carmelites have come to lead other women religious supporting the neotraditionalist teachings of the current Vatican. With the blessing of John Paul II, the sisters have become leaders in a battle against liberal Catholics in one wing of the American church—even as Mother Luisa's spiritual heirs in Mexico have appropriated her charism as a model for liberation theology.

The Filipino and Latino parishes to whom the Carmelites' neotraditionalism most appeals similarly define themselves in resistance to outright assimilation into Anglo-Protestant culture. The members of these communities are Catholics who articulate a cultural identity betwixt and between the United States and their respective homelands. The concept of "borderlands" will be employed in this study to signify the cultural identity of both Mexican Americans and Cuban Americans. Originally restricted to scholarship on Mexican Americans, the designation of a borderlands culture refers to a *mestizaje*, or "mixed," identity born of an appropriation and recombination of cultural elements from both the country of origin and the United States, sometimes reinforced by a "revolving door" pattern of migration to and from each country.[23]

Mexican-American identity has been fashioned in the meeting and exchange of two cultures, Mexican and Anglo-Protestant, primarily in the Southwest region of the United States. In Mexican-American historiography since the emergence of Chicano studies in the 1960s, the borderlands thus refers primarily and figuratively to a collective identity born betwixt and between two cultural centers. Given the geographical locus of Mexican-American culture, however, the borderlands can also be conceptualized literally as a geopolitical designation. Lacking such geological barriers as mountain ranges or oceans separating the southwestern United States from northern Mexico, the geopolitical locus of Mexican-American culture lies along a "borderlands" whose boundaries must be constantly maintained by nation-states on either side of an imagined international "line." Since the 1848 annexation of northern Mexico by the United States after the Mexican War, this line has in fact been patrolled by military personnel and police from both countries to offset what would otherwise be a natural movement of peoples across open plains. The cultural and geopolitical borderlands of the Mexican-American experience are mutually reinforcing. Scholars have pointed out that the physical proximity of Mexican and Mexican-American homelands offsets the unilinear "assimilation" of Mexican Americans into Anglo-Protestant culture. In short, the constant influx of Mexican immigration into the United States and the comparative proximity of relatives on both sides of the international border ensures the uninterrupted influence of Mexican culture on Mexican-American culture.

The extension of "borderlands" as a description for other Latino groups, such as the Cuban Americans of this study, returns to the cultural dimensions of the term. While the Cuban Americans of Miami are in fact geographically separated from their homeland, they are nevertheless a community fashioned by the influence of two different cultures. The history of Cuban Americans makes clear, however, the importance of geopolitical factors in shaping cultural consciousness. Such Cuban-American scholars as Gustavo Perez Firmat, for example, have argued that American-Born Cubans—physically separated from their parents' homeland, as well as politically barred from a return to the island—lack the bicultural sensibility of their parents.[24] Not unlike descendants of European immigrants to the United States, American-born Cubans are shaped primarily by the influences of Anglo-Protestant culture, in Perez Firmat's analysis. Clearly both geography and international relations between the United States and Communist Cuba play an important role in shielding American-born Cubans from a stronger Cuban influence. Notwithstanding the important distinction between the "borderlands" as it is applied to Mexican Americans and Cuban Americans, however, the Cuban-American community of this study is a bicultural one, insofar as the parameters of its identity are shaped primarily by Cuban-born respondents.

While scholarship in Filipino studies presently lacks a singular analogous metaphor to describe the identity of natives of and immigrants from the Republic of the Philippines, the findings of this study support E. San Juan's designation of Filipino Americans as a "diasporic" community. The history of what is today the Republic of the Philippines has been characterized throughout the modern era by a series of intrusive and disruptive incursions of colonial powers and economic power interests. Founded as a Spanish colony in 1565, the modern Philippines was subsequently ceded to the United States in 1898 following the Spanish-American War. While the Philippines emerged as a politically autonomous republic in 1946, the pressures of a global economy increasingly undermined its economic and political stability in subsequent decades, draining away from the archipelago its skilled and educated workers, many of whom came to settle in the United States. Even after its dissolution as an American commonwealth in 1946, the Philippines has experienced an onslaught of American cultural influences throughout the twentieth century, spawning a postcolonial nationalist movement to define Filipino identity without reference to United States culture. "There is a specific reason why the Filipino contingent in the United States . . . needs to confront its own singular destiny as a 'transported,' displaced, and disintegrated people," San Juan writes:

> The reason is of course the fact that the Philippines was a colony of the United States for over half a century and persists up to now as a neocolony of the nation-state in whose territory we find ourselves domiciled, investigated and circumscribed. The reality of U.S. colonial subjugation and its profound enduring effects . . . distinguish the Filipino nationality from the Chinese, Japanese, Koreans, and other Asian cohorts. We are still suffering the trauma from the incalculable damage inflicted by the forward march of white supremacy. To understand what this means is already to resolve halfway the . . . spiritual and physical ordeals that people of color are forced to undergo when Western settlers and powers fight to divide the world into spheres of domination for the sake of capital accumulation and populations are expediently shuffled around in the global chessboard of warring and collusive interests.[25]

Criticizing aspects of United States culture and in some cases expressing desires eventually to return to the Philippines, Filipino Catholics interviewed for this study articulated their version of an ethnic community analogous to Latino communities, imaginatively located somewhere between the archipelago and the United States. Despite the "Americanization" of the Philippines, they echoed the sentiments of Mexican Americans in the archdiocese and Latino Catholics in other parishes in their resistance to wholesale assimilation into Anglo-Protestant culture.

Unlike the "official Catholic" identity of the Carmelite sisters, lay parishioners' narratives of religious identity are not limited primarily to a defense of normative Catholic doctrine and rituals. For them, the Tridentine symbols preserved in the sisters' demeanor and devotions awaken memories of a shared Spanish Catholic heritage. Their religious identity is articulated not in relation to postconciliar battles between conservatives and liberals but in reference to their respective histories and everyday experiences of trying to preserve communal identity in America. Associating Tridentine symbolism with a Spanish Catholic past, lay Catholics see in the cloistered community of sisters a model for ethnic solidarity and cohesiveness, typically conflating theological and social concerns in their narratives of Catholic identity.

Taken together, the narratives of lay Catholics thus offer a more textured explanation of why and how neotraditionalism has taken hold in the religious imagination of Americans than those afforded by an exclusive focus on the order's ecclesiastical history or ongoing efforts to canonize their foundress (Chapters 1 and 2). The Filipino and Mexican parishes of the Los Angeles diocese who appropriate the sisters' cosmology struggle with problems of urban and social fragmentation (Chapter 3). In the last two decades, the perceptions and reality of inner-city gang members spreading indiscriminately through the city's suburban neighborhoods have become symbols of social disintegration. Here the Carmelites' semi-cloistered schools and houses become transformed into bunker-like safe havens for middle- and lower-middle-class families trying to raise their families and preserve the integrity of their neighborhoods and communities. The Los Angeles parishes also shed further light on the Carmelites' unflattering perception of the contemporary world. Though worlds away from Wojtyla's formerly occupied Poland or Mother Luisa's war-torn Mexico, Los Angeles nevertheless stands in its own unique way as a monument to failed progress. Even the one upper-middle-class parish in Los Angeles rejecting the Carmelites' neotraditionalist world view, San Marino, barricades itself in houses protected by elaborate security systems. Sisters and laypersons alike tell their own version of Los-Angeles-as-Dystopia, an urban myth with longstanding roots in American arts and letters.

Reflecting what is arguably the most important demographic shift in the American Catholic church since the 1960s, both of the other two American communities embracing the Carmelites' theology are predominantly Latino.[26] To the lower-middle-class Mexican and Mexican-American parish on the Arizona borderlands, and the upper-class Cuban-American parish outside Miami, neotraditionalist Catholicism speaks powerfully to the tensions in these communities' interaction with Anglo-Protestant America and modern nations more generally. In the first case, the borderlands city of Douglas/Agua Prieta has been left to eke out a future in the social and economic vacuum left by the closing of its huge copper-smelting plant. The Phelps-Dodge mining interest, once the community's largest employer, has left the area in pursuit of more lenient environmental laws in Mexico (Chapter 4). Having looked in vain to the United States and Mexico for support and guidance, Catholics of the "Twin Cities" have turned to the Carmelites' cosmology for meaning and orientation amidst their town's toxic slag piles and boarded-up thoroughfares. In this primarily Mexican and Mexican-American parish, the sisters' charismatic founder, Mother Luisa, also evokes powerful memories of hope and survival through previous trials in modern Mexican history.

From the parish of Coral Gables, Florida, comes a tale of Cuban-American Catholics struggling with mixed success to preserve traditional family structures and class status in the wake of political exile from Fidel Castro's Cuba (Chapter 5). The Miami diocese, under both Cuban and American leadership, has successfully galvanized religious and political identity by fostering yearly pilgrimages to and ceremonies at La Ermita, the shrine to Cuba's patroness, Nuestra Señora de la Caridad del Cobre. Exiles, prohibited both politically and pragmatically from a return to the island and resisting outright assimilation into Anglo-Protestant America, seek to articulate a new Latino identity, what Thomas Tweed has referred to as a "translocative identity."[27] Here the neotraditionalist vision of church and society reflects an exilic sensibility of being "in the world but not of it"—or more specifically, of existing symbolically between two worlds but part of neither one. As they do in the Arizona borderlands, the Carmelites' pre–Vatican II rituals and lifestyle leave a powerful impression on the Cuban-American Catholics in Miami, who were raised in a culture shaped by the Spanish church.

The translocative dimension of Cuban-American Catholicism is but one expression of the *mestizaje* religiosity of Latin American and Latino traditions more generally: the blending and recombining of myths and rituals into unprecedented forms in response to new historical and political circumstances. Both Mexican and Cuban Catholicism emerged as traditions defining themselves in relation not to a dominant Protestant culture, but rather to a Spanish Catholic New World. In Mexico, religious myths and rituals merged with the sacred places and beings of Aztec society, yielding shrines and saints that partly continued Amerindian traditions. In Cuba, where the indigenous Taino population was all but destroyed by disease in the earliest decades of colonialism, Spanish Catholicism merged with the New World marketplace culture concentrated in the sugar plantations. As ethnography from the Arizona borderlands and Miami suggests, Latino Catholics have appropriated the Carmelites' tradition selectively. Teachings on the fate of Anglo-Protestant America are less important than the continued observance of Tridentine devotions, which are received as a mnemonic link to a Spanish Catholic heritage.

There remain, however, two parishes where the Carmelites quite simply fail to win many converts. The first is the parish of Saints Felicitas and Perpetua in San Marino, California. It is in this predominantly Euro-American, upper-middle-class parish that I have recorded an understanding of postconciliar Catholicism most reminiscent of liberal American scholars like Harvey Cox or Andrew Greeley. For San Marino Catholics, the Carmelites' monasticism is both outmoded and antithetical to the decidedly Anglo-Protestant mores of individual "success," reflected in the academic competitiveness in the school. The second is the parish of St. Rose of Lima in Cleveland, Ohio (Chapter 6). Invited to Cleveland in response to the bidding of a theologically conservative priest and long-time ecclesiastical ally of the sisters, the Carmelites have been received as quaint at best and obsolete at worst, but in neither case relevant to communal problems. Notwithstanding this city's own share of postindustrial, urban malaise since the Second World War, parishioners of the Saint Rose Parish embody what Richard Rodriguez has characterized as Protestant America's comedic optimism. Lying close to the heart of what is implied by "progress," the theatrical term is employed by Rodriguez "as the Greeks used it, with utmost seriousness, to suggest a world where youth is not a fruitless metaphor; where it is possible to start anew; where it is possible to escape the rivalries of the Capulets and the McCoys; where young women can disprove the adages of grandmothers."[28]

In a fine example of comedic sensibility, Cleveland parishioners identify most passionately not with religion or politics but rather with the city's sports teams. Unlike lay Catholics from other regions of America, Clevelanders have not yet abandoned civic or national pride, celebrated in the ubiquitous athletic banners, flags, and stickers bedecking the school walls. When these Clevelanders speak about their urban problems, they do so pragmatically and empirically with an eye towards eventual solutions. Many of them are Euro-American Catholics who were raised on the outskirts of the Midwest, the cultural bulwark of Anglo-Protestant America. In Cleveland it does indeed seem possible to start anew, and against such optimism, dystopian prophecies of America's demise or apostasy in the liberal American church border on the sacrilegious.

Fieldwork among the Carmelites' lay constituents was greatly expedited by the order itself, particularly by its superior, Mother Vincent Marie Finnegan. My initial success in establishing a working relationship with her and the other sisters doubtlessly reflected the fact that this project did not begin as a study of postconciliar Catholic identity, which could have otherwise raised questions about my religious and political motives for conducting research. At the outset of the project, I was instead interested in exploring devotion to a popular Mexican "saint"—a designation given to Mother Luisa by a Mexican-American woman in Santa Barbara, California, who was aware of my scholarly interests and familiar with the Carmelites through her own research as a potential aspirant to their order. Following her suggestion, I telephoned and arranged to meet with Mother Vincent Marie at the Carmelites' central headquarters in Alhambra, California, in the spring of 1993.

The first meeting with the order's superior shaped the format of subsequent interviews. Probably because of the potentially polemical nature of scholarship on her order, she asked me to refrain from tape-recording our conversations, but was comfortable with my taking written notes during our session. And while I had specific questions about Mother Luisa—What was her life story? Had Catholics reported any "miraculous intercessions" since her death? Were there pilgrimages to her graveside or specific devotions to her?—it was immediately apparent that questions about the foundress led to issues not anticipated by my original scholarly interests. I decided thereafter to let interviewees explain to me the appeal of Mother Luisa and the present-day Carmelite order in their own terms, recording our conversations by hand and supplementing my notes at the end of a workday with memories of details not included in the original transcriptions. It was only by coincidence that I thus found myself in the midst of the order that had organized women religious into a conservative, nationwide council since Vatican II.

It was Mother Vincent Marie Finnegan who first told me enthusiastically about the popularity of the order in parishes outside Los Angeles, and sanctioned my visits to them. She would typically arrange both the place and the times of interviews, mandating that every teacher of each school meet with me. Depending on the size of the school, interviews with the staff took between one and three days. Like the first interview with the superior herself, my conversations with teachers—who were also local parishioners in the churches adjoining their parochial schools—invariably led to impassioned discussions about the meaning of Catholic identity in today's world. Unlike discussions with the sisters, however, there was typically a confessional tone to interviews with lay Catholics. Behind closed doors, they were concerned to give me the "real story" of their church and community: explanations that were not limited to theological or ecclesiological issues of why the Carmelites did or did not appeal to the parish.

Following the cues of these discussions, I would continue ethnographic research in an archdiocese or diocese for two to three weeks, exploring the histories of parishes and their communities in local libraries and museums, and visiting—where appropriate—Catholic shrines, graveyards, and pilgrimage sites. I also supplemented my initial interviews with visits to other parishioners and local church prelates, typically at their work places. Given my own interest in popular legends of Catholic saints prior to the study of the Carmelites, my attention was predisposed to detecting coherent narrative themes that ran through and recurred within individual conversations. I would make the decision to cease supplementary interviewing as soon as it became clear that discussions were becoming redundant, that I had already "uncovered the story" of the Carmelites' appeal in a given locale. The narratives of Catholic identity within a parish invariably incorporated aspects of local regional identities, a parallelism that helped me to contextualize the interviews within the broader contours of American Catholicism and culture.

A project that began as an intended study of devotion to a Mexican saint thus transformed into the present overview of neotraditionalist Catholic identity. The first two chapters recount the narratives of the Carmelite sisters themselves, who are concerned primarily with the history and future of the institutional church. The subsequent chapters record narratives of the order's lay constituents, whose Catholic identity is accentuated by themes reflecting particular communal and local histories. This is not, however, a story of "popular Catholicism," of a church distinguished by "official" and "unofficial" interpretations of neotraditionalist doctrines. While I was reconstructing ethnographic research into the following chapters, it became clear that communal identity is a consistent theme running through both the order's and the parishioners' articulation of Catholicism. No less than their lay supporters or detractors, the Carmelite sisters embellish their doctrinal positions in imagining a Catholic community infused with themes from their foundress's biography and their experiences in the present-day United States.

As I will show, the postconciliar history of Mother Luisa's Carmelites underscores the extent to which the contours of American Catholicism have shifted some four decades after the election of John F. Kennedy as the country's first Roman Catholic president. Not only is the church today split by liberal and conservative factions contesting the normativity of American culture as a model for church organization, but it also has been transformed by the addition of non-European Catholics to its fold. The story of the Carmelites includes parish histories of "borderland" and "diasporic" Catholics who self-consciously resist total assimilation into an Anglo-Protestant society or an Anglo-Protestantized church, allying themselves with the order in an attempt to define and protect their ethnic identity. The history of the Carmelite Sisters of the Most Sacred Heart of Los Angeles since the 1960s thus refutes former predictions of a unilinear democratization and Protestantization of the American Catholic church. Neotraditionalist Catholicism, once relegated to the sidelines of church history by contemporary liberal observers, has gained a foothold in the fissures and cracks of a reconfiguring Anglo-Protestant America.

Conservative
Catholicism
and the
Carmelites

1

The Emergence of a Neotraditionalist Order

I N THE COURTYARD of the Carmelites' American headquarters in Alhambra, California, stands a tall statue of Jesus, his arms extended in a welcoming gesture, and his "Blessed Heart" exposed to the dry heat and smog that forever envelop Los Angeles. "Come to me," letters engraved in the rock base declare, "all you who labor and are heavy laden, and I will give you rest." In 1926, as Mexican troops flushed Cristero guerrillas out of hiding places in Jalisco, the Los Angeles–San Diego diocese, in unison with the American church, extended its arms in welcome for Mexico's beleaguered Catholics, offering itself as a haven for religious refugees.[1] It was to Los Angeles, via Nogales, that Mother Luisa came on a Southern Pacific train with two companions in June of 1927. She stayed in the city for two years, laying the foundations for what would become the American order of the Carmelite Sisters of the Most Sacred Heart of Los Angeles.[2]

This chapter is an overview of the Carmelites "official" history, its development strictly considered as an order of women religious within the American church. Particular emphasis is given to the period of the Second Vatican Council (1962–1965) and its reception by Catholic sisters in the United States throughout the years immediately following the council. For it was during this period, some forty years after the Carmelites' arrival in America, that their present-day identity began to take shape in response to two mutually reinforcing influences. First, in keeping with Vatican II's own suggestion for religious orders to renew their identity in light of their founders, the Carmelite sisters discovered in the Mexican identity of their foundress a rationale to retain their traditional lifestyle. This conservative decision to resist ecclesial transformations marginalized the Carmelites to the sidelines of American church history for nearly a decade. Second, with the election of Karol Wojtyla as Pope John Paul II in 1978, the Carmelites found official sanction for their position from the Vatican, reconstituting themselves as a decidedly neotraditionalist order advancing a literalist interpretation of magisterial teachings. The dual aspect of Mother Luisa's American order as both Mexican and neotraditionalist has allowed them to emphasize different aspects of themselves depending on which context they find themselves within. While this chapter and the next will explore the Carmelites' role as defenders of doctrinal orthodoxy within the church, subsequent chapters recording the "unofficial" history of the order among lay Catholics will return to the importance of the sisters' association with Spanish Catholicism.

As this chapter will argue, however, the conflation of Catholicism and cultural identity figures implicitly even in the official history of the Carmelites. At the heart of their conflict with liberal women religious lies a disagreement over the normativity of Anglo-Protestant culture as a model for the American church. The liberal sisters accept the democratic ideal as a self-evident principle by which the postconciliar church should be organized. In contrast, the Carmelite sisters and the neotraditionalist orders that they represent fault radical egalitarianism as having led to the alleged demise of social cohesion and moral clarity in both the church and the contemporary United States. This disagreement surfaces in theological debates over the nature of magisterial teachings: liberal sisters emphasize the revelation of divine will in the conscience of individual believers, while neotraditionalist sisters insist that God has disclosed unchanging truths in the communal teachings of the church. In imagining the boundaries of the *ecclesia,* therefore, liberal sisters accordingly invoke Anglo-Protestant American ideals, while the neotraditionalists turn to both Europe and Rome for models of ecclesiological organization. While Mother Luisa's Mexican heritage was therefore important in delineating the boundaries of the Carmelite order immediately after Vatican II, her cultural identity has become less important for the sisters since that time—at least when they are defining themselves in opposition to liberals in the church. When Mother Luisa is invoked as a model for present-day Carmelite leadership, she is portrayed less as a Mexican than as a martyr persecuted by modern society.

After her initial arrival in the United States, Mother Luisa and her companions spent their first two months recuperating at the Hollywood convent of the Immaculate Heart of Mary order in Los Angeles. From there, diocesan bishop John J. Cantwell directed them to work in the parish of the Holy Innocents in Long Beach, where refugees from Mexico were arriving daily. Over the next year, dozens of sisters from Atotonilco and Guadalajara followed Mother Luisa to Long Beach, leading to the purchase of a house and establishment of a convent. Their apostolate expanded to catechetical education for Mexican exiles, while the foundress began a youth league of Mexican Catholic women. In January 1928, Mother Luisa and several sisters were siphoned off from their newly established convent in Long Beach to work as kitchen staff at Santa Maria College in Moraga, California. Mother Luisa returned after eight months to Long Beach, consoling the sisters in their homesickness until the turmoil in Jalisco lessened. In 1929, Mother Luisa was the first of her order to return to Mexico. Other sisters soon followed, while a core group stayed in Los Angeles.

The foundress did not live to see the purchase of the Alhambra residence in 1941. By that time, however, the Carmelites had expanded and taken root in distinctively American soil. A love for Carmel, rather than for Mexico, became the vital connection between Mother Luisa's order and the Los Angeles–San Diego diocese. Father Leroy S. Callahan, diocesan liaison to Mexican refugees and devotee of Saint Thérèse of Lisieux, had taken a particular liking to the foundress and her order ever since their first visit with Bishop Cantwell. When Archbishop Orozco y Jimenez of Guadalajara expressed his disdain for the menial assignment of the sisters at Santa Maria College during an unexpected visit in 1928, Callahan targeted Mother Luisa's Carmelites as the future staff for a tuberculosis clinic dedicated to Saint Thérèse he was then envisioning. The Carmelites subsequently left Santa Maria in 1930, and sisters were rerouted to the newly established "Saint Teresita's" clinic, a renovated farmhouse standing next to orange groves in Duarte, California. In 1939, it was Callahan again who prompted Sister Margarita Maria, then superior at the hospital, to initiate the founding of a retreat house—a plan, he reminded her, conceived by the foundress herself soon after her arrival in the country.[3] After an extended real estate search, a vacant twenty-six room estate, topped with Spanish tiles and surrounded by expanses of grassy, shaded lawns, was located in Alhambra. In spite of heated protests against the establishment of a Mexican Catholic institution in an exclusive Euro-American neighborhood, it was designated the Carmelites' headquarters and retreat house at a zoning meeting in July 1941.[4]

The official absorption of Mother Luisa's Carmelite order into the American church was completed in 1942 with the foundation of a United States novitiate, located in the newly purchased Alhambra mansion. American-born sisters had been received into the Carmelite order even during the foundress's lifetime, but a directive in 1936 by Orozco y Jimenez's successor,

Cardinal José Garibi y Rivera, to abolish the United States province had required new members to complete their novitiate in Guadalajara.[5] Even after the American Carmelites of the Sacred Heart were canonically established in Los Angeles in 1938, then, the mandatory formation period in Mexico stemmed the tide of new American sisters. Bishop Cantwell of Los Angeles thus made a direct appeal to Garibi y Rivera for an independent American novitiate, and with its granting, the American order began to grow as both a nursing and a teaching order. Saint Teresita's evolved into a modern hospital facility, and the Carmelites were asked, starting in 1950, by parishes in downtown Los Angeles, Wilmington, Long Beach, and La Puente to teach the children of families—mostly of Mexican descent—who had moved to Los Angeles during the wartime employment boom. Until the 1960s, Mother Luisa's American sisters were for all intents and purposes indistinguishable from other American orders with similar apostolates and lifestyles, except for their predominantly Mexican constituency.

With the convening in 1962 of the Second Vatican Council, however, women religious in the United States reached a critical juncture in their collective history. In the final year of the council, Rome exhorted religious orders throughout the world to re-examine the meaning of their essential monastic vows—poverty, chastity, and obedience—in the hopes of effecting both modernization and renewal. Vatican II's 1965 "Decree on the Appropriate Renewal of Religious Life (*Perfectae Caritatis*)" declared that such renewal involved "two simultaneous processes: (1) a continuous return to the sources of all Christian life and to the original inspiration behind a given community, and (2) an adjustment of the community to the changed conditions of the times."[6] The generalized language of *Perfectae* encouraged a decentralized grassroots reform, in which it was hoped that religious communities around the world would look back to their own founder or foundress as the "original inspiration."

Undergirding the directives of *Perfectae* was a much broader reconceptualization of the church that had already effected changes in the full spectrum of Roman Catholic teachings and observances. The Vatican II ecclesiology was decidedly more decentralized and inclusive of lay members than that of the preconciliar church. In particular, the Vatican II documents *Lumen Gentium* and *Gaudium et Spes* had deliberately incorporated scriptural references to the church as a community of the faithful—the "People of God"—united in a covenantal relationship with God.[7] Such a democratized notion of the church had been meant to temper the emphasis throughout the nineteenth and twentieth centuries on the hierarchical aspect of Roman Catholicism, epitomized by such teachings as Pope Pius IX's doctrine of papal infallibility and Pius XII's equation of the church with the Body of Christ.

Scriptural metaphors sanctifying ecclesiastical hierarchy, taken mostly from Pauline letters, had been invoked by the earliest church fathers. These metaphors included the church as the body of Christ, the eucharistic body of Christ, the bride of Christ, God's building, the New Jerusalem, and the fellowship of the Spirit; of these, corporeal images had lent themselves particularly well to explaining internal divisions of power within the church, likening ecclesiastical offices to various anatomical parts of the body, with the head being ever in charge.[8]

The democratization of the church was not the only result of the Vatican Council. Other fundamental changes included an emphasis on the church's self-proclaimed role as servant to the modern world, promises of increased participation by local parishes in shaping global polity, and goals of more tolerance for both non-Catholic and non-Christian religious traditions. Vatican II also directly challenged Pius XII's claim that the church represented the immutable and perfect manifestation of the kingdom of God in the world. The council had declared that the kingdom of God was forever revealing itself in history, so that the church's mission and identity in any given era was but one of its expressions and developments. Presentations of the church as continually transforming undercut Catholicism's historic claims as the bearer of ahistorical or eternal truths: as history and the kingdom continued to unfold, so too would the "pilgrim church."

No sooner had Vatican II adjourned than the national organization of American sisters, the Conference of Major Superiors of Women, responded to the directives of *Perfectae*. The conference distributed a questionnaire, the so-called Sisters' Survey, to approximately 140,000 sisters in 1966, asking 778 questions about their self-understanding as religious and opinions on the central vows of poverty, chastity, and obedience.[9] Following the collection of the surveys, an independent consulting firm—Booz, Allen and Hamilton—was hired to evaluate and make recommendations to American sisters in light of changing times and mores.[10] Notwithstanding the radical changes of Rome's own council, the papacy was not prepared for Vatican II's reception in the United States. Sisters were virtually united in their critique of poverty as the mystification of labor exploitation; chastity, carried to the extreme of lessened social contact, as psychological repression; and obedience as fundamental submission to male-dominated, institutional power. At its annual 1971 meeting, the Conference of Major Superiors of Women passed a new set of bylaws advocating a sweeping revision of monastic life, a kind of Catholic Declaration of Independence from the perceived tyranny of the European past. The bylaws sanctioned democratic polity, the adoption of more modern dress and lifestyles, and increased involvement in the affairs of contemporary society. Voting 356 to 39 to support the new bylaws, the conference even emerged with a new name, the Leadership Conference of Women Religious, avoiding any reference to hierarchical distinctions among its members. Close to 90 percent of American women religious subsequently joined the organization.[11]

Conciliar reflections on the role and meaning of the church provided American women religious in the 1960s with abundant images and theological rationales for the rejection of inherited understandings of their vows. If *Perfectae Caritatis* directed their reforms, *Lumen Gentium* and *Gaudium et Spes* sanctified them. One of the first and most widely publicized orders of American sisters to proclaim "self-determination by women" was the Sisters of the Immaculate Heart of Los Angeles, the community that had first welcomed Mother Luisa to the United States in the 1920s. In the preamble to their new 1967 constitution they declared:

> We see the church as the extension of Christ's body, instituted by Himself, meant to be of service and a yoke to no man. Christ . . . showed us by His own choices, by unhesitatingly transcending traditional categories and separations, that life is to be abundantly fulfilled only in the freedom to make difficult and consequential decisions which confound some of the people some of the time.
> . . .
> What all of this affirms is the pulpit message often preached but seldom perceived, that we have not here a lasting city, that we are pilgrims on the move. We must be ready to weigh the value of any change, and ready to choose it without regard to the cost, if such change appears to be in order.[12]

The order then proceeded to remove its habits, live outside of cloistered communities, and lessen restraints on its members' daily activities. The Vatican's conservative Sacred Congregation for Religious refused to recognize the canonical validity of these new decrees, ignoring pleas and arguments from the order. Three years later in 1970, after the congregation had stopped answering or acknowledging the sisters' correspondence and 150 members had left the community, 352 religious asked for and received dispensation from their vows.[13] Together with the Glenmary Sisters of Ohio and the School Sisters of St. Francis of Milwaukee—whose reforms had met with similar censorship from the Vatican—the Immaculate Heart Sisters were portrayed by the *National Catholic Reporter* as heralding a new type of American woman religious, who fought against the patriarchal oppression and political tyranny of the Roman church.

As battles over the control and expression of religious lifestyles raged outside their doors, however, Mother Luisa's Carmelite sisters decided to retain their inherited lifestyle and vows with minimal changes. The reason was simple enough: despite their increasingly diverse ethnic membership, the American Carmelites of the 1960s still represented a largely Mexican community made up of women who had sought in the United States freedom to observe traditional monasticism. In contrast, when the Immaculate Heart sisters looked back to their own Mexican foundress, they found but a hopelessly outmoded and culturally foreign blueprint for their future:

> Women, perhaps especially dedicated women, insist on the latitude to serve, to work, to decide according to their own lights. Our community's history from its beginning, including its early missionary activities in California and its eventual separation from a Spanish foundation which was inevitably removed and indifferent to peculiarly American conditions, speaks of our readiness to abandon dying forms in order to pursue living reality. It expresses, also, our willingness to seek human validity rather than some spurious supernaturalism.[14]

In the convent at Alhambra, however, Mexican Catholicism was neither felt as "removed and indifferent from peculiarly American conditions" nor perceived as "spurious supernaturalism." Older sisters' persecution during the Cristero years, the circumstances of their own foundress's arrival in America, and communal observance of inherited Mexican devotions assured that Mexican Catholic monasticism would continue in at least one Los Angeles order. In the words of the present-day mistress of novices, "the older [Mexican] sisters kept asking, 'They're not making us take off our habits again, are they?'"[15]

The habits of Mother Luisa's sisters were thus retained, though with alterations from wool to more comfortable blended cotton fabric, and the elimination of restrictive collars. The Carmelites also chose to retain the communal, cloistered organization of their society and reaffirmed the meaning of "obedience" as loyalty to the teachings of the church in Rome. In the meantime, Mother Luisa's heirs in Mexico responded to Vatican II by reinterpreting their charism as radically as had many of the liberal American orders. Inspired by Latin American liberation theology, the Carmelites in Mexico since the 1960s have emphasized the Gospel's preferential option for the poor, straining the relationship between American and Mexican sisters until recently. By the time the American order was granted congregational autonomy in 1983, therefore, it was as a community with a theological and ecclesiological emphasis clearly different from that of its Mexican sister order.

If Pope John XXIII, architect of Vatican II, and his successor Pope John VI, who presided over the council until its end, championed a democratized church in keeping with the liberal Leadership Conference's decentralized ecclesiology, the election in 1978 of Karol Wojtyla as Pope John Paul II could not have heralded a more auspicious turn for orders like Mother Luisa's Carmelites. Successor to John Paul I, who died after only thirty-three days as pontiff, Pope John Paul II came to be known to the church and the world as the church's postconciliar "reformer," a former Polish bishop who felt the decentralization spawned by Vatican II had left the church in a state of confusion and disarray. Despite his extensive participation in the drafting of council documents, particularly *Lumen Gentium,* John Paul II gave American Catholics one of their first hints that his was to be a more conservative papacy in a visit to the United States in 1979. Peter Hebblethwaite, former Vatican correspondent for the *National Catholic Reporter* and student of popes before and after the council, accurately forecast the future papacy in his analysis of remarks by John Paul II that may have appeared little more than oblique to the layperson.

Speaking of Catholic doctrine, the pontiff had quoted a famous statement of John XXIII's—but omitted a crucial sentence. "The greatest concern of the ecumenical council is this," Pope John II explained to American bishops, "that the deposit of Christian doctrine should be more effectively guarded and taught."[16] "This is true," observed Hebblethwaite, "But if one leaves it at that, one has only a defensive, apologetic, and conserving view of the council's work. . . . Pope John XXIII added something else: 'Our duty is not only to guard this precious treasure, as if we were concerned only with antiquity, but to dedicate ourselves with an earnest will and without fear to that work which our era demands of us.'"[17] In other words, Hebblethwaite explained, if council architects had envisioned an adaptation of the church to modern times, an application of traditional wisdom to new circumstances, the second postconciliar pope saw his role as preserving received tradition with minimal changes.[18] Hebblethwaite's early analysis of Pope John Paul II as "collegially conservative, socially progressive, and doctrinally restorationist"[19] was to be vindicated over the next two decades by a series of pronouncements and actions perceived as downright retrogressive by liberal Catholic theologians. Collegial conservatism was reflected in a series of silencings, condemnations, and excommunications of renegade theologians and priests; social progressivism was epitomized in Wojtyla's continuing critique of capitalism; and doctrinal conservatism was evidenced in the pontiff's defense of an "eternal essence" of Catholicism reflected in the new and universalistic *Catechism for the Catholic Church* in 1992, as well as an encyclical on moral theology in 1993, *Veritatis Splendor.*[20]

Before the publication of Pope John Paul II's *Essential Elements of the Religious Life* in 1983, however, Rome had not yet redressed in earnest what it considered the excesses of monastic renewal in various religious communities throughout the world, and particularly in America. The some 10,000

American sisters choosing not to join the Leadership Conference of Women Religious in 1971 had quietly banded together in an organization called the Consortium Perfectae Caritatis, initially organized by Father James Viall, present-day priest of Saint Rose of Lima church in Cleveland, Ohio.[21] As conservative sisters tenaciously held to the pre–Vatican II monastic lifestyle and theology, the Vatican went no further than to classify the reforms of the more liberal sisters as "experimentations." But with the publication of the *Essential Elements,* Consortium sisters could finally claim that their literalist interpretations of poverty, chastity, and obedience to the magisterium reflected normative Vatican teachings.[22] In 1989, Pope John Paul II appointed Archbishop James Hickey of Washington, D.C., as official liaison to the Consortium, which was granted canonical approval in June of 1992. Though still recognized by the Vatican, the liberal Leadership Conference could now no longer claim exclusive representation of American women religious.

In October of 1992, the consortium emerged from the sidelines of the American church with new leadership, vision, and support. Renaming itself the Council of Major Superiors of Women Religious, the organization held its first meeting in Techny, Illinois. "It is the specific purpose of this Council," the statutes declared, "to provide a clear, stable, and official channel through which major superiors, assisted by an Episcopal Liaison appointed by the Holy See, can share the vision, principles, and directives of the Magisterium of the religious life."[23] The Council of Major Superiors had been formed just in time for the pontiff's October 1995 Synod on Religious, held to conduct a thirty-year review of contemplative life since the issuance of *Perfectae Caritatis.* Together with Leadership Conference officials, three representatives from the neotraditionalist council were invited to Rome to participate in preliminary hearings. Replacing James Viall as president of the new council was none other than the mother superior of Mother Luisa's American order, Mother Vincent Marie Finnegan, who had been instrumental in drafting its bylaws.

It is unclear from the available historical documents exactly at which point Mother Luisa's order took on the countercultural status it has today as the leading order of the conservative council. But sometime in the early years following the Vatican II reforms—most likely between the closing of the council in 1965 and the birth of the Leadership Conference of Women Religious in 1971—what had started as a presumably innocent retention of Mexican devotionalism became a statement by an American order resisting assimilation into a church seen as theologically misguided and even hostile to the continuation of normative Catholicism. In and through this transformation of the order, the life of Mother Luisa has taken on new shades of meaning for the sisters. Today a candidate for canonization by the Vatican, the foundress is remembered no longer as simply a Mexican Carmelite but as a Catholic who was persecuted at the hands of anti-Catholic Mexican federalists. The preamble to her official biography clearly underscores this political dimension of her identity:

> In presenting to the Congregation for the Cause of Saints the profile of Mother Maria Luisa Josefa of the Most Blessed Sacrament (Maria Luisa de la Peña Navarro V. de Rojas) the Church wishes to place her before all else in her historico-ecclesial context, characterized especially by a religious persecution which witnessed the beginning and first development of the Congregation of the Sisters of the Sacred Heart [sic], founded by her. It is in this historic atmosphere where her heroic virtues are revealed and in which the reputation of holiness of the Servant of God is taking form.[24]

On this side of the Rio Grande, the mother superior of the American Carmelites, who is Irish-American, is fond of drawing comparisons between the Mexican national government, which fought against Cristero guerrillas in Mother Luisa's home state of Jalisco, and anti-Catholic forces in the United States, who are left unnamed.[25] Even a cursory glance at the history of American Catholicism since Vatican II leaves little doubt, however, as to whom she is talking about. The order's most heated battles in the last thirty years have been fought in the church, with other orders of women religious.[26]

If liberal sisters grapple with the ambiguities of Catholic identity in light of pluralism, postmodernism, and feminism, the Carmelites offer an unambiguous and simple message of salvation, claiming to supply eternal and unchanging answers to questions about life in this world and life in the next. Liberal critics often characterize such an essentialist theology as blind to the historical and cultural forces that shape and transform religious traditions. Neotraditionalist Catholics like the Carmelite sisters retort by arguing for the revealed status of their tradition and the divine guidance shaping the magisterium's interpretations of the faith. Behind these seemingly irreconcilable theological conflicts, however, looms an equally daunting dispute over the normativity of Anglo-Protestant American culture as a model for the church. For if the same Holy Spirit that allegedly directs the unfolding of ecclesial history also speaks through the conscience of individual believers in America—if, in other words, democracy itself can be sanctified—then the liberal sisters can implicitly assume that their theological interpretations are as inviolable as the magisterium's.

As Jay P. Dolan has discussed extensively in his overview of American Catholicism, two distinct and antithetical conceptions of the church have coexisted in the United States ever since the eighteenth century, each reflecting a different relationship between religious tradition and American culture. One ecclesiology, designated by Dolan as "republican," is so named for its incorporation of American republican conceptions of governance by the earliest Jesuit communities in the British colony of Maryland. The republican church thrived for a brief interlude after the American Revolution, as American Catholics—who had helped fight for independence—were eager both to respect church and state separation and to emulate their country's principles in and through church governance. This was a church eager, then, to model itself after the American nation, bringing together concepts of cultural traditionalism—identification with one's country—and religious traditionalism—identification with the Roman Catholic heritage.

When patriotic sentiments stemming from the American Revolution cooled, however, another ecclesiology—designated by Dolan as the "imported church" model—was introduced by fugitive clerics from France, who had opposed, with Rome's backing, the birth of the modern nation there. The imported church model of American Catholicism gradually gained ascendancy in the early decades of the 1800s, garnering support until the Second World War from the waves of European immigrants who themselves felt disenfranchised from American culture.[27] This was an ecclesiology that made sharp distinctions between Roman Catholic and American identity and that viewed the United States primarily as a mission field for Catholic proselytization. Starting in the late 1940s, however, notions of the republican church regained its former appeal as Americans experienced a new wave of patriotic fervor. Both the defeat of the Axis powers and the socioeconomic and educational ascent of Euro-Americans "up and out" of ethnic isolation rendered the vision of imported church an increasingly untenable model. American women religious of the mid-twentieth century—who underwent a mandatory period of "professionalization" as teachers and nurses—were themselves exposed to secularizing influences during their religious formation.[28] In the meantime, priests and bishops aligned themselves with the nation in its fight against atheistic communism, at the same time championing the separation of church and state in their Anglo-Protestant society. The election of John F. Kennedy as the country's first Roman Catholic president in 1961 symbolized for many American Catholics their coming of age and final inclusion into the country.

On the one hand, both liberal and neotraditionalist sisters can claim to be perpetuating "traditional" American Catholicism. The liberal sisters, who rode the wave of contemporary American patriotism in rallying the country's support for their changes, were advancing the model of the republican church into a new generation. The neotraditionalist sisters can find precedent for their conception of the American church as well by hearkening back to the era before the Second World War, when the imported-church model was still ascendant. On the other hand, the neotraditionalist sisters do not define themselves primarily in relation to an American past. When they invoke "tradition," they mean the heritage of European Catholicism and, most important, the magisterial lineage of the Vatican. In the final analysis, the Carmelite sisters seek to separate themselves from the American cultural milieu altogether, while the liberal sisters struggle to articulate an "indigenous" church modeled after the decidedly Anglo-Protestant mores of "public Protestantism": voluntarism, pluralism, and individualism.

The two pamphlets distributed to potential Carmelite novices concisely state the order's mission to as being perpetuate, in the United States, the normative Catholicism of Rome's magisterium and the tradition of Carmelite monasticism as formulated and expressed by European predecessors. "Our heritage," one of the brochures explains, is rooted "in the Gospels, the Church, the spirituality of Carmel and the charism of our Beloved Foundress."[29] Accordingly, the order continues the full range of devotions accrued throughout centuries of both European and American Counter-Reformation spiritual practice. The order is advertised as "affiliated to the Order of Discalced Carmelites and enjoy[ing] all the privileges, indulgences and other spiritual favors of the Order."[30] Meanwhile, the life and spirit of the Carmelites is described as "contemplation and constant prayer, both private and communal."[31] Daily eucharistic celebration, meditation, chanting of the Divine Office, recitation of the rosary, spiritual reading, and devotions to the Sacred Heart of Jesus and the Blessed Mother are prominently listed in the order's statement of its religious practice.

A second pamphlet unfolds like an accordion to present a series of the Carmelites' patron saints.[32] The front page displays the statue of Our Lady of Carmel, seated on a throne with the infant Jesus on her lap, her head crowned and surrounded by a circle of stars.[33] The image of Our Lady is followed by portraits of Carmelite predecessors Saint Teresa of Jesus, Saint John of the Cross, and Saint Thérèse of Lisieux; then the seal of Carmel representing Elias the Prophet; and finally a picture of Mother Maria Luisa Josefa. As photographs feature the veiled Carmelites at work in their various apostolates of education, hospital and retreat work, day care, and care for the aged, quotations taken from the writings of both Saint Teresa and Mother Luisa emphasize the order's first priority as the cultivation of prayer and contemplation. "Before talking to the children about God, talk to God about the children," the foundress's saying advises, next to a photograph of a sister in a computer laboratory.[34] Another description of retreat work highlights the order's central doctrinal concern in capital letters: "giving souls opportunity to speak with their Creator about the only problem: ETERNAL SALVATION."[35] "It was in the Providence of God," the brochure declares, "that

Reverend Mother Maria Luisa Josefa of the Most Blessed Sacrament should find religious sanctuary in the United States as she fled persecution in her native Mexico in 1927, and that this should lead to the establishment of the Carmelite Sisters of the Most Sacred Heart of Los Angeles."[36]

Membership in the Carmelite Sisters of the Most Sacred Heart of Los Angeles has held steady since Vatican II at approximately 120 women, with new members replacing though not surpassing the number of deceased religious.[37] Defying earlier feminist stereotypes of cloistered religious women as victims of a patriarchal church structure, the most recent novices and postulants are women in their twenties and thirties, most of whom hold at least bachelor's degrees and have had experience in the professional world. Precisely because the liberal Leadership Conference now offers a wide range of alternative religious lifestyles for women, entrance into the Carmelite order—like any affiliate of the traditionalist Council of Major Superiors of Women Religious—is a choice of a particular kind of religious life. Thanks to the women's movement of the past three decades, social roles for women have expanded beyond marriage, childbearing, and housekeeping, rendering monasticism but one option amidst many possible lifestyles.

Advertisements for the American Carmelites will not be found in mainstream Catholic newspapers; their reputation spreads through more grassroots channels, including word-of-mouth and local Catholic conferences. The vast majority of today's candidates to the order have learned about it from local priests. Given the national scope of the traditionalist Council of Major Superiors of Women Religious, however, these methods of recruitment manage to reach women far beyond the diocesan boundaries of Los Angeles. In the summer of 1995, for example, I interviewed the twelve newest postulants and novices—women between the ages of 21 and 32, both from the Los Angeles area and with origins as distant as Virginia and Kentucky—to ascertain their reasons for joining a neotraditionalist order in post–Vatican II America. Despite the variety of their cultural, economic, and geographical backgrounds, these women were united in the reason they gave for exploring the cloistered religious life: to separate themselves from American society and become members of an extraordinary socioreligious community. In and through this separation, they felt, Catholicism is rendered more visible against the backdrop of a secularized culture.

One sister who had once studied computer science at Saint Louis University spoke comfortably about the life and world she had left behind. "I enjoyed my former life while I was doing it, but now I don't miss it. It's not that the other's bad, it's just that this is better. God used my logical mind to realize there must be something more to life. I had a very personal relationship with my faith but they [my employers and colleagues] wouldn't know if I was Catholic or not unless I said something about it." She was particularly attracted to orders with an "essentialist" understanding of vows because, as she explained, "if I'm going to be a convert [to religious life] I might as well go all the way."[38] Another novice elaborated on the significance of essentialist monasticism by reflecting, "[T]here are essentials to a religious life, and that's what makes you different. Right now, people need to see the difference between religious life and secular life. We've crossed the boundaries. The orders have their own reasons for modifying their habits. But I don't see what witness that gives to people."[39]

Another postulant, a thirty-year-old woman who came to the Carmelites from the business world, similarly emphasized the importance, for her, of remaining separate from secular society. This woman had worked as a corporate tax examiner for the state of Connecticut but entertained the idea of religious life for several years before becoming a postulant, earning a graduate degree in moral theology and living as a third-order Dominican while working for the state. She had conducted extensive research on religious orders and had definite ground rules for joining one. "Number one, it had to be centered on the Eucharist; number two, if you're talking about the living-in-an-apartment thing, I was doing that already. And the habit was important to me. How can you be a witness if you don't know who you really are?" The Carmelites appealed to her for their lifestyle and emphasis on contemplation. "Without prayer, I'll just be a social worker," she said. "I'll bandage the wounds but not really heal them."[40]

A native Los Angeles woman who became a Carmelite revealed the power, for her, of the traditionalist monastic lifestyle in her designation of the Carmelites as "the cloister people," an expression she had coined for the sisters in her childhood. As a young girl, she used to pass the sisters' retreat house on her way from downtown Los Angeles to Mass in Alhambra. "There was something very nice about them [the Carmelites]," who came to assume for her an aura of mystery and intrigue. Several years later, as she was deliberating on the course of her future after high school, she made her first visit to the Carmelite motherhouse. "After I had graduated from school my mother told me she'd seen one [of the 'cloister people']," she recalled. "There was something about them—something the 'cloister people' had."[41]

Like the liberal women religious, Carmelite postulants and novices acknowledge the strains attendant on living a cloistered life in contemporary America—identifying obedience as the most difficult vow to honor. Obedience to ecclesial superiors is justified by them, nevertheless, as a necessity if their theological and ecclesiological ideals are to be made manifest in American society. "I don't have a problem with obedience," one woman told me. "Our Lord was obedient unto death." Because bishops and priests are the present-day instruments of God in the world, obedience to them, she explained, re-enacts Jesus' submission to God. Women's obedience to God also has ample scriptural backing. "The Bible makes it perfectly clear that men fled Jesus while the women stuck around," she noted, referring to the apostles' betrayal of Jesus before his death and the gathering of Mary, Mary Magdalene, and other female disciples during the scene at the crucifixion.[42] Another novice similarly explained, "It's not submitting to any person—I believe Sister Regina Marie [the Mistress of Novices] is the voice of God speaking in my life."[43]

The Carmelites' acceptance of essentialist monastic vows would thus seem to reflect nothing less than the choice to model their lives after a social ideal distinct from and, for them, even preferable to Anglo-Protestant culture. They are willing to submit themselves to the hierarchical structure of the order as a relatively small price to pay for inclusion in what they see as the kingdom of God on earth. "I'm more free than I ever was in the world," a novice reflected, "free to do what God wants." Looking back to her former career as a bonds trader, she commented that, as a corporate employee, she was a "slave" to her job as well as to societal expectations of success. While obedience challenged her, it nevertheless gave her "completely more freedom."[44] Similarly, when I asked one novice about submission to church authority, she responded, "That's funny, because that's talking about the freedom of the person. When I surrender myself to the person who created me, I have more power. If you look at it, everyone does that [surrender to authority]—in the world they have bosses, plus parents. For me, this is just a different focal point."[45]

Feminist critics of preconciliar Catholicism have oftentimes pointed to the "invisibility of women" as a glaring fault of the traditional Roman or "imported" American church model. Leading American feminist theologian Elisabeth Schüssler Fiorenza, for example, has summarized the liberal sisters' ecclesiology and theology as an act of "Breaking the Silence—Becoming Visible" in the title to an essay on women in the Catholic church. The monastic cloister in particular emerges in Catholic feminist scholarship as the symbol par excellence of the marginalization of women: the place where women are literally kept concealed from the public eye. In an article by Margaret Brennan, for example, the origins of the cloister in the Roman Catholic church are explained as a case of the androcentric usurpation of radical sexual equality in the New Testament church:

> The imposition of the cloister (enclosure) was a gradual development. It followed in part from a genuine concern of Church leaders to provide some form of structure and security for women whose cultural situation afforded them little autonomy and no place in public life. They were con-

sidered to be inferior, immature, emotional, incapable of logical reason-
ing, weak, and fickle. In spite of the insistence of the New Testament on
the spiritual equality of men and women, this androcentric view found
its way into the early Church where it was given theological justification.
Women, perceived to be in need of protection and vigilance, were placed
under the guidance and direction of men who, moreover, considered them
to be sources of temptation and ultimately responsible for the fallen condition of humankind.[46]

Upon closer inspection, however, such analyses that fault the Catholic
church for marginalizing women are ultimately rooted in an adoption of
the democratic *polis* as the normative model for Catholic ecclesiology.
Schüssler Fiorenza, for example, in elaborating upon her critique of the Roman Catholic church, follows the classicist Marilyn Arthur in returning to
Athenian democracy as the cradle of normative civilization.[47] For liberal
American sisters perpetuating the republican church model, the neotraditionalists' failure to democratize gender relations within the church approaches an apostasy that is as much cultural as theological. Neotraditionalist sisters are faulted as much for their oppositional relationship to
American democracy as they are for their literalist interpretations of church
teachings. In contrast, for neotraditionalist sisters who have already decided
that democratic ideals are not the last word in or the only model for ecclesiological organization, such critiques seem spurious and unrelated to their
more central concerns of "becoming visible" in an extraordinary social order of monastics.

In their unabashed demythologization of America as a social template
for the church, the newest recruits to Mother Luisa's American order fall,
according to most analysts, on the extreme right of American conservative
Catholicism. In his essay "The Triumph of Americanism," R. Scott Appleby
has argued that the ideals of voluntarism, pluralism, and individualism—
condemned by Pope Leo XIII at the turn of the twentieth century as antithetical to the Roman Catholic faith—have at last triumphed at the turn of
the millennium as a model for conservative and liberal Catholics alike. "We
are in an unprecedented position," he writes,

> in the sense that liberals and conservatives, despite their important differ-
> ences and vehement disagreements, share a basic orientation and set of as-
> sumptions about the United States and its worthiness as a model for the
> Roman Catholic Church. The conservatives . . . tend to apply the lessons
> learned in two hundred-plus years of U.S. political and economic history
> to Roman Catholic social doctrine, while the liberals tend to apply Amer-
> icanist insights to the ecclesiology, or internal governance, of the church
> itself. Nonetheless, the tacit agreement to lift up the American experiment

as exemplary, even revelatory, is striking to the historian. Even the original Americanists did not go this far.

While Appleby's generalizations are certainly applicable to liberal sisters in
the church and even "centrist" conservative Catholics, they do not easily fit
Mother Luisa's Carmelite order. Turning to a Mexican foundress as a model
for normative Catholic practice in the 1960s, defining their mission in reaction to liberal sisters throughout the subsequent decades, and supported by
a papacy at odds with Americanist principles, the Carmelites take pains to
define themselves in critical tension with the surrounding culture of the
United States. From the perspective of the cloistered Carmelite community,
it is the wholesale adoption of Americanist ideals as guiding principles for
church organization that is questionable. Ultimately, the failure thus far of
the Leadership Conference of Women Religious and the Council of Major
Superiors of Women Religious to enter into dialogue about social, economic,
or ecclesiological issues reflects a fundamental disagreement over the exact
status of the American experiment, an issue that will be explored further in
the conclusion to this book.

In the meantime, the Vatican has accepted Mother Luisa as a candidate
for canonization. Given the status of the American Carmelites as leaders of
the council, her potential sanctification would transform a Mexican Carmelite
into something of a patron saint for neotraditionalist sisters in the United
States. As incongruous as this might seem, this is not the first time that Pope
John Paul II has bestowed his blessings on Protestant countries by idealiz-
ing Catholic heroes normally excluded from the national fold. In his interaction with German Catholics, for example, the pontiff has strained *not* to
mention the nation's historic role in spearheading the Protestant Reformation. As Peter Hebblethwaite once noted:

> His Germany [is] peopled by Boniface, a Cornish monk who evangelized
> the place, St. Albert the Great, teacher of Thomas Aquinas, a few medieval
> mystics and then with a great leap of the pontifical seven-league boots, on
> to the 19th century and Bishop Wilhelm von Ketteler, the workers' friend
> and inspirer of Leo XIII, and so on to the heroic anti-Nazis who perished
> in concentration camps.[48]

As much as the pontiff would like to include all nations in his modern
Christendom—a dream that seemed to fade with the Berlin Wall's fall in 1989
and the weakening of Catholic nationalism in Eastern Europe—modern
democracies founded on Protestant principles, of which America is the pro-
totype, are deliberately excluded. The split between liberal and neotraditionalist sisters has given the pontiff a foothold, however, in Catholic Amer-

ica. Under his leadership, the Carmelites have become valorized as Catholic dissidents in a Protestant nation—clearly a status not reflected in their pre–Vatican II history—and Mother Luisa as a quasi-American patron of the neotraditionalist church.

The next chapter will continue an exploration of how Mother Luisa's American community has been transformed since Vatican II into a neotraditionalist order by focusing on the construction of her official biography by Vatican saint-makers. As we shall see, the profile of the foundress primarily as a martyr of anti-Catholic forces represents but one possible interpretation of her life. Consistent with other studies on canonization, an overview of Mother Luisa's ongoing review as a potential saint reflects political strategies within the Vatican to bolster and consolidate those Catholic factions that support magisterial objectives. Within the United States, Mother Luisa's order has undergone significant developments since Vatican II to become an important presence in the conservative postconciliar American church.

2

Mother Luisa's Canonization and the Sanctification of Neotraditionalism

O N THE DAY OF HER DEATH, it was said, Mother Luisa's corpse gave off the fragrance of roses, and sisters throughout Jalisco heard mysterious knocking sounds on their convent walls. Crowds gathered around her body in the city of Guadalajara to offer prayers, "asking and hoping to obtain favors, graces, and even miracles through her intercession. Some persons would touch rosaries, medals and other objects to her body."[1] It is clear from the pages of her official biography, completed by Vatican hagiographer Camilio Maccise in 1989, that the foundress was known to her contemporaries as something of a saint long before her passing in 1937. In a country recently torn asunder by battles between church and state, the outpouring of devotion prior to the funeral was charged with both religious and political overtones. The day after her death, Maccise notes, Mother Luisa's community "had to leave the rented house they lived in because the great influx of persons who went to pray before her body had revealed that they were religious. This was a cause for fear and confiscation, imprisonment and even death."[2]

Unfortunately for the sisters, the prevailing anticlerical mood of Mexico continued for many years, reducing them to extreme poverty as their public apostolic work—and means of livelihood—was restricted. It was not until 1967 that their superior general, Elisa Graciela Gonzalez, petitioned her local bishop in Guadalajara to initiate the formal canonization review of the foundress. The cause had also been delayed for lack of the necessary funds, the order's unfamiliarity with canonical protocol, and administrative disorganization in the archdiocese of Guadalajara. Cardinal Archbishop Don José Garibi y Rivera of Mexico advised the sisters to wait a few more years until Rome quieted down from the excitement of the Second Vatican Council.[3] In a trip to Rome in 1975, Mother Gonzalez at last brought Mother Luisa's cause to the attention of the Congregation for the Causes of Saints, and the official review began in 1977.

As we have seen, the Carmelite sisters in the United States remember Mother Luisa primarily as a martyr of anti-Catholic persecution, citing the circumstances of her arrival to Los Angeles in 1927, in flight from the violence of the Cristero Revolt. This memory of their foundress plays a central role in the construction of the American sisters' postconciliar identity today. For them, Mother Luisa was simultaneously a fighter, a victim, and a triumphant survivor in the face of the forces that threatened to destroy her. This portrayal is at once a backward glance at the past and a statement of the Carmelites' oppositional relationship to their present-day social context, particularly to liberal women religious in the church. As this chapter will attempt to show, however, the biographical details of Mother Luisa's life reveal a slightly more complex portrait of the Carmelite foundress. Mother Luisa was sixty years old when the fighting between Cristeros and Mexican federalists erupted in 1926, having already spent some twenty-two years as a Carmelite sister in Jalisco. Prior to the Cristero conflict, she was most renowned as a local saint to the members of her hometown of Atotonilco. Here she was neither fighter nor martyr, but a member of high-class society whose holiness was observed even before she entered the cloister in her outreach to the sick and the poor.

The model of Mother Luisa taking an active stance to remedy social problems in her contemporary society inspired the founding of the Saint Teresita's tuberculosis clinic in Duarte, California, and the willingness of American Carmelites to teach and catechize the children of poor Mexican immigrant families in the less politicized years prior to the council. It is also most likely a model of sanctity that inspires the liberation theology of the Carmelites in Mexico, who continue their foundress's example of identifying herself as one of the poor and marginalized. Nevertheless, Mother Luisa's official biography chooses to highlight the oppositional relationship between the Carmelite order and modern society. The countercultural magisterium of Pope John Paul II's Vatican thus lends its support to the American neotraditionalists' ecclesiology through its particular construction of her sanctity. Consistent with Kenneth Woodward's study of official canonization, the preliminary stages of Mother Luisa's review would suggest that saints are not so much discovered as made, in light of the political objectives of particular papacies.

The formal canonization of Mother Luisa continues a Catholic procedural protocol dating back to the sixteenth century. Veneration of saints and martyrs dates back even farther, to second-century meetings at the gravesites of those martyred by Rome, where prayers, commemoration of the deceased's "baptism in blood," and celebration of the Eucharist were observed on the anniversary of their death. Following the halt of state persecution with the conversion of Constantine and the Christianization of the Roman empire in the fourth century, asceticism came to replace death at the hands of the state as the highest path to Christian perfection, and monastics superseded martyrs as objects of local veneration. While the sanctity of martyrdom had been unquestioned within the early church, the holiness of deceased ascetics admitted to more ambiguity. Hence, as early as the fourth century, bishops were frequently consulted to help determine the authenticity of saints. By the fifth century, both laity and episcopate expanded their criteria of holiness to include thaumaturgic powers, channeled through the saint's gravesite and relics, as palpable confirmations of alleged virtuous deeds and moral acts.

It was not until 993, however, when Pope Benedict VI was sought by local prelates of Augsburg to bless their recently deceased bishop, that popes became involved in the designation of saints. Over the next two hundred years, Rome increasingly involved itself in identifying local saints, until Pope Alexander II made it official in 1170 that a saint could not be venerated without the Vatican's approval. Still, it would not be until the Reformation that the Roman Church standardized its canonization procedures, in reaction to Luther's lambasting of devotional excesses. In 1588, the papacy established the Congregation of Rites for the sole purpose of the canonization of saints, and in 1684, Urban VIII codified the official saint-making process in his *Decreta Servanda in Canonizatione et Beatificatione Sanctorum*. The *Decreta* became part of the Code of Canon Law in 1917, remaining the official guideline for canonization until Pope John Paul II simplified the review procedures and changed the hagiographic format in 1983.

The standardized and centralized "saint-making" bureaucracy of the Counter-Reformation has remained intact, however, leaving the Congregation for the Causes of Saints with total and final control in judging posthumous sanctity. Ever since the sixteenth century, canonization law has stipulated that a candidate for sainthood cannot be the object of a local cultus prior to beatification, lest the judgment of the laity usurp the Vatican's designation of who is or is not a saint. Local bishops of the modern church have consequently been left in the rather delicate if not paradoxical position of having to prove to Rome that there is enough, but not too much, popular devotion to their nominees. The wedge thus driven between local and universal churches has made possible new ecclesial uses and abuses of making saints: despite local veneration, the congregation can deny causes; or, conversely, the congregation can venerate local saints attracting minimal local support.

The official cause for Mother Luisa's canonization successfully has met the preliminary standards for ecclesiastical review. On the one hand, her Carmelite order could easily find enough evidence of local devotion to support its petition to the Vatican. Not only did local Catholics consider her a saint by the time of her death, but they have attributed to her intercession a total of twelve posthumous graces and favors. These include seven physical healings, the revitalization of one man's Catholic faith, the verification of a religious vocation, the waiving of one woman's mortgage debt, the avoidance of death by passengers in a major automobile accident, and—unquestionably the most spectacular claimed miracle of all—the rerouting of a cyclone:

> Towards the end of October, 1976, an announcement from the government was heard through the radio, that a cyclone was coming towards this direction at a great speed. This notice was transmitted every five minutes during eighteen hours, with the insistent recommendation to take every kind of precaution, and to be furnished with the necessary supplies to confront the imminent danger. It was eleven o'clock at night and the call of alarm was growing each moment.
> At that time our religious community got together in the chapel accompanied by lay persons. I had the inspiration of commending our need to Mother Luisita so that she would obtain from Our Lord the grace to be saved from the cyclone.
> Because of fear, no one was able to sleep throughout the night, until five o'clock in the morning, when a tranquil day and clear sky was announced, with the radio's confirmation that the cyclone had taken another route. Afterwards it was learned, through the newspaper, that the cyclone had hit other places causing real disasters.[4]

While implicating the foundress as a powerful intercessory, these stories are not clustered so densely around a particular locale as to suggest unofficial veneration. Canonization would doubtlessly revitalize devotion to Mother Luisa in Atotonilco, as the powerful corpse would at last become acknowledged as sanctified.

On the other hand, the official canonization process is primarily an intra-ecclesial affair. According to bureaucratic protocol, Mother Luisa must progressively assume one of four identities along the legalistic road to holiness. A candidate becomes a "Servant of God" if a local bishop can collect sufficiently persuasive eyewitness accounts of his or her moral virtue to merit a case. If the congregation deems these accounts authentic, the client is deemed "Venerable." In order for the person to become "beatified" and bear the title "Blessed"—the next step—the Vatican must find evidence of an authentic miracle, which is typically a physical healing that physicians cannot attribute to natural causes or theologians cannot attribute to the intercession of other saints. At this point in the process, the church allows both pilgrimages to the candidate's grave and prayers of intercession within the local diocese. Finally, the beatified becomes a "Saint," worthy of veneration throughout the church, if a further miracle can be proved. Today Mother Luisa is considered a "Servant of God," as her case is still awaiting an official review by saint makers in the Vatican.

Mother Luisa's official life story was completed in 1989 by the Vatican biographer Camilio Maccise, with the unadorned and bureaucratic title *The Life and Work of Mother Luisa Josefa of the Most Blessed Sacrament, Foundress of the Congregation of the Carmelite Sisters of the Sacred Heart of Guadalajara, and of the Institute of the Carmelite Sisters of the Most Sacred Heart of Los Angeles.* While the opening preamble of this work stated that the foundress's life was "characterized especially by a religious persecution," the collection of testimonies, biographical details, and moral virtues contained in its main text reveals that during her life Mother Luisa embodied two distinct notions of sanctity, only one of which could be considered oppositional. Before 1924, Mother Luisa was a local saint who blessed and sanctified her home town, Atotonilco. Her portrayal primarily as a victim of religious persecution selectively focuses on the last twenty years of Mother Luisa's eighty-year-long life, suggesting that the sanctity of the foundress has been constructed in such a way as to maximize her chances for elevation to at least "Venerable" status by the conservative Pope John Paul II.

On the evening of Maria Luisa de la Peña's birth on June 21, 1866, Mexican society could be described as a modern nation-state comprising many medieval-styled villages and cities. Many townships like Atotonilco retained much of the feudal social structure first introduced by Spanish conquistadors in the sixteenth century. The important terms of this relationship had been codified in the sixteenth-century policy of *Patronato Real,* royal patronage, granted by the papacy to Spanish royalty. In short, Spain had been executor in the colonial New World of a host of responsibilities previously reserved for the papacy, including the appointment of clergy and bishops, allotment of church lands, and, in return, the collection of a portion of church revenues. Even more radically, the Council of the Indies, the governmental overseer of Spanish colonization in the Americas, reserved the final decision regarding which papal bulls could be sent to the American colonies. In return for royal protection, the church became, from the Spanish perspective, the "civilizing" force in the New World, responsible for the spiritual conquest of indigenous American peoples.[5]

From its inception, the federal government's policy of regulating the church swung periodically between the poles of toleration of and conflict with the church. Thus, while the senate voted in 1826 to continue the state's protection of the church as outlined in the *Patronato,* liberal clergyman José Maria Luis Mora's anticlerical party concurrently lobbied for the widespread curtailment of the church's social activities. These restrictions included the elimination of church-run schools and male monastic orders, and separate laws of jurisprudence for clergy; they contained, as well, close state monitoring of ecclesiastical finances. Many of these regulations were incorporated into Mexico's constitution in 1857, catalyzing widespread revolt throughout the country. President Benito Juarez temporarily succeeded in crushing the insurgence and enacted a host of laws further restricting the clergy in his Laws of Reform, nationalizing all church property in the process. Then, in a dramatic counterattack, supporters of the church in 1864 invited Maximilian of Hapsburg to reign as king in Mexico, and, with the military support of Napoleon III, Catholic monarchy was established for a brief time in the country. Finally, in 1867, nationalists succeeded in killing Maximilian, and Juarez returned from exile in the United States to resume power. In spite of further insurgence throughout the 1870s, the Laws of Reform were grafted onto the constitution in 1873, irreversibly depriving the church of its colonial powers and privileges.

Notwithstanding the relationship between church and state on the national level, small agricultural towns like Atotonilco El Alto in the rolling hill country of southeast Jalisco retained much of their colonial blending of the social and religious order throughout the nineteenth century. Under the presidency of Porfirio Díaz (1876–1911), the Laws of Reform remained but were not enforced, and the church actually experienced a resurgence of activity. By order of Pope Leo XIII's Apostolic Delegation to Mexico, four new ecclesiastical provinces and eleven new dioceses were established under Díaz's leadership.[6] Numbers of priests and bishops increased, and formerly exiled monastic orders returned to the country.

The de la Peña family into which Maria Luisa was born as one of nine siblings was a particularly wealthy, landholding family of Atotonilco, and the constant maintenance of class identity constituted an important dimension of their social life. Bonds of patronage and philanthropy in particular were crucial in maintaining connections between the family and the lower classes of Atotonilco. Maria Luisa's father, Don Epigmenio de la Peña

Ibarra, is described in the foundress's biography as "something like the pa-triarch of the town" and portrayed accordingly: he is the host of frequent and lavish festivals, which seem to have been intended as an important part of Maria Luisa's informal education as a member of Atotonilco's aristocratic class.[7] As an adolescent she was once invited to pose as the queen of a bullfight, the typical accompaniment to the fiestas still allowed during the Díaz era. Her accouterments were decidedly Spanish, reflecting her family's place in Mexican society, stratified since colonial times into descending ranks of Spanish, creole, *mestizo,* and Indian heredity. Accompanied by a retinue of Atotonilco's most attractive teenage girls, Maria Luisa, her complexion described in another biography as "very fair, with an almost transparent qual-ity,"[8] appeared before the town as an Iberian vision, "wearing the back comb and Sevillian mantilla, the fan and bouquet of carnations."[9]

The festivals did not, however, seem to produce their desired effect of socializing Maria Luisa; on the contrary, her taste for the religious life, which began to emerge in adolescence, was inextricably tied to distaste for these obligatory rituals of class identity. One particularly poignant story related by Maccise portrays the adolescent feigning sleep rather than endure yet an-other evening serenade at the de la Peña family home after a day's fiesta. "Luisita would be there, apparently asleep. [But] someone stated that she was awake since she was heard saying: 'My God give me a holy heart with a pure intention to please You.'"[10] This crucial tension between the obliga-tions of social aristocracy and the yearning to escape the restrictions of class identity followed Maria Luisa into her marriage. At the age of sixteen she became the bride of a physician by the name of Pascual Rojas, aged thirty, a member of the Mexican upper class as well. "The same social position of the doctor and Luisita drew them to feasts and reunions that finished mold-ing the young girl in the relationship with the people of her class, although certainly she never lost her aversion for the luxury and hustle and bustle of these parties."[11]

It was, ironically, Maria Luisa's agreement to marry Pascual Rojas that in time led to her identity as a Catholic religious. After learning they could not have children, Maria Luisa and Pascual together decided to devote their energies to establishing a hospital in Atotonilco. While Dr. Rojas solicited the donation of a house through his class connections, Maria Luisa joined together with other women of Atotonilco to form a *cofradia,* or confrater-nity of volunteers, to nurse the sick in their homes. The donated house was "solemnly blessed in the presence of almost all the people of the town" in January 1892.[12] The confraternity itself had been established canonically in November of 1891 as the Conference of Saint Vincent de Paul under the aus-pices of the parish priest. For the next fourteen years, Maria Luisa assumed a leadership role in the conference and accompanied her husband on his rounds. As her biographer explains, "The activity, continual contact with people, and the unfavorable situations which at times were not few had intensely changed Luisita's character. She no longer was a delicate and shy young lady. She became a strong woman in full action who knew how to take advantage of opportunities, and she kept in her heart the treasures of daily experience."[13] And so this life continued for Maria Luisa until the untimely death of Pascual in 1896, at which time she took vows of chastity and returned home to the de la Peña ranch. From there she resumed her duties as a member of the confraternity, nursing the sick in their homes.

In 1904, eight years after Pascual's death, Maria Luisa left Atotonilco to begin her formal religious career as a cloistered Carmelite nun. It could be argued, however, that the aspects of Mother Luisa's character leading to posthumous claims of her sanctity had been shaped and expressed even before her taking of vows. Maria Luisa's apparently deep-rooted distaste for aristocratic fanfare, her desire to work both before and after her husband's death amidst the lower classes of Atotonilco, and her status as a woman in the traditional Mexican social order characterize the foundress as what Victor Turner would classify as a "liminal" being. Barred from assuming a public role of power and choosing not to identify with traditional class-based roles assigned to her by her family, the young woman Maria Luisa lived even before her official religious life largely "betwixt and between" the social boundaries of her inherited culture. There she could mingle with the disenfranchised, weak, and oppressed members of her local village in support and solidarity, momentarily to obliterate or even reverse traditional hierarchical distinctions of social ranking in what Turner calls "communitas."[14]

Mother Luisa's biography offers a particularly graphic profile of her status as a leader among the marginalized members of Atotonilco society in the twilight Marian devotions she began organizing soon after Pascual Rojas's death. The same workers whom she had visited throughout the mornings would regularly descend from the town's hills in the evening and gather at the de la Peña ranch, where Maria Luisa would lead them in Marian prayers as well as distribute material assistance to those in need. It is recorded that some of these peasants would arrive with gifts of flowers for the young widow. "The peasants still remember how happy Luisita was when, in the evening, they would arrive for the recitation of the rosary," Maccise writes. "They would present their bouquets of wild flowers. 'Every flower is like a Hail Mary to the Blessed Virgin,' Luisita would say as she received the humble gifts for the Most Holy Virgin."[15]

With Maria Luisa and Marian prayer as the focal point of the villagers' pilgrimage, the role of these gatherings was not, as in her father's conspicuously lavish and public fiestas, to reinforce social differentiation, but rather to level hierarchy and diffuse tensions between workers and overseers on the hacienda. With the implicit blessing of the aristocratic widow, workers could express their displeasure at the hacienda overseer through the use of Catholic rituals themselves: "As everywhere, also in the haciendas were found the less fervent, like the rigid administrator who felt hurt by the acts of mortification performed by his subjects under the orientations of the Servant of God. However neither he nor anybody else could have denied the benefit that Luisita's presence meant to the peasants."[16] During the course of the day, children of the workers felt comfortable playing with Maria Luisa on her hacienda porch swing and even eating with her in the ranch at night.[17]

Maria Luisa's decision to work with her husband had doubtlessly reflected a desire to live beyond the strict limitations imposed upon her as the wife of an aristocrat. Far from being restricted to the healing of the sick, the hospital in the Catholic history of Mexico addressed the needs of the poor and infirm of all kinds. In the early years of the hospital, Pascual and Maria Luisa extended their aid to include moral and financial assistance. Under Mother Luisa's leadership, the hospital continued to function as more than a medical station. After taking formal religious vows, Mother Luisa would expand the institution to include a school, which her order staffed until 1910; Archbishop Orozco y Jimenez declared at that time, however, that "teaching and the care of the sick were ... incompatible" and restricted Mother Luisa and her sisters to teaching.[18] Before this decision, however, the hospital served as a formal institution through which Mexican women, otherwise defined socially as mothers and wives, could serve their society in a number of ways.[19] For Maria Luisa, daily contact with the poor and downtrodden both reflected and reinforced her identification with Atotonilco's marginalized members.

And as the pages of her biography reveal, it was precisely in the marginal and concealed places of Mother Luisa's society that religious power coursed and flourished. As virtual custodians of the private, domestic world, women in particular were spiritual leaders within their families and close circles of friends. Maria Luisa's own spiritual formation was shaped not in the public institutions of the church, but by her childhood tutor, Agapita. Requested by the de la Peña family to educate the young Maria Luisa, who was too sickly to attend school as a child, Agapita not only prepared her for the first Holy Communion but imparted a mystical belief in the power of prayer and a vision of the world as infused with a spiritual presence. Mother Luisa would remember Agapita much later in life; according to one interview, Mother Luisa related stories of her religious tutelage to a fellow sister as they hid from federal troops in 1926: "At the end of that happy day [of my religious profession], both Mother and I went into hiding together in the house of Victoria Alatorre where we remained for some time. She spoke to me about Agapita, her old servant and companion of her childhood, the one who taught her how to pray, how to contemplate the flowers of the field and the morning dawns and sunsets."[20] In another interview, Mother Luisa is remembered "continually praising God for the beauty the fields presented at dawn, for the flowers and birds" as she and a group of sisters fled on foot through the hills from Atotonilco to nearby San Francisco in 1925.[21]

In his exploration of the power of liminality, Turner has suggested that, despite their purportedly dangerous and threatening abilities, the lives of sanctified individuals ultimately uphold the very social structures from which they distinguish themselves. Mother Luisa and the apparently charismatic women with whom she surrounded herself certainly worked to support the status quo of Atotonilco through their traditional Catholic teachings. A few brief glimpses into Mother Luisa's teaching orders in Atotonilco suggests an interdependent relationship between the female-controlled, liminal, religious power and the male-controlled, public, social power of her village consistent with broader analyses of Mexican Catholicism. One account of life in a Carmelite schoolroom records, for example, that the "Blessed Sacrament was exposed after Mass, and the students took turns in adoration before the Blessed Sacrament. The most deserving two students occupied the special kneelers as the rest of the students adored from the pews."[22] Another reveals that "every first Friday of the month, the students attended Mass and received Holy Communion. This day the report cards were distributed by Mother Luisita who would add a small gift, such as a medal or holy card, among the students who had the highest marks. There would be a procession with a statue of the Infant of Jesus carried by the awarded students who had the privilege to keep the statue in their classroom all day."[23] Consistent with Turner's analysis, Maria Luisa's initial flight from the fiestas of Don Epigmenio paradoxically led to her orchestration of a similar sanctification of rank in the classrooms of her village.

Had events in Mexico's national history not taken their fateful course toward revolution, Mother Luisa may well have remained something of a local religious heroine, attracting attention and favor to her town while living and praying on its social margins. The biography suggests it was natives of Atotonilco who first recognized her most clearly as an extraordinarily spiritual woman—whose alleged powers were only intensified by her commitment to a monastic life:

> In this town of Atotonilco, Mother Luisita was known as a religious who was very close to God, very loving and always available to anyone who sought her wise and concerned advice. When I was a student [at the school

run by the Carmelites,] the principal of the school announced a visit of Mother Luisita to the convent. She said that a representative from every grade would be chosen to welcome Mother Luisita on her arrival. I wished very much to be one of those chosen for this privilege. However my disappointment was great when I heard that the teachers had selected girls who might have a possible vocation to the religious life. I felt hurt, and tried to hide my discontentment with an apparent indifference. *I thought to myself, they say that Mother Luisita is a saint; if that is so, she will know that I want to be a religious.* I went back home from school pondering these thoughts in my mind. Not very long after I arrived home, Tomasito the faithful servant of the hospital came saying that Mother Luisita wished to see me. *Immediately I went to the hospital filled with joy, and at the same time with fright, realizing that Mother was indeed a saint, since she knew that I wanted to see her. As I arrived at the hospital a sister presented me to her. I greeted her trying to avoid her glance.* [italics added][24]

The story continues with Mother Luisa anticipating the girl's desire to become a religious and consoling her that, despite her reputation as a "little imp," she would become a religious if her vocation was authentic. The foundress's legendary reputation, charisma, and allegedly supernatural powers had apparently developed during her upbringing and early life in Atotonilco, where today her grave remains a site of sporadic pilgrimage.

Conflicts between church and state on the national level, however, would eventually come to affect and transform the course of events in Mother Luisa's religious career. Until the overthrow of Porfirio Díaz in 1910, the Mexican church had been making a steady comeback in political involvement, spurred on by Pope Leo XIII's encyclical letter *Rerum Novarum* of 1896. Citing the new social inequities created by industrialization, Leo XIII had exhorted clergy and nation-states alike to address the needs of the working class. In Mexico, the letter spawned the organization of hundreds of Catholic Worker circles dedicated to uplifting the economic condition of both Indians and industrial and agricultural workers. In 1911, Díaz's successor, Francisco Madero, permitted the formation of the National Catholic party. It succeeded in popular elections over the next two years, sending four senators and twenty-nine federal deputies to the national congress, as well as electing governors and winning control of state legislatures in both Zacatecas and Jalisco. In the Jalisco legislature, National Party delegates enacted laws mandating employer-sponsored accident insurance for workers and enforcing Sunday as a work-free day of rest. While the renewal of political involvement brought a new identity to the church as a co-worker, it also set the stage for a new era of anticlericalism.

In 1913 Madero was assassinated in a coup d'état by the Mexican military, led by Victoriano Huerta. Unfortunately for the church, Catholic leaders had withdrawn their support for Madero in the wake of their own political successes just prior to his assassination. Thus, when the forces of Venustiano Carranza succeeded in ousting Huerta and assuming the presidency, anticlericals within the new administration suspected the church of conspiring with the coup. It was therefore under Carranza's presidency that, in 1917, the 1857 Constitution was updated with new articles aimed against the church. Despite their initial nonenforcement, articles 5, 27, and 130 became the rallying points for subsequent church-state battles. These amendments explicitly prohibited monks and nuns from taking monastic vows, the church from buying or selling any property, and priests from claiming rights as Mexican citizens, respectively.

In the meantime, Catholic clergy and laity alike had been mounting a defense against the Carranza administration. Jalisco, again, came to play a central role in Catholic organization: in 1913, under the leadership of a former Guadalajaran philosophy professor, the Asociación Católica de la Juventud Mexicana (Catholic Association of Mexican Youth) was established to educate Mexican youth in the evils of secularization and the necessity of Catholic principles in establishing a morally sound society. The association spread quickly throughout the nation, and in 1918, Anacleto Gonzalez Florez, a former charismatic leader in the National Party born and raised in Mother Luisa's home province of Los Altos, founded the Unión Popular (Popular Union) to supplement the association's educational activities with a program of Catholic social action. The Union flourished predominantly in Jalisco, with approximately eighty thousand subscribers to its weekly paper, *Gladium,* by 1924.[25]

It took two decades before the escalating tensions between church and state interfered directly with Mother Luisa's religious career. After a brief stay in 1904 as a cloistered Carmelite in Guadalajara, she had received permission from the archbishop of Guadalajara to return to Atotonilco, where, together with six other women from the local parish, she quietly resumed work among its sick and poor. Over the next five years, the group was transformed into a new, private religious community, culminating with the reception of its own rule in 1909 from the archbishop. The first winds of change had been felt in Atotonilco in 1920, when the newly appointed Archbishop Orozco y Jimenez of Guadalajara, following Vatican directives to consolidate and centralize the Mexican church, instructed Mother Luisa to affiliate her local community with an extant third order.[26] Subsequently, she and her congregation had taken the profession of vows with the Third Order of Carmelites, and the foundress was renamed Mother Maria Luisa Josefa of the Most Blessed Sacrament in 1921. Resuming their teaching mission with no further interruptions, the newly reconstituted Carmelites went on to expand their order beyond Atotonilco, to Guadalajara in 1922 and San Francisco Los Altos in 1924.

It was with the ascendancy of Plutarco Elías Calles to the Mexican presidency in 1924 that Mother Luisa and her order were abruptly thrust into the spotlight of the nation's religiopolitical conflicts, signaling an end to the foundress's previous life as a local saint and beginning a new chapter in her vocation as a religious. Calles made the fateful decision to enforce aggressively the anticlerical articles of the 1917 constitution, raising antipathies between zealous Catholic and national leaders to a boiling point. Following a takeover of a church in Mexico City by governmental agents disguised as priests, the Liga Nacional de Defensa Religiosa (National League for Religious Defense) was formed in 1925 to defend the church from government persecution. While the League stopped short of explicitly advocating violence to resist further military excursions, it warned that the government's activities were precipitating conflict. It also became the umbrella organization uniting the Catholic Association of Mexican Youth and the Popular Union, which pledged support days after its establishment. While no single military event marked the beginning of the Cristero Revolt—as the fighting between League and the Mexican government would come to be known—Calles's mandate to state governors to enforce the anticlerical articles effectively started armed conflict in February 1926. Rebellion was nationwide but concentrated in Jalisco, where both popular support and organizational infrastructure were strongest. Archbishop Orozco y Jimenez categorically withdrew his support for any use of violence among Catholics and went into hiding somewhere in Jalisco between 1927 and 1929.

Like the majority of Catholics in Mexico and even in Jalisco, Mother Luisa and her order were trapped in a conflict over which they had little control. Notwithstanding the large army of Cristero guerrillas, constituted primarily of *rancheros,* or ranch owners, the vast majority of Mexican Catholics shrank from military involvement, as revolutionary and Catholic intellectuals polarized church-state issues and vilified each other. Pages of the foundress's biography are filled with stories of the Carmelites' flight from federal raids, dispersion into smaller groups, and hiding in private homes. A contemporary sister related one such incident in 1926 to Mother Luisa's biographers:

> One day, about 3:00 P.M. the Federal forces entered Atotonilco. The Mistress of Novices, Mother Manuela of the Conception, gave orders to all the novices to leave the house. My companion and I, both of us novices, fled immediately in anguish and fear trying in vain to find refuge from the bullets crossing above our heads. All the houses had their doors closed. Suddenly we met a servant of the hospital who took us to the place where

Mother Foundress and other professed sisters were hiding. This was a hiding place about a yard and a half covered with a block of straw. There sequestered was our Mother Luisita with fifteen professed sisters and two novices. Also hiding there were the statues of Our Lady of Mount Carmel and of our Mother Saint Teresa of Avila, as well as the vestments used for the Mass, and the sacred vessels. The space was so small that we had to squeeze together in a space on the floor for someone to sit for awhile and rest. Thus we were, when we heard the Federals coming into the house. They brought their horses and were trying to find food for their animals. This was indeed a big worry for Mother! To suppose [sic] they should take away the straw that covered the entrance and find us there! Fear and anguish showed on her face and she said: "What are we going to do, my daughters! Place yourselves in the Hands of God and make an act of contrition. If they find us, they will certainly kill us!" . . . Meanwhile the shooting between the Federals and the Christian troops could be heard in the distance, and the voices of the soldiers threatening the owner of the house for the purpose of getting food for their horses could be also heard. Nothing happened! The soldiers went away without doing any harm. After a whole day of prayer, fasting and good preparation for death, we left the house at dusk time.[27]

As the hostilities mounted, the sisters found themselves increasingly in hiding or fleeing to nearby villages for protection. In 1926, the Carmelites' house in San Francisco was shut down, and the following year the Atotonilco community relocated to Guadalajara. To conceal their identity as religious they shared an apartment with a family and were visited periodically by a priest pretending to buy food from the tenants. By June of 1927, even Guadalajara was too dangerous for the sisters. Mother Luisa, together with two other sisters, boarded a Southern Pacific train headed toward Nogales, Arizona.

Over the next two years several Carmelites followed their foundress to the United States. In Los Angeles the sisters were in high demand by the church, as countless other Mexican exiles had fled across the border to escape hostilities. Some sisters continued their original work among Mexican refugees, first in Long Beach and later in downtown Los Angeles, while others were sent to the newly opened Santa Maria College in Moraga, California, to perform menial chores. The biography records a visit to the sisters during these years by Archbishop Orozco y Jimenez—whose whereabouts were unknown at this time to the government of Mexico. After paying a visit to Santa Maria College, the archbishop announced that menial labor was "certainly not meant for . . . [the] community."[28] Accordingly, the sisters would be rerouted by the diocese in 1930 to Duarte, California, where the foundress established a tuberculosis clinic. In October 1929, Mother Luisa returned to Jalisco, leaving behind sisters who soon began accepting American-born postulants and novices from the diocese.

The final years of Mother Luisa's life were characterized by the expansion of her order to include additional Mexican chapters outside Jalisco. Relations between church and state continued to be tense in Jalisco, with the arrest and temporary imprisonment of five sisters in 1932. Archbishop Orozco y Jimenez emerged from hiding in 1929, only to be asked by the government to leave the country lest his presence help continue antirevolutionary sentiments. He accepted the request, returning to Guadalajara only in 1935 in anticipation of his own death, which occurred the following year. As the Carmelite order continued to grow, its novitiate moved to Guadalajara, while the motherhouse remained in Atotonilco. After her return from the United States, Mother Luisa made Guadalajara her new home, while circulating periodically throughout her houses in both Mexico and the United States. Early in the morning on February 11, 1937, after longstanding health complications caused by diabetes, she died in Guadalajara, leaving the Carmelite Sisters of the Third Order to continue her charism.

Even as it attempted to ease tensions between church and state, the Vatican unwittingly did its share to exacerbate tensions between Mother Luisa's order and the Mexican nation-state by uprooting the order from its ties to the local community of Atotonilco. The "Romanization" of the Carmelites from a local community into an affiliate of the Third Order Carmelites in 1920 was a last-minute effort by the church to shield the sisters from mounting political turmoil, part of a broader reversal in 1918 of Mexico's colonial *Patronato* privilege. Rome asserted its unchallenged sovereignty in establishing new religious communities, a claim never before made in the country's history. Pre-existing Mexican congregations like Mother Luisa's Atotonilco sisters were incorporated into extant communities directly accountable to the Vatican, giving Rome a way to bypass the independent bishopric in its control of monks and nuns. In the meantime, Rome pursued an increasingly conciliatory course with the Mexican government, urging bishops to submit peacefully to state sovereignty despite its initial condemnation of the anticlerical articles of the 1917 constitution. By 1921, the Mexican government was extending a warm welcome to Rome's new apostolic delegate.

What the Vatican underestimated, however, was the centrality of place and community in the Mexican Catholic tradition. From the earliest days of colonialism, the saints of Spanish Catholicism had taken up new homes amidst the ruins of the Aztec civilization, blessing both the settlements and local societies of New World Mexico. Like the Mexicans themselves, the new saints were *mestizos*, Spanish in name but Indian in their association with local traditions, as exemplified in the legend of La Virgen de Guadalupe, national patroness and most beloved intercessor. According to the traditional tale, on December 12, 1531, Juan Diego—a recent Nahuatl convert to the Spanish faith—was walking past the sacred hill and sacrificial site of To-nantzin, mother of the Aztec gods. A brown-skinned visage appeared on the summit, revealing herself as the Virgin of Guadalupe, a Catholic virgin named after a local village in Spain. He hurried to tell the bishop of the miraculous sighting, but the story fell on deaf ears. Following a second appearance and another failed attempt to convince the prelate, La Virgen appeared again amidst a flowering rose bush miraculously blossomed in the dead of winter. Diego appeared to the bishop a third time, unfurling his cloak to spill flowers upon the floor and revealing an image of the Virgin emblazoned upon the cloth. This was enough, it was said, to convince the church of an authentic miracle.

In official church teachings, La Virgen is none other than the Virgin Mary, mother of Jesus, who appeared to bless the faith of the pious Mexican converts. In popular observance, however, she has been adopted as the mother of Mexico. Today the alleged cloak of Juan Diego hangs in a church in Mexico City near Tepeyac, drawing thousands of pilgrims each year to the former Aztec capital, Tenochtitlán. Throughout the country, local Catholic saints have similarly come to incorporate myths and rituals of Amerindian holy beings, typically fusing elements of both Spanish Catholic and Nahuatl cultures in their legends. It is this fusion of Catholic and communal identity, more than any development in the country's institutional church, that has undermined the modern nation's claim to embody Mexican identity. But when Rome withdrew its support of local orders like Mother Luisa's Atotonilco community in 1920, it left a vacuum in the religious imagination that antifederalist Catholic nationalists easily filled. For the faithful, Mother Luisa had to belong somewhere, and to some people. The Cristeros simply adopted her into a new and larger community, whose boundaries extended to include all of Mexico.

An especially revealing illustration of the foundress's emerging nationalist symbolism can be found in an account of her 1924 reception by the residents of San Francisco, where she had traveled to open the first of her schools outside of Atotonilco. This village was the birthplace of Anacleto Gonzalez Florez, founder of the Popular Union and main leader of the Cristeros, who was captured and executed by Mexican federal troops in 1927 as he declared, "I die, but God does not die. Viva Cristo Rey!"[29] As the Carmelites from Ato-tonilco made their way to San Francisco on foot and by donkey, they encountered an unexpected welcoming party:

> On their way, the travelers made a stop at the foot of an oak tree to recite Evening Prayer and Compline. They put on the holy habit, and continued

on their way. A short time later, three cars met the sisters coming to pick them up. The cars were beautifully adorned. The emblem of the Carmelite Order formed with daisies was displayed in front of one of the cars. Another car was showing a monogram of Mary, and a third one was also beautifully decorated. In these cars came the pastor [sic] of San Francisco, Don Ramon Ugarte and Don Ignacio Valezquez respectively. As the Sisters arrived at a place called La Loma Piedra, they found a double row of men on horseback, which constituted the escort of the cars. At the entrance of the town, the ladies of San Francisco were formed in perfect lines ending with the boys and girls of the town. Then the peal of bells was heard, and the ground appeared carpeted with flowers. As the religious entered the town, Don Ignacio Valezquez shouted at the top of his voice, "Long live the benefactors!" At this, the whole town applauded with enthusiasm. It was then that Don Ramon Ugarte, recalling the triumphant entry of Jesus to Jerusalem, said: "Today is the triumphant entry, Good Friday will follow!" The religious came out of the cars and went immediately to the Parish Church. The image of Saint Francis of Assisi, which had been covered before, was unveiled. The Pastor took the Sisters to the sanctuary. The Magnificat was intoned at the end of which all the people sang the Salve Regina.[30]

In a blending of local Catholic ritual reminiscent of Don Epigmenio's fiestas and decidedly militaristic regalia—parade-like columns of men, women, and horse; a procession of decorated automobiles—the reception of the Carmelites in this one village reflects their unwitting adoption into the nationalistic Catholic movement mounting in Jalisco at the time.

The biography of Mother Luisa thus contains not one but two portrayals of sainthood that both sanctify a certain ideal of religiopolitical community. The first model is that of the local saint whose holiness serves to sanctify the existing social boundaries of her native Atotonilco. The second is a model of the national saint vying with the modern state for political support of the modern community. This transforming meaning of Mother Luisa's sanctity compressed in the course of a few months a similar change in the meaning of European sainthood that unfolded over centuries. Documented again in the work of Victor Turner, the shift from medieval feudalism sanctified by Catholicism to democratic nation-states sanctioned by the Enlightenment inevitably changed the political meaning of Catholic sanctity in the modern West.

> Despite obvious resemblances and historical connections between archaic, medieval, and modern pilgrimages, we would argue that there is a significant difference between pilgrimages taken after the Industrial Revolution and all previous types. In the scientific and technological age, pilgrimage is becoming what [Clifford] Geertz . . . has described as a "meta-social commentary" on the troubles of this epoch of wars and revolutions

with its increasing signs of industrial damage to the natural environment. Like certain other . . . genres of symbolic action elaborated in the leisure time of modern society, pilgrimage [and devotion to saints] has become an implicit critique of the life-style characteristic of the encompassing social structure. Its emphasis on transcendental, rather than mundane, ends and means; its generation of communitas [i.e., egalitarian community]; its search for the roots of ancient, almost vanishing virtues as the underpinning of social life, even in its structured expressions—all have contributed to the dramatic resurgence of pilgrimage [in the modern era].[31]

The great European pilgrimage sites of the nineteenth and twentieth centuries upon which his work is based—La Sallette and Lourdes in France, Medjugorje in Bosnia-Hercegovina—are thus centered on places where visionaries have received messages urging modern society to repent and return to a life based on older Catholic teachings, lest the wrath of God destroy it. These messages are invariably delivered by the Virgin Mary, a Catholic image of universal appeal, rather than by a local saint known to and acknowledged by a few.

Recognizing the volatile power of such religious symbolism, the modern Mexican nation-state, victorious in its battles with the Cristeros, has been extremely vigilant of the church ever since the end of the revolt in 1929. Religious orders like the Tertiary Carmelite Sisters of Guadalajara survived only by becoming invisible; clerics and religious alike were forbidden to wear ecclesial dress in public until 1991. As the Mexican nation ushered in its own saints—revolutionary heroes and martyrs—the Catholic saints thus disappeared or left the country, some to the more welcoming shore of the Rio Grande. The American order founded by Mother Luisa during her exile to Los Angeles retained the Tridentine habits and devotions of their foundress, blending indistinguishably with other orders of women religious in the United States. They also continued the order's charism of service to the local community, a prominent feature of Mother Luisa's own vocation during her years in Atotonilco. Since the transformations in American culture and religion since the 1960s, however, the foundress's later status as an enemy of the state has been emphasized by Los Angeles sisters and Vatican II biographers as part of a larger effort to redefine the ideological contours of the church.

With the rise to power of Pope John Paul II, official canonization has become a popular means for the conservative papacy to define the limits of normative Catholicism in the wake of the more liberal Vatican Council. As of 1994, Pope John Paul II had granted no less than 596 beatifications and 267 canonizations, an astounding number when compared to the records of previous pontiffs (Table 2.1).[32]

TABLE 2.1

Pope	Reign	Beatifications	Canonizations
Pius X	1903–1914	7	4
Benedict XV	1914–1922	3	4
Pius XI	1922–1939	11	26
Pius XII	1939–1958	23	33
John XXIII	1958–1963	4	10
Paul VI	1963–1978	31	21
John Paul I	1978 (33 days)	0	0
Total:		79	98[33]

Between beatifications and canonizations, by the mid-1990s the current pontiff had conferred his blessing on almost five times as many Venerables as his predecessors combined. Indeed, in a July 1994 meeting with his cardinals to discuss the papal celebrations of the year 2000, John Paul promised that a defense of his canonization record would constitute one of its main themes. In his preliminary statements, John Paul explained that his enthusiasm for making saints was nothing more or less than a result of Vatican II's understanding of sanctity as a "universal vocation to holiness."[34]

It is not too difficult to see, however, how the pontiff's penchant for making saints reflects his more general "restoration" of the church. John Paul has discovered the effectiveness of the "communion of saints" as a symbol banding together the increasingly decentralized churches of the post–Vatican II church, as well as a powerful ritual linking local churches to Rome. He is the first pope in Catholic history to preside at canonizations outside of the Vatican; in 1984, for example, the first beatification in North America was conducted with the beatification of Venerable Marie-Leonie in Montreal.[35] And while popes are not themselves solely responsible for the making of saints, they do, like American presidents appointing Supreme Court justices, wield the power to shape the ideological contours of the Congregation for the Causes of Saints. Former Congregation prelate Cardinal Pietro Pallazini, for example, was both a champion of the conservative Opus Dei movement and an outspoken critic of John XXIII. Under his leadership from 1980 to 1989 and under the guidance of his successor, Cardinal Angelo Felici, the doctrinal conservatism of candidates has been all but assured.

As the decidedly backlogged Congregation for the Causes of Saints has not yet reviewed her case, Mother Luisa remains today a Servant of God. In his study of modern canonization, however, Kenneth Woodward has concluded that, under the conservative papacy of John Paul II, "the general principle is clear: once a cause is accepted by Rome, the expectation is that the candidate will at least be declared heroically virtuous [i.e., Venerable] or a martyr."[36] He has further concluded that "the more conventional and in-nocuous a candidate (typically, founders of religious orders), the better his or her chances of eventually being declared a saint."[37] Mother Luisa's review will center on her official biography and will emphasize the events of her life after 1924, the year the Mexican church became embroiled in the politics of the Mexican Revolution. This is certainly the aspect of the foundress's life that has most interested the American sisters, not only because she came to Los Angeles in flight from the Revolution, but also because the opposition between church and state that characterizes their order today is most pro-nounced during this period.

Pope John Paul II has good reasons of his own to accentuate the perils of modern life rather than its promises. Having experienced anti-Catholic persecution under both Nazi and Soviet regimes, the pontiff enthusiastically endorses a vision of the church both in tension and in battle with the forces of the world, and is thus predisposed at least to declare venerable if not to beatify or even canonize the foundress of the countercultural American order. As the last two chapters have demonstrated, issues of cultural and re-ligious identity intersect at every important juncture of the Carmelites' post-conciliar history. The split between liberal and neotraditionalist sisters clearly emerged in the 1960s, when Mexican Carmelites living in the United States chose to retain their traditional lifestyle and devotions. This decision was quickly politicized, however, as the liberal church—refashioning itself in im-itation of the democratic culture of Anglo-Protestant America—associated such culturally specific practices with an outmoded and culturally irrelevant past. With the election of Karol Wojtyla as Pope John Paul II, however, the sisters found support in a pontiff whose own Catholicism had been shaped by the contingencies of Polish history. In the ongoing canonization process of Mother Luisa, Mexican history itself has been read selectively to support an oppositional view of the modern church.

The next four chapters of this study will turn to an overview of the Carmelites' reception in four parishes in the present-day United States, con-tinuing to illustrate the mutually reinforcing relationship between Catholic and cultural identities. Through their interaction with lay Catholics in Los Angeles, the Arizona borderlands, and Miami, the Carmelites have found support for their neotraditionalist church in communities descended from Spanish Catholic, New World cultures. Like the older, Mexican-born women of the Carmelite order, the parishioners in these places see the Tridentine lifestyle and devotions of the sisters as a continuation of their normative Catholic tradition, embellishing stories of the Carmelites' tradition with the details of local history and culture. While such elaborations are part of the "official" Carmelite history itself, the cultural features of the lay narratives are more pronounced and ultimately more central to their understanding of Catholic identity. Finally, the two parishes for whom neotraditionalism holds little appeal—SS. Felicitas and Perpetua in San Marino and St. Rose of Lima in Cleveland—turn like the liberal sisters to the symbols of Anglo-Protestant culture in imagining a more democratic or socially heterogeneous model of church community.

3

The Urban Cloister:
Religious and Ethnic
Identity in Los Angeles

S MALL, BUBBLING FOUNTAINS and statues of saints add to an aura of serenity and holiness at the Carmelites' motherhouse in Alhambra, California. Together with its northern neighbors San Marino and Pasadena, the Los Angeles suburb is self-consciously named and designed to reflect the ideal of single-home ownership in a stress-free environment reminiscent—in the Anglo-Protestant imagination—of Mediterranean cultures. Surrounded by a black, wrought-iron fence, the hacienda-style motherhouse is well located to serve both as a retreat center for Catholic laypersons and the center for the spiritual formation of Carmelite novices. Situated just four blocks off a busy main thoroughfare, the Carmelites' upper-middle-class neighborhood is nevertheless quiet and still, while its location reverberates with historical significance in the world of American Catholic monasticism. East Alhambra Road earned its designation on the arcane map of American monasticism as the site of the first Carmelite monastery in the United States. Today it is home of Mother Luisa's American Carmelites, a Carmelite-staffed parish next door to the motherhouse, and a cloistered Carmelite monastery for men.

Located ten miles to the east of downtown Los Angeles—the gateway to the San Gabriel Valley, as the bridge underneath Interstate 10 proudly declares—Alhambra continues to stand in the city as a monument to the American Dream, Los Angeles style. Like the Midwestern immigrants to Los Angeles before them, Chinese and Armenian families today aspire to live in

bedroom communities like Alhambra, which, despite showing signs of en-
croaching gang violence, still represent a vast improvement over the poorer,
more oppressive environments that are also Los Angeles. Built atop the bar-
ren deserts of southern California, the Los Angeles metropolis is an intri-
cate geographical labyrinth carefully marking the racial and class status of
its citizens in alternating scenarios of opulence and destitution. Not all neighborhoods are graced with the architectural finesse and serenity of East Alhambra Road.

It is clear enough from an overview of the Carmelites' postconciliar history that the identity of the American Carmelites has been shaped by both
the aftermath of Vatican II and the transformation of their foundress by Vatican biographers. This observation is not to suggest that the Carmelites are
misleading themselves or the public in their claim to be continuing a lifestyle
and advancing a theology that has roots in the preconciliar church. What it
is to suggest is that the order's emphasis on boundaries—their defense of
the official doctrinal teachings of the magisterium, and the monastic "essentials" of poverty, chastity, and obedience—has come to dominate its identity and mission since the Vatican II council. As Eric Hobsbawm has suggested in his study of the "invented traditions" of nationalism and ethnic
identity in the modern era, self-conscious claims of tradition commonly arise
as a defensive reaction precisely to those historical situations where change
and erosion of the past are accelerated. The neotraditionalist Carmelites have
made it their mission to counteract what they see as unmanageable and de-
structive changes in the American church since Vatican II by highlighting
the "unchanging essentials" of Roman Catholicism.

What is less clear from the Carmelites' ecclesiastical history are the reasons for the appeal of neotraditionalist Catholicism in most of their American parishes, which today include four communities within the Los Angeles diocese, as well as three others outside California. Designations of
Catholicism as liberal, conservative, or even neotraditionalist, which may
clarify theological positions within the church, are not particularly helpful
in explaining the appeal of neotraditionalism to the laity. Those communities that have appropriated the Catholicism of the sisters are all descended
from Spanish Catholic, New World cultures—Filipino, Mexican, and
Cuban—and have appropriated neotraditionalism as part of their normative socioreligious pasts. The maintenance of boundaries is a common
theme uniting lay parishioners and the sisters, but it is a maintenance of ethnic and social boundaries—rather than theological or ecclesiological ones—
that dominates the interviews with the sisters' constituents. In those parishes
where the doctrinal conservatism of the Carmelites goes uncontested, lay
Catholics recount narratives of traditional cultural mores undergoing changes

in the United States, weaving together perceptions of the traditional sisters with reflections on the fate and future of their communities. And where the Carmelites are rejected, parishioners discuss the incompatibility between neotraditionalism and their own idealizations of community, which invariably extol Anglo-Protestant values of individualism and/or ideological pluralism.

In Los Angeles, the order's decidedly dystopian analysis of American society is easily incorporated by parishioners into moralistic narratives about urban violence, poverty, and disenfranchisement from the hegemonic Anglo-Protestant culture of the city. The predominantly Filipino parish of Carson welcomes the Carmelite order as a model of normative Catholicism for its children and a shelter from local gangs. The Filipino parish of Long Beach similarly looks to the sisters for safety and also for spiritual support in the economic hardships of relocating to the United States mainland. In La Puente, the predominantly Mexican-American parish has embraced the order as an advocate for the Latino family and also as a shelter from gangs and gang-related violence. In all three of these parishes, the cloistered society of the sisters is embraced as a model for a safe and secure ethnic community, an ethnoreligious enclave described alternately as an "oasis" and as a surrogate family. In contrast to these communities, the affluent, Euro-American parish of Saints Felicitas and Perpetua in San Marino dismisses the Carmelites as hopelessly anachronistic, in a portrayal reminiscent of liberal sisters' characterizations of preconciliar monasticism. Parishioners there retain the Carmelites for their professional acumen as educators, but reject neotraditionalism as undermining their own ethnoreligious enclave: the Los Angeles suburb founded on the allegedly self-evident truths of individual liberty and the uncensored pursuit of happiness.

It is primarily through their work as school teachers and administrators that the Carmelite sisters have become known to parishioners of American dioceses. Their vocation as educators began in Los Angeles in the 1950s as a response to teacher shortages within church-staffed schools throughout the metropolitan area, which followed the population growth in Los Angeles during a World War II economic boom. Prior to this time, the Carmelites had restricted their social outreach services to work at the Saint Teresita tuberculosis clinic in Duarte, California, as well as to retreat work centered in the Alhambra motherhouse. In 1958, the Carmelites came to staff and administer both the Saint Philomena Parochial School in Carson and the Holy Innocents Parochial School in Long Beach; in 1968, they came to staff and run Saint Joseph Parochial School in La Puente. Saints Felicitas and Perpetua Parochial School in San Marino was added as a Carmelite school in 1981.

Of the four Los Angeles County parishes, Saint Philomena in Carson has arguably lived through the most tumultuous demographic changes since its original staffing by the Carmelites in the late 1950s. For the first decade, the parish was located in a mixed Euro-American and Mexican-American residential community marked by single-family homes and light agriculture. Rapid industrialization transforming much of coastal southern California—from Los Angeles south to San Diego—came to change the profile of Carson, however, beginning in the mid-1960s. Agricultural land was converted into industrial parks and strip malls, apartment complexes were built to house lower-income workers, and the ethnic constitution of the neighborhood changed. Filipinos in particular were drawn by employment in Carson's medical device industry. According to interviews with local parishioners, many of the Filipino families who came to Los Angeles during the 1970s were spurred to leave the Philippines for Carson by social and political turmoil in the archipelago. Since the election of Ferdinand E. Marcos as president of the Philippines in 1965, both political and religious freedoms had been progressively curtailed by the state, culminating in the imposition of martial law in 1972. Driven from an oppressive political climate that lasted in the Philippines until the election of Corazon C. Aquino in 1986, and pulled by a thriving economy in southern California, Filipinos arrived in townships like Carson supported by relatives who had migrated to Los Angeles since the 1920s in response to earlier political upheavals.

The Mexican origins and Tridentine observances of Mother Luisa's order have proven fortuitous for the sisters' positive reception at Saint Philomena. Far from representing a neotraditionalist or reactionary Catholic presence to Filipinos, the Carmelites at Carson are seen simply as a continuation of the Catholicism they observed in their homeland. Under the auspices of King Philip II, for whom the archipelago is named, the modern Philippines were founded in 1565 as a Spanish colony fashioned after the sociopolitical and religious image of Spain. Dominican, Augustinian, Jesuit, and Franciscan orders—backed militarily by Spanish armies— carried out the forced conversion of Filipino natives throughout the sixteenth century in what they saw as a spiritual war against demonically inspired animistic practices and worldviews. Notwithstanding either the transfer of the Philippines to the United States in 1898 or the complex interplay of Asian, African, South Pacific, and American cultures in shaping modern Filipino identity, Spanish Catholicism has remained a constant and pervasive aspect of the archipelago's culture throughout the modern era.[1]

In the Carson school and parish, Mother Luisa's Carmelite sisters are met with a mixture of both respect and awe by the laity, who commonly ascribe to them a supernatural and even thaumaturgic status. Native-born Filipinos are apt to kiss the hand of a Carmelite or press her hand to their heads for blessing and to seek out the order for spiritual direction in their private devotional lives.[2] In the words of one lay Catholic, "to know a Carmelite is to know an angel. To me, they're almost like saints."[3] Another parishioner similarly remarked, "The effect they have on people here is phenomenal—they mesmerize people," adding that the Carmelites had restored a sense of mystery to the church that she had not hitherto seen in the Los Angeles archdiocese.[4] Parishioners commonly seek out the sisters to help heal diseases, and the Carson community even boasted an alleged miracle of its own, which one sister speculated might be submitted to Rome for review in Mother Luisa's canonization process. In August of 1995, a local couple approached a sister, asking for the order's prayers in healing the woman's brain tumor. The afflicted parishioner was given a prayer card with a photograph of the aged foundress's face, while the entire school of Saint Philomena commenced praying for the husband and wife. On the night of the woman's surgery, the Carmelites even conducted an all-night prayer vigil in Alhambra. While remains of the brain tumor were detected in postoperative checkups, the purported miracle was said to come as the woman was about to receive chemotherapy: signs of the tumor had vanished without a trace. Additionally, the couple soon thereafter conceived a child together, even though they had previously complained of infertility.[5]

Lay Catholics in Carson saw reflected in the cloistered lifestyle a model of communal solidarity and protection from the dangers of life in contemporary Los Angeles. Parishioners and staff members cited drug addiction, vandalism, and particularly gangs and gang violence as pervasive threats to their neighborhoods and children. Within the boundaries of the Carmelite school and adjoining parish, however, such dangers are perceived to diminish. "We're like a little oasis here," one of the sisters summarized, "surrounded by people who are on our side."[6] Her comments were echoed by lay Catholics who characterized the school as "a great big family"[7] and as providing "a sense of belonging, of love."[8] When gang-inspired insignia began to encroach on the school in the mid 1990s on student notebooks, the Carmelites were quick to write to parents, successfully putting an end to the widespread craze.

In the eyes of Carson parishioners, economic pressures necessitating dual-income families diverted adults away from their responsibilities as parents and family members. The newest and most prominent gangs in Carson in the late 1990s comprised Filipino and also Samoan teenagers, children of two recent immigrant groups that had come to work in the community's light-industry factories. Lay Catholics feared that gangs had flourished in their neighborhoods as surrogate families, filling a gap that overworked parents could not address. "There is a five-year-old child here [at Saint Philomena] who doesn't get picked up here until five or six o'clock," one man told me to illustrate his concerns with familial disintegration.[9] In the final analysis, however, parishioners pointed not to economic pressures but to moral causes in explaining the perceived erosion of their families. Unbridled materialism, portrayed as a dominant feature of life in contemporary Los Angeles, was particularly faulted for luring parents away from their children. One teacher generalized, "In this parish, both parents are usually working—but they don't have to. They just want to keep up with the standards. They want their children to have more. But the more they have, the more they want."[10] For them, this was a moral issue that the Carmelite sisters could and did redress. Lay Catholics described their choice to patronize the Carmelites' school as a strategy to shelter children from the materialistic values allegedly reinforced in Los Angeles public schools.[11]

The history and contemporary profile of the Long Beach parish parallel those of Carson in two noticeable ways. First, the neighborhoods immediately surrounding Holy Innocents school in Long Beach—located several miles inland from the coastal beach and tourist attractions, and several miles north of the more affluent neighborhoods of Orange County—have undergone demographic changes since the 1970s, reflecting Filipino migration into a formerly Mexican/Mexican-American neighborhood. The parish today is made up of a Filipino majority, with Mexicans/Mexican Americans accounting for approximately one-third of its members.[12] Second, Long Beach has undergone accelerated industrialization since the 1960s, becoming a home to manufacturing plants producing aircraft parts and medical devices. Skilled workers employed in the factories subsequently take up residence in or near the factories. The Filipino Catholics who have come to work in Long Beach and now patronize the Carmelites' Holy Innocents School spoke of themselves as less rooted in the United States than the middle-class parishioners of Carson, however. They had arrived on the mainland more recently and thus had less to say about their new home in Los Angeles. More beset by poverty and more besieged by the violence of the neighborhood, they have turned to the sisters for spiritual support in the hardships of relocation, frequently invoking comparisons between their life in Long Beach and past experiences in the Philippines.

In Long Beach the neotraditionalist Carmelites commanded no less respect amongst parishioners than they did in Carson. "The sisters are as closely identified with God as they can get," one parishioner summarized.[13] Another Filipino layperson reported feeling "frightened" and "overwhelmed" by the sisters before she came to know them personally, adding that their appearance as traditionally clad monastics "put me in my place—I had to be good."[14] "I know that our goal is to bring all the students to be citizens in heaven.

That makes our school very special," another teacher stated. Students taught by lay teachers were reported as "being in awe" of the traditionally clad Carmelites when they came to visit their classrooms, and adult parishioners cited the sisters as an "inspiration" and as reminders of their belief in a supernatural dimension to life.[15]

The "miracles" effected by the sisters in Long Beach have pertained to the everyday struggles of economic survival. One teacher attributed her job at the Carmelite school to divine aid. A former teacher in the Philippines, her first job in Long Beach was at a local fast-food restaurant. "I was in tears all the time," she said, and she prayed a novena to the Virgin Mary to find a job at a school. The next Sunday she went to Mass at Holy Innocents parish, and was approached unexpectedly after the service by a neighbor, who asked her if she knew any teachers who wanted to work at the Carmelites' school. Another layperson, after relating a story of a young woman in the church who could not afford shoes, found consolation in the power of prayer to overcome even the most practical obstacles. "Have you heard this saying: 'If you know how to pray, then there's no problem at all'?" she asked me. One woman, whose lapsing Catholic faith had been revitalized by the Carmelites, had recently returned to praying the rosary "not to make the problems go away, but [for] the strength to deal with them," alluding to previous health and economic difficulties.[16]

Filipino Catholics in Long Beach also looked to the Carmelite sisters for physical protection from violence. The boundaries of Holy Innocents have demarcated a safe haven within a decidedly dangerous neighborhood. One Carmelite sister recalled the morning when the Long Beach principal was alerted to news of an approaching gang. Accompanied by the eighth-grade teacher—an advanced student of Judo—and a dog, the sister dissuaded the youths from entering school property by yelling through a bullhorn.[17] Another parishioner recounted being robbed at gunpoint as she and her two children entered their car just blocks away from Holy Innocents. From time to time, she reported, media equipment is stolen from the school.[18] Neighborhood and individual watches have come to supplement police protection throughout the parish. Notwithstanding these incursions of violence into parish territory, however, parents still felt that their children were protected by the Carmelites—both physically and morally. Like the parishioners of Carson, Filipinos in Long Beach drew sharp contrasts between their Catholic school and public schools in Los Angeles. One woman who had moved, in her words, to the "Land of Opportunity" to save money for her own family and relatives in the Philippines summarized, "The Philippines are rich in natural resources, but we [my family and I] didn't have the money. For money we came to America. For the future of my kids, I send them here."[19]

Parishioners at Long Beach described Los Angeles primarily as a place of economic opportunity, a city to which immigrants had come to make money. In articulating their cultural identity, however, lay Catholics located themselves somewhere between the United States and the Philippines. Lay Catholics spoke of sharing their earnings with relatives in the Philippines, and some even hoped for an eventual return to the Republic.[20] One parishioner recounted religious protests against the Marcos government in explaining the power of the rosary to overcome hardships in Los Angeles: if prayer could topple a tyrannical government, surely it could help her earn a living in the United States.[21] Seeing in the Carmelites a cultural bridge between the islands and the mainland, lay Catholics commonly referred to the sisters' version of Catholicism as "Spanish." While the laity did not cite biographical details of Mother Luisa's life, they did know that she was from Mexico, portraying the Carmelites as members of a Spanish Catholic, rather than neotraditionalist American, order.

Considered together, the Carson and Long Beach parishes offer a composite profile of the Filipino-American Catholic constituency served by the Los Angeles Carmelites. The neotraditionalist lifestyle of the sisters resonates with the laity as a continuation of Filipino Catholicism familiar to them and/or their relatives in the Philippines. In light of the specific political and economic contingencies of Filipino history, this retention of traditional religion cannot be likened to the celebration of "popular Catholicism" by earlier, European Catholic immigrants. Consistent with other studies of Filipino Americans, the interviews in Los Angeles record a culture defining itself in self-conscious opposition to Anglo-Protestant society, with little expressed desire to "assimilate" completely into the United States.[22] If parishioners of Long Beach frequently imagined themselves as temporary sojourners in the United States, Catholics in Carson, more rooted in American soil, were critical of certain aspects of hegemonic Los Angeles culture, and sought to shield their children from its influences in the sisters' school. Catholics of both townships characterized the public school as an institution inculcating values that threatened to disintegrate the traditional family and/or encourage violence in their neighborhoods, appropriating neotraditionalism selectively and strategically, as a practical resource to cope with contemporary social problems. Uniting the parishioners of both townships was a shared belief in the thaumaturgic powers of the monastic person, an emphasis that one observer of Filipino Catholicism has suggested has roots in the "densely populated spirit world of pre-Hispanic Philippine religion" as an expression of the "Philippinization" of Spanish Catholicism.[23] In Carson, this was a power that parishioners accessed to ward off disease. In Long Beach, lay Catholics sought association with the Carmelites to shelter themselves and their children from physical danger, and they incorporated the sisters' devotions into their daily lives to surmount poverty.

If the recently industrialized landscapes and the changing ethnic composition of Carson and Long Beach speak of changes in the archdiocese, Saint Joseph school and parish in La Puente preserve many features of the Los Angeles neighborhoods originally served by the Carmelite order. In the late 1990s, La Puente was still a residential neighborhood and Saint Joseph still the Mexican-American parish it had been when the Carmelites arrived in 1968. Here, Mother Luisa's Mexican heritage is well-known and proudly embraced as part of the local culture, while the Virgin of Guadalupe—the devotional center of Mexican Catholicism and foundational symbol of cultural identity—is routinely incorporated into religious instruction classes. Attendance at the two Spanish Masses offered on Sundays is usually full—"not at the beginning, but by the end"—while the one English Mass is poorly attended.[24] And if the term "family" is used metaphorically in Carson to describe the ambiance of the Carmelite school, in La Puente it is a more literal designation. By one estimate, 85 percent of the parish is related, while the staff includes relatives of schoolchildren and former students of the school.[25]

La Puente has not been immune, however, to rapid social changes in the greater metropolitan area. It is no longer the agrarian community it could claim to be until the 1950s, when farm land was converted into rows of tract housing. And leading the list of parishioners' concerns is the ubiquity of Mexican/Mexican-American gangs with their attendant violence, first noticed by parishioners in the mid-1970s. A former resident of La Puente related arguably the most spectacular miracle story recorded in ethnographic research, a legend of a "bullet-proof rosary." One morning several years ago, she recalled, a Carmelite sister was kneeling in prayer at the convent in La Puente, asking God for guidance with a decision to stay with or leave the order. The convent abutted a park that was infamous in the community as the scene of showdowns and shoot-outs between local gangs. In the midst of the sister's prayers, the early morning stillness was suddenly broken by the sounds of gunshots. A stray bullet allegedly pierced the wall, hit the prayer stall, and ricocheted directly toward the sister's body. Miraculously, instead of striking her dead, the bullet glanced off a small metal medallion hanging from the end of the sister's rosary, leaving in its trace just a small scratch. "She was absolutely glowing when she came to Mass that morning," the woman concluded. "When I asked her why she was so happy, she told me what had happened and showed me the rosary and said, 'Well, I guess God answered my prayer.'" The alleged manifestation of God's power convinced the sister she would be safe continuing to work in La Puente.[26] While she could not verify the legend of the bullet-proof rosary, the Carmelites' mother superior related a similar anecdote. One of the sisters in La Puente had momentarily left her bed a number of years ago to use the washroom, only to find upon returning a fresh bullet hole in the wall where her head had been lying.[27]

The park next to Saint Joseph's School in La Puente continued as a theater for ritualized gang fights and initiations in the 1990s. In the course of ethnographic research, witnesses shared the details of a recent initiation rite in which a local gang of girls beat up a new member in the park. The young woman, her face covered with blood, walked away from the ordeal unshaken, and even, according to some, smiling. Such scenes are a commonplace feature of everyday life around the school, parishioners assured me. As if to underscore the ubiquity of urban chaos around her, the La Puente principal recited a litany of automobile accidents that had occurred at the busy intersection outside her office: a car once crashed into the fourth-grade classroom; a woman had recently been hit and killed while crossing the street; another car crashed on the sidewalk at five o'clock the previous Christmas morning.[28]

In both legend and fact, however, what one parishioner called "Carmelite turf" is a safety zone in otherwise dangerous neighborhoods.[29] Several teachers in La Puente attributed the protective powers of the Carmelites to the strong taboo in Mexican gangs against attacking "their own"—since the Carmelite order is perceived as an extension of *la familia*.[30] Funerals of local gang members have been conducted regularly at Saint Joseph parish with no incidents of retaliatory drive-by shootings.[31] Catholics in La Puente portrayed gangs primarily as surrogate families in a radically fragmented society. They emphasized the disappearance of public support for children, the curtailment of after-school programs, and the erosion of the family by economic hardships as the real dangers to civic life, and they saw gangs as merely symptomatic of these deeper problems. Like the parishioners in Carson and Long Beach, they were quick to add that the materialistic and individualistic mores of Los Angeles have helped contribute to the family's demise, epitomized for them by the entrance of women into the workplace and the pursuit of happiness in the glitzy lifestyles promoted by advertisers. One longtime resident who now teaches at Saint Joseph thought she would have joined a gang had it not been for the afternoon programs at her school, which are no longer offered.

The Carmelites, in turn, have extended themselves in La Puente as a surrogate family, banding together against the hardships of the outside world. Their most commonly distributed photograph of Mother Luisa—or "Mother Luisita" as she is affectionately remembered by sisters and parishioners alike—taken six months before her death, presents the foundress as a gentle and compassionate grandmother. Appearing on school bulletin boards, official prayer cards, and even the patterns for children's puppets used in classrooms, the photograph projects an idealized image of maternal love that her American heirs work hard to promote. Within the Carmelite cloister, the distinctively Mexican Catholic familial custom of blessing a "family member" before she leaves her "home" continues to be observed, while private devotions to the Virgin of Guadalupe, observed by older Mexican and Mexican-American sisters, help transform the community into a domestic—and Mexican—space. Outside the cloister and within the boundaries of Saint Joseph parish, school and church alike are transformed into a kind of extended Mexican Catholic family banding together for strength and support, and more than willing to welcome gang members into its fold should they choose to change lifestyles.

No less than the Catholics of Carson and Long Beach, parishioners in La Puente appropriate neotraditionalism to preserve and in some cases rebuild aspects of their Mexican-American identity threatened by urban violence and the allegedly corrosive influences of individualism and materialism. They praise the Carmelites for their resistance to postconciliar changes in religious life. "For those of us who are older," one woman explained, "we feel we have lost the stable parts of our own lives. The rest of our lives are changing; we don't want change when we go to church. We're losing our jobs, we're losing our children, we're losing our spouses. We don't want to go to Mass where there's a heavy metal performance. This community is conservative; we don't want change."[32] Another Mexican-American woman who has been a Carmelite sister for more than forty years invoked memories of the early years of the order in Los Angeles, when sisters staffed the Saint Teresita tuberculosis clinic in Duarte, California, "beside the chicken shacks," drawing sharp contrasts between a more halcyon past and an overly materialistic, dangerous present.[33]

In their common emphasis on the moral decrepitude of greater Los Angeles, Filipino and Mexican Americans do their part to reinforce the apocalyptic sentiments of many Carmelite sisters, who embrace Pope John Paul II's antimodernist indictments of "the world." Expressing it more often through innuendo and passing comments than through official teachings, many sisters are apt to interpret social problems and even natural disasters in southern California as signs of God's anger toward a morally decrepit society. The mother superior once pointed out to me that a recent earthquake had wrought disproportionate damage in a neighborhood housing pornographic bookstores.[34] "Satan is angry," one sister in La Puente explained while reflecting on the increase in urban violence. "He wants to grab the place that was once his. But we can't say it's the end [of the world]. Whether or not the world gets better or worse depends on us."[35] Another sister, reflecting on the legalization of abortion and "euthanasia" and the sanctioning by some churches of homosexual marriages, concluded, "The world is in a bad state right now, and we are living in a very bad time—especially in America. We are doing what the Roman Empire and Nazi Germany did."[36] Echoing the perceptions of their lay supporters, the Carmelites particularly fault the public schools for disseminating allegedly anti-Catholic mores, even suggesting their unwitting collusion with the forces of evil.

Such social problems as gang violence and family disintegration are interpreted differently, however, by lay Catholics and Carmelite sisters. While Filipino- and Mexican-American Catholics band together with the support of the Carmelites primarily to defend and maintain themselves against the materialism and individualism of Anglo-Protestant culture, Carmelite sisters cite the urban fragmentation in Los Angeles as sufficient proof of a spiritual battle unfolding in the streets. Notwithstanding these important differences of interpretation, however, sisters and laity recount a similar narrative of Los Angeles as a dystopian city. In the final analysis, the Carmelites and their supporters join in perpetuating an urban mythology with longstanding roots in the local Anglo-Protestant culture, despite their efforts to distinguish themselves from their contemporary society. A virtual jeremiad exposing the sleaziness, violence, and immorality of Los Angeles came to emerge as a popular portrayal of the city, beginning in the early twentieth century and accelerating after the Second World War. In the cinematic depictions of film noir and their literary counterparts, Los Angeles has been portrayed as the myth of Manifest Destiny inverted. The metropolis is a symbol of the West as the mockery of life, liberty, and the pursuit of happiness, Anglo-Protestant ideals that drove settlers westward in the nineteenth century.

As the terminus of westward expansion, Los Angeles has elicited from its inception much speculation about the transcendent meaning of the country's destiny. To the first Anglo settlers, the city was a monument to the nation's "progress," rescued from the control of the semi-savage Mexicans in the Mexican War. Less than a century later, however, movies and books were revealing the opposite indictment: America had run its furthest course to the Pacific Ocean, only to be revealed as a nation wracked with evil and sin. Legendary detective fiction writer Raymond Chandler—many of whose Los Angeles-based stories became plots for noir films in the 1930s and '40s— painted a vivid picture of dystopian Los Angeles in his 1950 essay "The Simple Art of Murder":

> The realist in murder writes of a world in which gangsters can rule nations and almost rule cities, in which hotels and apartment houses and celebrated

restaurants are owned by men who made their money out of brothels, in which a screen star can be the finger man for a mob, and the nice man down the hall is a boss of the numbers racket; a world where a judge with a cellar full of bootleg liquor can send a man to jail for having a pint in his pocket, where the mayor of your town may have condoned murder as an instrument of money-making, where no man can walk down a dark street in safety because law and order are things we talk about but refrain from practicing. . . .

It is not a fragrant world, but it is the world you live in, and certain writers with tough minds and a cool spirit of detachment can make very interesting and even amusing patterns out of it. It is not funny that a man should be killed, but it is sometimes funny that he should be killed for so little, and that his death should be the coin of what we call civilization.[37]

Hidden behind smiles and handshakes and the sunny suburbs of southern California lurked a tawdrier Los Angeles, and, by extension, a more disturbing national character. If not exactly marked for divine destruction, Anglo-Protestant society in the noir imagination seemed to merit its moral condemnation. Subsequent portrayals of Los Angeles have been even darker and more violent than Chandler's depictions. By one estimate, Los Angeles has featured in books and movies as the setting for divine or cosmic destruction by earthquakes, floods, monsters, nuclear bombs, and even extraterrestrial beings on the average of three times a year since the early 1900s.[38]

In recent years, gang violence in particular has become the symbol par excellence of dystopian Los Angeles narratives in the local press. Concluding his overview of gang-related news coverage by the city's most widespread—and Anglo-controlled—newspaper, the *Los Angeles Times*, writer Mike Davis has observed: "In Los Angeles there are too many signs of approaching helter-skelter everywhere in the inner city. Even in the forgotten poor-white boondocks with their zombie populations of speed-freaks, gangs are multiplying at a terrifying rate, cops are becoming more arrogant and trigger happy, and a whole generation is being shunted toward some impossible Armageddon."[39] On the one hand, accounts of gang violence recorded in interviews with Filipino and Mexican Catholics are real enough. Especially in Long Beach and La Puente, parishioners can point to robberies and drive-by shootings as hard evidence of the encroachment of gangs in their neighborhoods. On the other hand, depictions of Los Angeles as a gang-infested metropolis often carry a metaphorical meaning as well. In the interviews with parishioners in Carson and La Puente, gang violence is both real and symbolic of civic fragmentation, which the Carmelites and their supporters attribute to the individualistic and materialistic mores of the hegemonic urban culture.

A *Times* article that appeared on the front page on March 26, 1992, underscores the ambiguous meanings of gang violence in Los Angeles. Sixty-year-old Jane Guin, the newspaper reported, had just settled down in her armchair to watch television one fateful evening when the sounds of nearby gunshots startled her. Unbeknownst to Guin, two factions of the local El- don Street gang—consisting of young Mexican-American men—had been dueling in a high-speed chase that ended outside her home on Moccasin Street. As she retreated from the danger outside, a stray bullet shattered the den window and lodged itself fatally in the back of her skull. "June Guin was killed by a stray bullet over the weekend in the gang-torn La Puente neigh- borhood that she planned to soon leave," the article began, "[and a] little piece of the American dream died with her."[40] The coverage proceeded to weave details of the shooting with the image of the Guins' camper, their in- tended retirement home, parked in the driveway. Contrasting the Los An- geles of the late twentieth century with La Puente in the 1950s, "when wal- nut groves began to give way to neat bungalows with tidy lawns," the article concluded:

> Such scenes would have been unthinkable in 1957, when the Guins pur- chased their three-bedroom, two-bath dream home with a *faux* fireplace with a plastic, light-up log.
>
> "Our biggest problem back then was whether a coyote was going to come by, running across the wheat fields," said David Guin [June's son], a communications major at Cal State Fullerton.
>
> Grudgingly, June Guin had come to recognize just how much things had changed.
>
> On Sunday, a lifetime of knick-knacks still sat in packing boxes, some marked "Mom and Dad." On the walls were ghostly shadows where pho- tos of their children and five grandchildren once hung. Their camper, their ticket out of La Puente, remained parked in the driveway.[41]

The death of seventeen-year-old Jesus "Diablo" Calletano, another resident of La Puente killed by a bullet that evening, was reported in a few disinter- ested sentences at the end of the article. The *Times* mentioned fellow *cholos* defacing property on Moccasin Street, spray-painting a eulogy, "Rest in Peace, Diablo," on a wall, and holding a car wash in his honor.[42]

No less than the Carmelites' or lay Catholics' own reflections on gang violence, the article clearly arranged the mélange of journalistic details in a recognizable narrative about the demise of Los Angeles. The tragedy of June Guin's death for her family and friends became subsumed by the *Times* in a narrative about the passing of the Anglo-Protestant suburb, a decidedly idealized community comprising "neat bungalows with tidy lawns," intact nuclear families, and neighborhoods cleansed of unruly Latin youth. Thus, whether the city is imagined as a madhouse of materialism and individual- ism-gone-awry, an apocalyptic theater where Jehovah battles Satan, or a monument to Anglo-American suburbia threatened by violent "foreigners," narratives of a fallen Los Angeles share an attempt to make sense of a rapidly changing metropolis by articulating clear social boundaries delineating the contours of safety and danger, purity and impurity.[43] What the Carmelites and their supporters have in common with the *Times* is a vision of a homogeneous society that is equated with security and stability. Where the neotraditionalist Catholics and the Anglo-Protestant newspaper part ways is in their prescriptions for maintaining utopia: in the first case, theological and moral consensus ensure communal purity; in the second, ethnic homogeneity staves off chaos. Filipino- and Mexican-American Catholics articulate a vision of ethnoreligious community that falls somewhere in between these two extremes. Equating the unchecked intrusion of Anglo-Protestant values into their neighborhoods with chaos, they turn to theological essentialism to maintain ethnic boundaries.

The one parish where the Carmelites have virtually failed to make inroads into the hearts and minds of the laity, however, is the parish school of Saints Felicitas and Perpetua in San Marino, a stronghold of Anglo-Protestant culture in Los Angeles. In this affluent neighborhood of quiet streets, with tastefully understated shopping malls located just a few blocks away from the Carmelites' Alhambra mansion, both neotraditionalist theology and essential monasticism are received coolly, if at all. Saints Felicitas and Perpetua was the last school in Los Angeles County to be staffed by the sisters, who came in response to an invitation by the theologically conservative Monsignor Lawrence J. Gibson, the local pastor, in 1981. The order was also welcomed at the time by parents eager to provide their children with the top-rate educational services offered by the sisters. What neither parishioners nor Carmelites anticipated, however, was the extent to which ideals of academic competition espoused by the parents masked ideals and mores fundamentally at odds with the sisters' emphasis on intellectual submission to church dogma and social conformity to moral teachings. One particularly vocal teacher and local resident, who was "furious" she could show only "G"-rated movies in her classrooms, equated the sisters' neotraditionalist Catholicism with an inability to think critically and thus to succeed academically. "I need to know where these eighth grade students are at," she said. " These kids here are like me—they can think for themselves. They don't care if someone's wearing a habit and it'll be, 'Yes, sister, what'll it be [she folded her hands demurely across her lap].'" Characterizing the Carmelites as "the modern-day Jesuits," she went on to generalize, "a lot of the parents here think they're a little wacky. Some of the sisters can't stand it here, because people think for themselves."[44]

The Carmelites are tolerated in San Marino primarily for their excellent teaching and administrative skills. In the words of one local resident, whether or not the sisters wear habits or live in community is inconsequential so long as they know "how to run a tight ship."[45] Exceedingly high educational standards have left the order with little time for other objectives. A kindergarten teacher with previous experience in public schools, for example, estimated her students to be reading at a second-grade level. "Some of the parents have had their children in school since they were two," she explained.[46] The current principal described her arrival to San Marino from Long Beach as "quite a shock": she characterized San Marino parents, in contrast to her former parishioners, as "very defensive," scrutinizing the order's administration of the school. "To prepare a parents' meeting here," she said, "you have to do your homework really well, to back up everything you say."[47] Another teacher, a native Los Angeleno from working-class Echo Park, said his students' parents would "constantly test" his professional authority, but he "kept his chin up."[48]

The few staff members at San Marino supportive of the sisters' cause have found themselves unable to convince students or parents of their views. A Ukrainian teacher, whose parents had fled their Communist country to live in the United States, has tried in vain to instill a zeal for religious freedom in her fifth-grade students. "I feel like an alien here sometimes," she said. "I think the way the sisters do, but especially in today's society they are going against the grain. Society doesn't allow you to be simple, and sometimes it's difficult."[49] Another teacher, identifying herself as "a very strong Christian and a very strong Catholic," criticized what she called the "New Age perspective" of the parents. "They think they're masters of their own destiny," she said; "everything can be explained through psychological factors. . . . They question the reality of spirituality—'Are heaven and hell real? Are angels real?' Since [they] can't see it, [they] don't believe it."[50]

The Carmelites find it difficult to carve a space for themselves even amid the conservative Catholics of the church, the contingency that supports the local priest . "Part of the parish here is very, very, traditional—almost *too* traditional," one Carmelite explained. "I ask myself, 'Are they being loyal to the Pope, or do they think they're better than the Pope?'"[51] In addition to their boycotting of such Vatican II liturgical changes as exchanging the peace with fellow parishioners or standing during prayers, the conservative faction of Saints Felicitas and Perpetua has taken to distributing pamphlets reprinting medieval papal pronouncements of eternal damnation for all non-Catholics and to boycotting the selling of ice cream during Lent. Dismissing these concerns as "the non-essentials rather than the essentials" of Catholicism, the sister distinguished her order as "with the Church—not with the people who think they are the church."

The most revealing observation of the Carmelites' failure to win con-

verts in San Marino, however, evoked not theological disputes over normative Catholicism but the sociocultural profile of the Saints Felicitas and Perpetua parish. A teacher who had previously taught in a Mexican-American
neighborhood in Highland Park made a sharp contrast between her teaching experience there and her job in San Marino:

> This [school] is not typical of Los Angeles. In Highland Park, my students
> came from gangs and drugs and booze. We used to have "Mad Dog" drills,
> preparing for the drive-by shootings. But as tough as it was, those were
> probably the most rewarding years I had teaching. I took them on field trips.
> They didn't even know their own neighborhood. They were near the zoo—
> I took them there. Another time I took the kids to see *Cats* at the Schubert
> Theater. We had to have two parent meetings to convince them it was O.K.
> to go out at night.[52]

A native of upper-class South Pasadena, she would share her own childhood
stories with the students of Highland Park. "They loved my stories," she said.
"It was like I was from Never-Never Land." In turn, after transferring to the
Carmelite school in San Marino, she taught her students about the conditions of everyday life in Highland Park—the crowded conditions of the
apartments, the noise level in the streets, the ubiquitous gang activity—and
"the kids were amazed." Asked why her teaching experiences in Highland
Park were more rewarding, she replied: "I loved it. They were so easy to im-
press. Their school was the haven—not the home. It was just the opposite
of how I grew up. For us, the home was the haven."[53]

As the ubiquitous security alarms protecting the private homes of San
Marino might suggest, this neighborhood marks its turf with threats of retribution no less than any gang. San Marino approaches the idealized Anglo-
Protestant suburban paradise whose passing is eulogized by the *Los Angeles
Times*.[54] Unlike the parishioners of Carson, Long Beach, or La Puente, the
Euro-American Catholics of San Marino did not associate the lifestyle and
theology of the Carmelites with a Spanish Catholic heritage—either their
own or anyone else's. Much like Sisters of the Immaculate Heart, who spear-
headed reforms in women's religious orders during the 1960s, laypersons in
San Marino saw in the American descendants of Mother Luisa a model of
community incompatible with their own sociocultural ideals. Yet notwithstanding their emphasis on critical thinking, parishioners in San Marino reject the neotraditionalist Carmelite order for reasons more mythic than rational. An air of defensiveness surrounded lay Catholics' reflections on the
Carmelites' presence at Saints Felicitas and Perpetua; indeed, some parishioners even seemed to view my interviews with them as an incursion into
their community.

The teacher in San Marino who characterized the "school as a haven" for Mexican-American children accurately summarized the sentiments of parishioners in Carson, Long Beach, and La Puente, who see in the Carmelite order a protective "oasis" or surrogate family. For the Filipino- and Mexican-American Catholics served by Mother Luisa's order, the parochial school is less of a replacement for the home than an extension of it, and the cloister is as much of a model for the ethnically homogenous neighborhood as a neo-traditionalist religious order. And while the home is indeed the haven for the affluent community members of San Marino, ethnicity is a bonding element in social life no less for them than for the Catholics of the other three schools. In their embrace of the single-family home and success through academic competition and prowess, however, San Marino Catholics extol the very Anglo-Protestant ideals of individualism and material acquisition that are faulted by Catholics in less affluent and non-Euro-American neighborhoods. San Marino can be seen, in short, as an Anglo-Protestant socioreligious enclave, whose totem is not the cloister but the private home, and whose mores celebrate individual success over communal or familial solidarity. Here the neotraditionalist teachings of the Carmelites make as little sense as the underinvested Mexican *ranchos* did to the city's first Anglo-American planners and architects of the suburbanized metropolis.

For their part, the Carmelites dismiss San Marino parishioners' protests as signs of "spiritual poverty," a basic ignorance of their ultimate dependence on God that is masked by material wealth and creature comforts. More accurately, the theological gulf between the Catholics of San Marino and those of La Puente, Long Beach, and Carson tells "a tale of two cities." Two distinctive socioreligious narratives of Los Angeles reflect the divergent urban experiences of Los Angeles Catholics living inside and outside the Anglo-Protestant fold. Since their earliest days working among Mexicans and Mexican Americans, the Carmelites have lived on the cultural and economic margins of the city. Looking back to the inspiration of their foundress after Vatican II to renew their charism, they found sufficient reason to highlight her oppositional relationship to the modern world. Since that time, the Carmelites have received ample support for their order from Filipino- and Mexican-American Catholics in Los Angeles, where efforts to distinguish ethnic identities from Anglo-Protestant culture have merged with Catholic neo-traditionalism. Thus, it is in the parish most closely resembling the Anglo-Protestant ideal of suburban Los Angeles that the essentialist theology of the sisters falls on deaf ears.

Situated along the Pacific Rim as a gateway for Asian immigrants, and north of the international border between the United States and Mexico, Los Angeles has become a home to transnational communities like the Filipino-

and Mexican-American parishes served by the Carmelites. Despite Anglo-American portrayals of the city as the terminus of westward migration, Los Angeles is more accurately described as a microcosm of global culture. The parishes of Carson, Long Beach, and La Puente understand themselves less as peripheral communities orbiting around an Anglo-Protestant center than as socioreligious centers in their own right, resisting assimilation into Anglo-Protestant America in part through their retention of a Spanish Catholic heritage.

The next two chapters, based on ethnographies in the Mexican/Mexican-American borderlands of southern Arizona and in Cuban-American Miami, will record similar narratives of countercultural Catholic identity. Unlike the Filipino- and Mexican-American parishioners of Los Angeles, however, lay Catholics in these two parishes narrate their disenfranchisement from Anglo-Protestant culture in less oppositional terms. In communities where the local culture is predominantly Latino, parishioners incorporate the Tridentine symbols of the neotraditionalist sisters and draw upon memories of their own homelands to articulate a Catholic identity.

4

Underground Carmelites: Catholic Identity in the Arizona/Sonora Borderlands

A PPROXIMATELY ONE HUNDRED MILES southeast of Tucson, the adjacent cities of Douglas, Arizona, and Agua Prieta, Sonora, first appear to the traveler on Interstate 80 like a continuous mirage shimmering on the mesquite-and-cactus-covered plains of the Sulfur Springs Valley. As the road gradually descends some 1,800 feet from the former regional headquarters of the Phelps-Dodge Mining Corporation of Bisbee, Arizona, the white buildings of the "Twin Cities" slowly take on discernible shapes and contours against the backdrop of the Mule Range mountains. But the international border between Douglas and Agua Prieta remains invisible to all but the most scrutinizing observer. A few miles outside Douglas, Highway 80 grazes close to the chain-link fence running alongside the Southern Pacific railroad tracks, dividing the United States from Mexico. The pale green Broncos of the United States Border Patrol can be seen stealthily rolling through clumps of desert grass, their drivers hoping to surprise the unsuspecting family or individual from Mexico or Central or South America who is attempting undocumented entry into Arizona. Perhaps the large white "D" surreally inscribed in one of the cities' outlying and pristine hills suggests other efforts to distinguish American from Mexican territory; but without these most conspicuous signs of an international divide, Douglas and Agua Prieta appear to the inbound traveler as a single settlement, and indeed, the only sign of human civilization in this corner of southeast Arizona's abandoned mining kingdom. The "border" here is minimized by both Anglo and

Mexican residents as "the line," while family bloodlines pay no attention to arbitrary distinctions between Mexican and American territories; as of 1996, 85 percent of the population in Douglas descended from Mexican ancestry.[1]

When the Carmelite sisters came in 1987 to live in Douglas—their first assignment outside Los Angeles—to run and staff an ailing diocesan primary school, they entered into the landscape and culture of the Mexican border-lands. Here they have been received enthusiastically by the predominantly Mexican and Mexican-American community as both spiritual guides and competent teachers who might help the children of this locale to escape the poverty that has come to characterize the "Twin Cities" of Douglas/Agua Prieta since the closing of the local Phelps-Dodge smelting plant in the late 1980s. In contrast to Los Angeles, where sisters and laity bunker down in eth-noreligious "oases, " here there is no need for either sisters or parishioners to articulate clear boundaries between themselves and an Anglo-American church or culture. In a landscape and culture that are predominantly Mex-ican, the Carmelite school in Douglas has tapped into something of an underground root system of interconnected Mexican Catholic pilgrimage sites, shrines, graveyards, home altars, and historical markers that has nur-tured and strengthened their mission. In this chapter the history of the Car-melites in Douglas/Agua Prieta will be reconstructed from interviews and contextualized within the broader cultural and religious landscape of the Ari-zona borderlands. The story of the Carmelites here cannot be understood in relation to issues discussed in earlier chapters: it is neither the triumph of neotraditionalist over liberal Catholicism nor the resistance of a Latino com-munity to Anglo-American culture. It is rather a record of the perdurance of a distinctive regional Catholicism that predated the Carmelites' arrival and that will outlive them should they leave. The inclusion of the borderlands in this study broadens the discussion of neotraditionalist Catholicism be-yond intra-ecclesial politics and the oppositional construction of ethnic iden-tity by moving its center to the fringes of the Anglo-American world.

It was in response to an invitation by the bishop of Tucson, Manuel Moreno, that the Carmelites first came to assume administrative leadership of the Virgin of Loretto school on the west side of Douglas. As a former res-ident of the California southlands himself, Bishop Moreno had attended school in Los Angeles with young women who would later become Carmelite sisters. Later in his life, during his work as priest in the Los Angeles arch-diocese, Moreno came to know the order on a professional basis, growing so fond of the sisters as to invite two Carmelites to Rome for his ordination to the bishopric.[2] After being reassigned to Arizona, Moreno personally asked the archbishop of Los Angeles that the California sisters staff Loretto. Like the bishop himself, the Carmelites were immediately adopted into their

largely Mexican and Mexican-American parish, effecting a dramatic transformation in both the school and the church. Shortly after the departure in
the late 1960s of a Dominican community, the last religious order to staff
Loretto before the Carmelites came, the school's attendance and condition
alike had begun to plummet. According to one resident, "There was a distinctive difference in the way the Mexican people looked at the school when
the lay people came here [after the Dominicans left]." Once the Carmelites
arrived, however, "they started sending their children back."[3]

The neotraditionalist sisters have awakened powerful religious sentiments in the community. A local resident who sometimes accompanies the
Carmelites on shopping trips likened them to "movie stars." In their errands
outside the cloister and school, the sisters are approached by parishioners
and strangers alike, who ask for blessings and confessions, or simply make
passing conversation.[4] Shopkeepers offer them merchandise at lowered
prices. In some contexts, the Carmelites can provoke fear and awe. The
school's principal remembered a Sonoran parent breaking down in tears of
embarrassment after learning that her child had earned her dishonor, while
a parishioner recalled a kind of spiritual showdown at Loretto in which an
irate Sonoran father suddenly stopped his tirade against a silent and mo-
tionless sister, apologized, and sheepishly retreated down the stairs. "I've seen
grown men shakin' and quakin' in their boots [in confrontations with the
sisters]," one Anglo resident of Douglas recollected with Wild West flair.[5]

When the Carmelites first arrived in the Twin Cities in 1987, however,
Loretto was a mere shadow of what it had once been. Originally built in the
1920s during the heyday of Douglas's glory as a smelting center in southeast
Arizona, Loretto fulfilled the hopes of the city founder, William Brophy, to
add a Catholic school to the emerging pioneer city. Brophy donated a plot
of land marked for Loretto in 1915, leaving fundraising in the hands of the
local Catholic community. In 1922, after Brophy drowned during a fishing
trip in Mexico's Guaymas Bay, his wife Ellen extended a sizable donation to
the building fund and enabled the school's immediate construction. The
completion of the school as the second largest building in town was proudly
heralded on the front page of the August 2, 1924 edition of the *Douglas Daily
International:* "Completion of Structure Marks Addition to Douglas Property of Perhaps Largest Structure to Be Built in Past Decade; Mottled Pressed
Brick With Terra Cotta Trimmings Used in Construction; All Modern Features Are Provided," the paper boasted, quoting the local priest's assessment
of it as "one of the most modern Catholic institutions in the Southwest."[6]
The Sisters of Loretto, the school's original staff members, invited families
of all denominations to send their children to the school, and initial enrollment filled the Loretto classrooms to full capacity. Amidst much hoopla and

hope for the local future the school was thus founded, seeming to redeem even the premature death of its benefactor and the city's founder.

Bishop Moreno had warned the sisters that Loretto had deteriorated considerably in the decades since its construction, but descriptions of the school's condition had not apparently done justice to what they first beheld that September. Sisters remember feeling stunned and overwhelmed by the extent of the school's institutional and physical dilapidation. Not only had Loretto's student attendance fallen to an all-time low, with an approximate 50 percent enrollment, but the three-story brick building was in shambles. Its broken windows were stuffed with newspapers, the paint of its interior walls was peeling off in large flakes, its once shiny hardwood floors were covered with years of unwashed grime, and its rooms were infested with roaches. Rising doggedly to the task, the sisters worked tirelessly over the next several years to orchestrate the badly needed physical repairs and to upgrade the school's curriculum. In the mid-1990s, less than a decade later, the building was all but completely restored, and the enrollment had rebounded from 180 students in 1987 to its maximum capacity of 300—with a long waiting list of families eager to enroll their children.[7]

The deterioration of the Catholic school was just a small part of a greater crisis in the Twin Cities by the late 1980s. In 1987, the same year the Carmelites arrived, the Douglas Phelps-Dodge smelting factories closed, marking the end of an era that had hitherto shaped both the economic life and the public image of the cities. Douglas/Agua Prieta had come into existence as a corporate community in the 1880s, shortly after traces of ore were discovered in what is now Bisbee—Douglas's northern neighbor—by two members of the United States Army pursuing a band of Chiricahua Apaches across the plains. Reports of the ore's discovery prompted the Phelps-Dodge mining interest to purchase claims for the land. A quarry was soon opened, and Bisbee rapidly swelled from its former desert outpost status to become a bustling industrial site attracting laborers from around the world. But copper ore remains useless until it is first refined of its impurities, and as the quarry's output increased, plans for a new and larger smelting plant sent company engineers scouting for a new refining site. The ideal locale was discovered at Whitewater Draw some twenty miles due west of Bisbee, where natural supplies of water would aid in the smelting process and a lower elevation would allow carts of ore to roll down the hills along railroad tracks running out of the quarry. In 1900, five men—including the geologist Dr. James S. Douglas—bought claims for the site in anticipation of the smelter. Within two years, they had submitted a grid-like map of a proposed town to the Cochise County headquarters, naming it after Douglas. Soon after they began the orchestration of their city's development, keeping pace with the economic development fueled by the two refining plants begun by Phelps-Dodge in 1902.[8]

Technological developments in late-nineteenth- and early-twentieth-century America made copper mining in the southwestern United States a thriving and lucrative enterprise, and during these years the Twin Cities thrived. America's entrance into the "electrical age" demanded huge amounts of the mineral for wiring and set the mines and smelters of Bisbee and Douglas on an economic course that seemed to have no end. As late as 1976 one local historian, Ervin Bond, concluded his portrayal of the community with a rather optimistic rhetorical question: "'What will Douglas, the Climate Capital of the World, be like by the turn of this century when the town reaches its first 100 years?' Predictions are that it could reach a population of 50,000 or more."[9] Bond's prognosis was not at all unreasonable; copper processing had continued steadily in Douglas through the twentieth century, peaking during periods of war.

What the historian did not foresee, however, were the implications of the perpetual clouds of smoke that the Phelps-Dodge smelters billowed into the Sulfur Springs Valley. They gently blew with natural wind currents northward in the daytime, southward into Mexico in the evening, and occasionally hovered still over the carefully gridded streets and parks of the city. By the mid-1980s, both Arizona state and national legislatures were pressuring the mining company to comply with basic environmental standards of clean air. The territory bounded by the Douglas smelter and its two sister plants in Cananea and Nacozari, Mexico, had earned the designation of "the gray triangle." Phelps-Dodge responded by taking a route well trodden by American corporations: claiming substantial losses to profit, it closed the Douglas plants in 1987, while keeping open the smelters in Cananea and Nacozari, where environmental standards could be avoided.[10]

The closing of the smelting plants in 1987 signaled the end to predictions of a bright economic and social future for Douglas. The economic vitality of the borderlands community ground to a halt, and the population stabilized at a modest 15,000 people.[11] But the final blow to Douglas was yet to come. In an episode still recounted by residents with all the drama and pathos of local legend, Phelps-Dodge decided in January of 1988 to detonate the abandoned smokestacks of its former factories. In the stillness of a cold Sunday morning, townsfolk on both sides of the border heard an explosion as the two five-hundred-foot chimneys collapsed, their bases pulverized into clouds of dust. Not a person who heard the blast has yet forgotten exactly where they were or what passed through their minds at the time of the dynamiting. The reaction of one woman from Agua Prieta identified the symbolic import of the smokestacks' destruction for most of the Twin Cities' residents: "When I heard that explosion," she told me, squinting her eyes and pressing her hand to her heart, "I thought, 'Well—that is the end of Douglas!'"[12]

It is hard to dismiss today the sharp contrast between the recently renovated Loretto school and its surrounding environs. A once bustling main street has been reduced to a mere two or three blocks of locally owned businesses, the rest of its storefronts boarded up or put up for sale. In order to stave off economic devastation, the state of Arizona has built a brand new prison facility just north of the city, while on the southernmost edge of town, private investors have funded the construction of a huge shopping mall. In spite of these efforts, Douglas has been declared an economic disaster area by the state of Arizona, together with the border community of Nogales to its west. In the mid-1990s, the unemployment rate hovered at 20 percent, having doubled since 1980.[13] On the east side of town, the former Phelps-Dodge factory buildings have been left to crumble and the slag piles left to stagnate.

In the meantime, for families on both sides of the border, Loretto has emerged under the Carmelites' direction as a gateway to upward economic and social mobility for their children. The staff members and parents I interviewed at the school were virtually unanimous in citing the school's excellent academic reputation as a primary incentive drawing enrollment from both sides of the line. Loretto graduates, it was pointed out, tended to succeed in their subsequent secondary school careers, approximately 95 percent continuing on to college, with the University of Arizona at Tucson a popular destination. "That in itself," a local reporter declared in a feature article for National Catholic Schools Week, "is taken by the Carmelite nuns and lay teachers at Loretto as a ringing endorsement of the quality of the education they have to offer."[14] The principal of the school offered further impressive statistics vindicating the school's academic excellence: two Loretto graduates, now at the University of Arizona, were recently ranked in the nation's upper second percentile for mathematical ability.[15] The school has placed second in national spelling competitions, even though Spanish is the first language for many of its students.[16] One man went so far as to state that there was "very little absorption of religious values" at Loretto, referring especially to the Mexican patrons as "snobs."[17]

In spite of the sisters' efforts to erase it, Loretto did not completely lose its local reputation as "a Mexican school," even though the citizenship of most of its students is American. The students who daily cross the international border to attend Loretto, children of Agua Prieta's wealthier families able to pay Loretto's monthly tuition, were typically born in American hospitals and thus can claim United States citizenship despite their Mexican residency. Constituting approximately half of Loretto's student body, they represent Agua Prieta's ranching and small-business-class families, whose homes are conspicuous in Agua Prieta for being the largest and best constructed, clustered along the chain-link border fence on the northernmost edge of town. The other half of Loretto's students, with the exception of a few Asian-American children, are Mexican-American residents of Douglas. In fact, Loretto has become, under the Carmelites' direction, a symbol of prestige for Mexican families. One teacher recounted Mexican parents lining up to register their children at three o'clock in the morning one year; residents from Douglas, though given first priority to enroll their children, were slightly less enthused.[18]

While the Carmelites' dedication and labor were instrumental in rebuilding the school, it was above all else their charisma as traditional Carmelite sisters that elicited both piety and material assistance from the Mexican and Mexican-American community. The Knights of Columbus, for example, helped to install the some two hundred windows needing replacement at the school, while according to the testimony of Loretto staff members, local politicians and businesses made what contributions they could to further facilitate Loretto's recovery. Parents from both sides of the border agreed to pay one hundred sixty dollars monthly tuition—a costly investment for Mexican families in particular, given the devalued worth of the peso next to the dollar.[19] In return, of course, the Carmelites made good on the community's investment by providing an excellent educational program, vouched for by the success of its graduates, without which the school would doubtlessly slide back to its former neglect. Nevertheless, the economic and spiritual revival of Loretto was sparked long before its graduates started leaving the Twin Cities for college. The equation seems simple enough: when the Carmelites arrived, parents started sending their children back to the school.

The six sisters who staff Loretto all speak Spanish, but only one is of Mexican descent. What they do share with their Mexican constituency is a common religious heritage symbolized by the same lifestyle and devotions that their foundress from Jalisco once observed. As one woman in Douglas put it, "I don't think it matters where they [the Carmelites] come from once they put on that habit."[20] In their own school and residence, the sisters sanctified the main entrance with a plaque to their patron, La Virgen de Loreto, and a large ceramic statue of the Blessed Mother, draped in a blue mantle, extending her arms in invitation at the end of the long hall. In the library they hung images of Mexico's patroness, La Virgen de Guadalupe, and they placed her statue at the foot of the stairwell leading up to their living quarters. Today the sacrament is periodically exposed in an ornately designed monstrance for devotions, while votive candles are lit to Guadalupe and to likenesses of Saint Anthony and the Infant of Prague enshrined in the back of the room.

The Carmelites are the first to acknowledge the impetus that the surrounding Mexican culture has given to their mission in the Twin Cities. There is more parent involvement in Douglas, they said, than in any one of their schools in Los Angeles.[21] Their students seemed more receptive to their theological teachings. "Kids here have an open heart and they know there is a God!" one sister said.[22] Another contrasted the musical tastes of the students in Los Angeles and the Twin Cities to illustrate what she saw as the basic moral integrity of Mexican culture: the favorite music of Agua Prieta students was traditional *cumbias,* devoid of the allegedly immoral lyrics suffusing American pop.[23] And of course the Carmelites looked fondly on the religious festivals in both the Mexican and the Mexican-American communities of the Twin Cities. Seeming to correlate Catholic culture with a more rarefied spiritual atmosphere, an older Carmelite added, "The first thing I noticed when I came here from Los Angeles was the silence. Both outside, and inside."[24]

To borrow a phrase from Keynesian economics, the sisters seem to have "primed the pump" of Loretto's revitalization, drawing from the rich underground waters of Mexican Catholic devotion permeating the local culture and landscape and predating the arrival of the Phelps-Dodge smelting plants. This is the transnational Mexican/American space known as the Pimeria Alta, dedicated to its local patron, Saint Francis Xavier, or "San Francisco" as he is known.[25] Between the mission church of San Xavier del Bac—south of Tucson, Arizona—and a church dedicated to him in Magdalena de Kino in Sonora, thousands of local Catholics conduct pilgrimages each year, marking and sustaining a social and cultural space much older than either nation-states or multinational corporations.[26] Any given day of the year can find the Spanish colonial baroque churches of San Xavier crowded with pilgrims and tourists. In the mission church south of Tucson, a carved wooden statue of the saint in the repose of death draws to its side Anglo, Mexican-American, and Indian pilgrims who touch the prostrate image—modeled after Francis's allegedly incorruptible body entombed in Goa, India—and cradle its wooden head in their hands.

On the opposite side of the church to the right of the altar, candles burn by the hundreds underneath a statue of the Virgin Mary. The likeness of Saint Francis is the center's primary attraction, evidenced in the hundreds of *milagros*—tokens of gratitude for alleged miraculous intercessions—pinned to the blanket draped atop him. On his body the devoted have pinned hospital bracelets, notes asking for the physical healing or spiritual edification of loved ones, photographs of men, women, and children, and even CAT-scan pictures of fetuses in utero. Outside the church, pilgrims purchase relics in gift shops or fried bread from small stands, while O'odham Indians may engage in more specialized commerce, purchasing glass picture frames manufactured in Sonora, which they hold to imbue their images with spiritual power.[27]

Between San Xavier's shrines in Arizona and Sonora, the Pimeria Alta is literally covered by markers of more local or private pilgrimages. The headstones in Agua Prieta's graveyards, as well as those in the Mexican-American sections of Douglas's cemeteries, are decorated with plastic flowers and votive candles testifying to the faithful visitation of the living—most lavishly during the days before *El Dia de los Muertos,* or the Day of the Dead, on November 2. Local roads are dotted by the occasional makeshift shrine to a victim of an automobile accident. In Douglas, the shrine room in Saint Luke's parish, a Catholic church directly behind Loretto School, vividly reflects local beliefs in the miraculous intercession of saints and the superconcentrated presence of God in the church's sacraments, especially the transubstantiated bread and wine. Even more concealed from the public eye, home altars and religious images sanctify the domestic spaces of the traditional Mexican Catholic world, symbolically uniting the intimate dwellings of families with the more public spaces of church sanctuaries and commercialized pilgrimage centers.

With their arrival in the Twin Cities in 1987, the neotraditionalist sisters seemed to have transformed the Loretto school into one more pilgrimage site in the landscape, tapping into a pre-existent source of socioreligious vitality that the more publicized rise and fall of the Phelps-Dodge culture can perhaps eclipse. In folk tales recorded from the Pimeria Alta as early as 1948—during the heyday of Phelps-Dodge activity—it is clear that the mining interests of Anglo-American investors have long been subsumed for Mexicans and Mexican Americans in narratives of local Catholic identity. Legends collected by the University of Arizona from the Patagonia region just west of Douglas/Agua Prieta reveal saints and ghosts alike meddling in the landscape and affairs of a more publicized mining industry:

I was newly wed in the year 1915. I was loading ore for the 3 R Mine at Bloxton and it was about 11:30 at night when I was passing by the old rooms of a house about a mile this side of Bloxton, where the Circle Z Ranch is now. Just down the hill was a railroad switch. And when I was passing by those rooms I heard Chinese talk and I stopped and when I stopped the talking stopped. So I looked all around to see if I could see someone but I saw nobody so I started walking again and the talking started again as if it were a

long ways from me so I stopped again and the talk stopped again. Then I
got scared and my hair went straight up and I came straight home.[28]

Legends like these record the time of the mines as an era not of progress
and profit, but of a dangerous intrusion into a pre-existing spiritual cosmos.
The landscape has been rendered threatening and unnerving. The dead ha-
rass the workers, while the saints cast a disparaging eye on the filthy lucre
extracted from the earth. In one story about the local patron, San Francisco,
a man discovered a "buried treasure" and offered half of it to the saint at a
church. Kneeling before the patron's image, the man discovered he could
not get up until he took the bag of treasure away with him.[29]

In angry and malicious personifications, numerous stories of haunted
or spiritually inhabited caves recall local Indian beliefs in the more-than-
human presences dwelling within the land. These places are identified as the
most deadly areas of the surrounding landscape to those foolish enough to
approach them.

> There is a cave where it is said that at night they will throw rocks at one
> passing in a car or walking. One day one of my friends was passing in his
> car when he heard a crashing sound and he turned back and saw the rear
> window of the car broken. The cave is on one side of the road on the way
> going back to the Washington Camp School.
>
> There is a cave on the side of the road that goes to the Duquesne Camp.
> In the past years they claim that a woman comes out of the cave at mid-
> night. If somebody was passing she would not let him pass until he gave
> her five cents, Mexican money. If one didn't give her the five cents, she
> would throw some cotton at him and in the cotton there would be a poi-
> son dart.
>
> Somewhere near Wilcox there is a cave, they say. In this cave is supposed
> to be lots of money and if you go in there you will hear a voice say, "Take
> all or none." Well, there were three men who went in the cave one day. All
> three of them heard the voice say "Take all or none." They filled their pock-
> ets full of money and started to walk out when they were shot. It is said
> that you must take all the money to come out alive, or none of it.[30]

In light of such portrayals of the angry and oftentimes feminized earth,
it is no surprise that Catholics should turn to a divine source for protection.
In folk tales like these, the land seems to resent the forays of miners, demanding payment in return and cleansing itself of all traces of capitalist incursions. While earthly women are forbidden access to the mines—"because
the mine is a woman and she . . . gets jealous and makes a serious accident
happen"—the Virgin Mary is cited as the patron of local miners.[31] The unfortunate miners who are nevertheless struck by accidents go on to inhabit

the shadowy realm of the ghosts, continuing to scream out for help from within the inaccessible recesses of their graves.[32]

In Douglas, the Irish-American priest of Saint Luke Church continues to find himself appropriated as something of a local wonder worker in a landscape that is still haunted and charmed in the religious imagination of local parishioners. His own "best ghost story" from years of frequent exorcisms comes from the blessing of a home where a dark, shadowy figure allegedly haunted one of the rooms. A year after performing the ceremony, the priest found himself responding to another request for an exorcism at the same house by different tenants. After listening to their descriptions of a dark figure in the back room, the priest was shocked to learn the couple had scrupulously avoided any contact with the former renters, reputed to be drug dealers, claiming no knowledge of either the previous exorcism or the house's rumored hauntings. The priest has also been frequently sought out to interpret portentous visions, like the dream of one parishioner who in a coma beheld her deceased grandmother relating details of the afterlife. Always careful to proclaim faith as the greatest miracle a Catholic could hope for, the Irish-American native of Hyannis, Massachusetts, has nevertheless won widespread support and popularity for taking the teachings and rituals of the church into the homes and haunts of the local landscape, where mothers and grandmothers continue their families' devotions with the candles he has blessed.[33]

The borderlands culture of the Pimeria Alta distinguishes itself both from the Anglo-American corporate culture of the former Phelps-Dodge empire and from the Mexican nationalist identity perpetuated in political rhetoric of the Revolution and promises of "progress." The withdrawal of the Phelps-Dodge smelting plants from southern Arizona signaled the end of an era when the "West was won" not only for economic development but also for Anglo-American domination of Indians and Mexicans.[34] Markers of the Anglo-American West abound in southern Arizona: entire towns, former military and economic outposts, have today been transformed into theme parks. Tombstone has embalmed its downtown in an attempt to preserve the architectural and cultural complexion of Wild West days, offering tourists a wide array of gift shops where they may purchase cowboy hats and boots, saloons where they may drink under stuffed animal heads mounted on walls, and even stagecoach rides along the main street, where ghosts of former outlaws seem to linger on. Bisbee, the former Phelps-Dodge capital, has taken a more gentrified approach, offering its consumer base a tasteful selection of art galleries and espresso bars. Situated close to Mexican territory, Douglas falls outside the orbit of this tourist zone, having been left to struggle with economic depression and cultural anomie with few distractions.

The curator of the Douglas-Williams Museum in Douglas, a shrine in its own right to the mythic history of the Wild West, characterized the history of the Twin Cities as ending with the departure of the smelting plants. Describing himself as a "raw-bone, Western, rope-'em, brand-'em, and ship-'em-out kind of guy," the longtime Douglas resident described his fellow residents as stunned and disoriented by recent economic downturns. "They're still waiting for another 'Papa Dodge' to tell 'em what to do and where to go," he said.[35]

On the one hand, his perception seemed to reflect accurately the widespread pessimism of local residents irrespective of national or cultural or religious background. Parishioners at the Loretto School shared grim prognoses for their community's present and future: "The whole make-up of Douglas has changed," one teacher lamented. "It's a whole different class of people here now. The people who worked in the smelters came from richer families."[36] Another staff member added that laborers in the Twin Cities today "are transient."[37] The community was described as "scary economically," a "place of no opportunity," and infiltrated by the international narcotics trade.[38] Epitomizing the danger and chaos of the present-day Twin Cities are the factual stories, well circulated, of children disappearing "over the border" into Mexico.

On the other hand, in light of the racist ideology and political objectives of Anglo-American colonizers, Mexican Americans have good reason to remember the era of the smokestacks as something less than halcyon. Indeed, part of the reason for building the Phelps-Dodge smelting factory on the Mexican border seems to have been to ensure a steady influx of cheap labor into the plant. In the Phelps-Dodge corporate hierarchy, surface labor jobs both paid less and were less prestigious than underground mining work, which was typically reserved for Euro-American workers.[39] One prominent Mexican American in the Douglas community characterized the company as "a dominating, smothering presence," adding that the local newspaper—a primary mouthpiece of local cultural identity—was little more than a vehicle for Phelps-Dodge interests.[40] And while the Chicano movement of the civil rights era has little currency in Douglas, "a fair amount of entrenched bigotry, which breeds reverse bigotry" still characterizes the city today for many residents.[41]

In the meantime, federal institutions on the Mexican side of the line stand like the Douglas slag piles as monuments to failed promises. Pemex, or Mexican Petroleum, whose stations distribute gasoline on Agua Prieta street corners, has failed to usher Mexico into the promised era of prosperity; it is victim to the worldwide oil glut and to falling petroleum prices. The local banks are also government owned, but the value of their pesos has been steadily falling since 1976. A hospital owned by Social Security earns a local reputation for being "a circus."[42] A city that named many streets in honor of the Revolution—Independence Day Avenue, Revolution Day Street, Cinco de Mayo Avenue—Agua Prieta has long welcomed *maquiladoras,* the "dual plant" factories owned mostly by American investors, to help push the economy along. The workers of Zenith, Telmex, and Takata commonly earn subsistence wages, however, and fill the drab row house apartments modeled after Communist Cuba's workers' housing. Just a few blocks south of the attractive storefronts and restaurants geared to American tourists, paved streets give way to dirt roads and grid-patterned neighborhoods to shantytowns of squalid shacks in this city of some 120,000 residents. The infrastructure is thin: liquid gas is delivered in tanks to individual houses, as is water to the residents of Agua Prieta's poorer neighborhoods. Residents of the city have expressed their disappointment with the corruption and unmanageable debt of the ruling revolutionary party, Partido Revolucionario Institucional, by voting in overwhelming majority over the last decade for Mexico's rightist opposition party, Partido Acción National, but to no avail.[43]

Residents of the Twin Cities further betray their distrust of the Mexican government by keeping alive memories of the Cristero Revolt, a local cultural trait that clearly works to the advantage of Mother Luisa's American Carmelites. The priest at Saint Luke declared that the "Cristero Revolt is very much alive here. I have seen older parishioners choking up at 'Viva Cristo Rey!' [the Cristero anthem]."[44] Even among the younger generation, in his opinion, "the Persecution Days are not so much a memory, but they've left a cultural imprint," reflected primarily in a strong sense of Catholic cultural identity. The relatively low participation at Saint Luke's Sunday Masses did not particularly seem to change this impression. "[T]he difference between here and Hyannis [his native home] is that the 60 percent who don't show up at church there don't think about religion at all. Here, everybody keeps some Catholic identification—whether they go to church or not."[45]

The priest's impressions were strongly echoed in the reflections of one woman from Agua Prieta, who explained that the reappearance of the traditionally clad Carmelite sisters awakened among many of her fellow Mexican parishioners dormant memories of Mexican Catholicism pitted against government anticlericalism. "The Carmelites have become symbols of what *we* stand for," she explained, pitting an allied local church and populace against the Mexican government. "You could really hear people talking when they came."[46] Her own reflections on the Carmelite sisters wove together impressions of the contemporary condition of Douglas/Agua Prieta with memories of her university days at a Catholic school in Mexico City. More than two decades after the Revolution, teachers held Masses in their classrooms, donning their robes in defiance of extant anticlerical laws, while students stood watch outside the doors. The priests' clothes and religious articles were stored in an armoire, she said, that was spun around to reveal a faux bookcase when classes were in session or a public official approached during services.[47] Keeping a clear distinction between the Mexican state and the Mexican people, she concluded, "They say one thing, we do another. What can they do? They look the other way."[48]

Residents of Douglas/Agua Prieta speak of their isolation from both the United States and Mexico in references to the Twin Cities as "an island surrounded by a sea of dirt."[49] University of Arizona folklorist James S. Griffith has documented a host of jokes, legends, and religious practices that similarly subverted both United States and Mexican jurisdiction in the state's six borderlands cities. In local lore, the six ports of entry on the Arizona-Sonora border—Douglas/Agua Prieta, Naco/Naco, Nogales/Nogales, Sasabe/Sasabe, Lukeville/Sonoyta, and San Luis/San Luis Rio Colorado—are not defined as borders or peripheral regions to either country, but as centers in their own right. Dismissive references to the international border include designations of its chain-link fence as an *alambre,* or "wire"; "illegal aliens" or "undocumented workers" as *alambristas,* or tightrope walkers; or the border itself as "the line."

Decidedly poetic protests of the international border include the volleyball tournaments related by James Griffith, held near Naco in the 1980s. "Each team played in its own country, with the chain-link border fence serving as the net," he writes.[50] Douglas/Agua Prieta displayed a similar genius back in 1957, when hoof-and-mouth disease forbade the importation of horses into either country for a race. Upon the advice of a United States Customs agent, the race was held nonetheless along a deserted stretch of the fence, with *Relámpago,* or "Lightning," running on the Mexican side and *Chiltepin* (a local, wild chile) on the American side of the border.[51] In 1993, the Twin Cities were home to a more overtly political demonstration after the local border patrol proposed the construction of a steel-plated wall between Douglas and Agua Prieta. A one-thousand-member organization calling itself Hermanos Unidos en Contra de la Pared—Brothers United against the Wall—quickly and effectively mobilized protest from both sides of the border to halt its construction.[52]

In May of 1990, Douglas/Agua Prieta once again became the site of what has arguably become the most colorful and sophisticated subversion of international law so far. From the front line in the "war on drugs" came the report that two local customs agents had just discovered a 250-foot, subterranean tunnel crossing the international border that was used to traffic narcotics. Buried thirty feet underground, the tunnel linked a house in Agua Prieta to a cement warehouse in Douglas. Described by one customs agent as "like something you'd see in a James Bond movie," "El Túnel" was accessed on the Mexican side by lowering an entire floor of the residential home—suspended on a system of compression-operated hydraulic jacks—to the underground level.[53] Not only did the tunnel receive coverage in the *New York Times* and on *Sixty Minutes,* but it quickly became a prized trophy of the United States Customs Service.

The editor of Douglas's newspaper complained to a California journalist just two months later, "'They're parading every possible dignitary through the tunnel—senators, representatives; they've had media days for chiefs of police, justices of the peace, mayors, you name it—telling them what a wonderful job they're doing."[54] In the meantime, Twin Cities residents memorialized the tunnel for themselves; two Mexican *corridos* about "El Túnel de Agua Prieta" were composed, while José and Nereyda Teran of Douglas started a line of tunnel T-shirts. Some six years after its unearthing, the tunnel is still discussed in Douglas/Agua Prieta. "You must have heard about the tunnel here?" people at Loretto would ask me in an attempt to locate Douglas on the American map, while a woman from Agua Prieta let me in on some local tunnel humor: *Question*—"Where the hell is Douglas?" *Answer*—"At the end of the Tunnel."[55]

The burgeoning narcotics trade in Douglas/Agua Prieta during the years the tunnel was used offered a tempting and infinitely more lucrative alternative to the legal economies that had come to fill the vacuum left by Phelps-Dodge. American residents lacking sufficient education or job training have been left with a choice of working for the new prison facility to the north of Douglas or in one of the many low-paying retail jobs in the gargantuan shopping plaza less than a quarter of a mile from the international border. Built on the southernmost edge of the Phelps-Dodge property, the mall draws a quarter million Sonoran shoppers each week to its J.C. Penney department store, the largest Safeway supermarket in Arizona, and a host of smaller shops and fast-food franchises. Otherwise pious Catholics at the Loretto School reluctantly admitted to the economic contributions El Túnel had made to their community. "I hate to say this, but at least the tunnel kept some money coming into this community," one teacher confessed.[56] Another woman noted that the Twin Cities' locally owned businesses, now struggling to compete against the shops of the mall, profited indirectly from the illegal revenues, concluding, "You could notice a difference after the tunnel was shut down."[57]

Against the backdrop of a once flourishing Anglo-Protestant culture and economy and a once triumphalist Mexican state, the local Catholic world of the borderlands shares something of the subaltern character of El Túnel even today. The transnational community of the Pimeria Alta has continued to thrive underground amidst the corporate and governmental control of the local landscape throughout the twentieth century. Until 1991 the wearing of habits was no less of a punishable offense on the Mexican side of the border than drug trafficking, and Tridentine devotions were kept alive in the privacy of homes under predominantly female leadership. In the Anglo-American Southwest, the late-medieval, Tridentine Catholicism of Mexico was seen as the legacy of an unenlightened and superstitious people, but Mexican Americans retained their religious practices and beliefs nonetheless. But as a new millennium dawns and former powers seem to weaken, older spirits rise from the earth and reclaim the public spaces. In Douglas/Agua Prieta, the Carmelites arrived at a critical juncture in local economic and social history, assuming the status of both rebels and saints.

The sisters also came to the Twin Cities as ghosts from a distant Mexican past, before the years of anticlerical legislation and the nation's struggle to join the modern global economy. For Anglos and Mexicans alike, the past lives on in the meanings attributed to the people, places, and things of the borderlands landscape: smokestacks are monuments to eras gone by, and haunted houses link the living to the restless dead. The Carmelites fail to elicit in Douglas/Agua Prieta the apocalyptic sentiments so common among parishioners in Los Angeles, who read in their own streets and buildings a dystopian story of Anglo-Protestant America. Here the Carmelites evoke instead images of saints from colonial Spanish times, holy persons who worked to uphold and bless the extant social order. Catholics of the Twin Cities do not so much fight against the modern world as include it in their narratives of a sanctified landscape. Like other expressions of the Arizona/Sonora borderlands, the history of the Carmelites speaks to a local sensibility of *mestizaje*, cultural mixture and recombination in which ancient and modern, Catholic and Indian, Mexican and American, and spiritual and material worlds coexist in ambiguous tensions.

Regardless of what the future holds for the borderlands, there is little doubt among local Catholics that the Pimeria Alta will endure and outlast all other obstacles. "Are we scared?" a Mexican teacher at Loretto asked rhetorically. "No! We are survivors. We will eat beans and potatoes until the times get better!"[58] As custodians of traditional devotions, the Carmelites have been adopted into a subaltern and subversive Catholic landscape that is charged with both supernatural and social power. While they faithfully carried out the orders of Bishop Moreno to rebuild Loretto, small necklaces of legs, eyes, and heads began to appear on the Infant of Prague, left as *milagros* for physical healings in the back of Saint Luke's shrine room. Money, materials, and support began to appear at the steps of the school. At Loretto, 1987 will be remembered not for the closing of the smelting plants, but as the year the Carmelite sisters miraculously resurrected the Mexican school.

Through their adoption into the pre-existing Mexican and Mexican-American Catholic culture of Douglas and Agua Prieta, the Carmelites lose their status as either a countercultural or a neotraditionalist order. In an area of the United States where the influence of Anglo-Protestantism is mitigated and offset by a longstanding Latino culture, there is no need to accentuate the tensions between the Carmelites' appearance and lifestyle and that of the surrounding environs. Here the Carmelites are in fact "traditional," blending naturally into what might be called a Tridentine Catholic landscape that pre-dates the sisters' arrival. Against the plains of the Pimeria Alta, dotted with shrines and mission-style churches, it is Anglo-Protestant culture and postconciliar theology that seem spurious and remote.

5

Betwixt and Between: Catholic Identity and the Reconstruction of Ethnic Identity in Miami

*I*T IS NOT WITHOUT A LITTLE IRONY that Mother Luisa's American Carmelites, affiliated with the order of Discalced—or "shoeless"—Carmelites, came to Coral Gables, Florida, in 1991 to minister to parishioners of the Church of the Little Flower. Built in 1926, Coral Gables, the bedroom community of Miami, was designed by George E. Merrick, one of the self-proclaimed "fathers" of Miami, to reflect both the indulgent opulence of the Gilded Age and grandiose Anglo-Protestant fantasies of the Spanish Mediterranean. "The lush tropical beauty of hibiscus, poinciana, banyan and bougainvillea frame stately Spanish colonial architecture on quiet streets that seem to come from another time," a current brochure of the city declares rather accurately. "In Coral Gables, the timeless grace and grandeur of 18th century Spain comes together with the excitement and energy of the Americas. Coral Gables is an elegant, easygoing residential community and a new world capital of international commerce. It was planned like no other city in the country and has evolved like no other city in the world."[1] While mansion-lined streets—their Spanish names marked understatedly on small, white stone markers—make up most of today's "City Beautiful," Merrick also bequeathed to posterity two renowned institutions: Coral Gables's University of Miami and the Biltmore Hotel. Without doubt the city's pièce de résistance, the recently renovated hotel towers in baroque splendor over sprawling square miles of golf courses, attracting the world's wealthiest tourists and business people to its halls.

Just four blocks down the street from the Biltmore, the Church of the Little Flower, where the Carmelites work, sits on land donated by Merrick himself. The church was built to seat no less than 1,200 people and modeled in the Spanish mission style. A 1927 full-page advertisement in the *Miami Daily News and Herald* listed its dedication to Saint Thérèse of Lisieux, the "Little Flower," as the second such ceremony in a week, "instancing again that the spiritual keeps pace with the material in this city, where you may live in beautiful homes and surroundings and where your children may participate in the finer things in life."[2] Saint Theresa's parochial school, originally named Saint Joseph's Academy, has also adjoined the church since its opening. It is now run and partially staffed by the Carmelites, who replaced the Sisters of Saint Joseph upon their arrival. Notwithstanding the awkward fit between the medieval austerity of the order and the tropical opulence of their surroundings, Mother Luisa's sisters not only have fared well in the epicenter of "Miami's Riviera," but have literally come for many parishioners of the Little Flower as godsends.

The Cuban Americans of Saint Theresa share with the residents of the Arizona borderlands discussed in the last chapter a *mestizaje* Catholicism that weaves together elements from both Anglo-Protestant and Spanish Catholic cultures. Reflecting what Thomas Tweed called the "translocative" nationalist identity of Cuban exiles, the narrative of Catholic identity reconstructed in this chapter is the story of a community trying to orient itself somewhere between a Cuban past and an American future. On the one hand, parishioners will admit that the Carmelites' school is "secluded—the ideal," or compare the sisters to the traditional Cuban *chaperonas* who escorted young women on dates.[3] In descriptions reminiscent of the urban narratives from Los Angeles, public schools especially are portrayed by Miamian Catholics as hotbeds of gang activity, security problems, sexual promiscuity, drug abuse, and egocentric mores. The Carmelites' image of themselves as a surrogate Mexican family, another central component of the Los Angeles narratives, also resonates deeply with Latino parishioners in Coral Gables. On the other hand, as members of the exile community who have met with overwhelming economic success in Miami, Coral Gables parishioners can only run so far from Anglo-Protestant culture. They are especially aware that the fragmentation of the traditional Cuban family has already introduced social fragmentation into the heart of their own community. The parents who "*think* the children are protected here" should know better.[4] In the shadow of George Merrick's Biltmore Hotel and splendid Spanish mission church, local Catholics live uneasily between two worlds, struggling to preserve a distinctive Cuban heritage for themselves and their children even as they enjoy the fruits of prosperity in America.

The transformation of Miami since the 1960s from an Anglo- and African-American southern city to the cultural and religious capital of Cuban Americans has fulfilled the dreams of the original city planners with a twist that they probably did not imagine. Millionaire speculators in the Roaring Twenties inaugurated Miami as signaling the "new day of the American South," the decisive end to Dixieland's defeat in the Civil War and subsequent, humiliating reconstruction at the hands of Yankee "carpetbaggers." If northerners looked back to England for their historical and cultural roots, the southern designers of Miami chose Spain and even Rome to be the mythic predecessors of their invented new world—even though the original city had been named after and built beside the Seminole Indians' Tamiami Trail snaking westward into the Everglades. In Miami, the founders envisioned, Anglo-Protestant culture would be revitalized and "sweetened" by contact with adjacent Caribbean cultures, and "changed . . . as were the Longobards and the Normans in Italy. New England will probably remain as our Scotland. But our Italy and Spain will evolve and mellow with the passing centuries. Indeed, in all our southland our race is destined to go on in this refining process. It is to be one of the major cultural evolutions of western culture."[5] Future American settlement would accordingly re-enact "the immemorial movement of northern peoples towards sunnier lands."[6]

With the outbreak of Fidel Castro's Cuban Revolution in 1959 and the subsequent exile of the white upper-middle class from Cuba to Miami, however, the southern city was transformed from an idealized center of Latin culture to what some observers have characterized as the commercial gateway to Latin America. Racial and cultural tensions between Anglos, Cubans, and African Americans—epitomized in the Miami race riots of the 1980s— have tarnished the earlier Anglo romanticizations of "Latin culture." Many of Coral Gables' former Irish-American residents have fled the neighborhood in distaste for real Latino culture, ceding the city's most coveted real estate gem to the former ruling class of Cuba, and transforming Saint Theresa into a predominantly Cuban and Cuban-American parish. In the meantime, the archdiocese of Miami has more than welcomed the influx of Cuban Catholics into its fold. The arrival of Castro-hating Catholics on the shores of Miami has effected a dramatic religious revitalization in this corner of the American Catholic landscape.

In the Miami archdiocese, the politics of Cuban exile have merged with the myths and rituals of the Catholic tradition, transforming the archdiocese into one of the world's last battlegrounds between the forces of the church and godless Communism. Ever since exiles smuggled a three-foot statue of her likeness via Panamanian and Italian embassies to Miami, Cuba's patron saint, Our Lady of Charity, has become a powerful symbol fusing Catholic and Cuban exilic identity in the United States. According to legend, three sailors rowing their boat across eastern Cuba's Bay of Nipe one morning after three days of storm-swelled seas found the statue of Our Lady floating on a wooden plank. The image—a dark-skinned manifestation of the Virgin, wearing a mantle and holding the Christ Child in her arms—allegedly had the power of disappearing and reappearing at will, and after vanishing from the sailors' sight revealed herself to a girl in nearby Cobre on the village hillside. There, a permanent shrine was built to La Virgen de la Caridad El Cobre. In 1916, amidst growing support for a Cuban nationalist movement led by the Freemasons, local Catholic prelates successfully petitioned Rome for canonical recognition of Our Lady of Charity as the patroness of the entire island.

Relocated to the United States in 1960, the facsimile of the original Virgin immediately began to draw tens of thousands of exiles to her annual diocesan Masses on September 8 in the Miami Stadium. In 1966, the local archbishop announced during the ceremony his plans to dedicate a permanent shrine and pilgrimage center to the Virgin on the shores of Miami's Biscayne Bay, appointing Cuban-born priest Augustin Roman director of the project the following year. Describing his own childhood as "unchurched," Roman worked tirelessly both to build and to sustain paraliturgical devotions to "La Ermita," personally inviting representatives from each of Cuba's 126 *municipios* to ensure the Virgin's exposure to the whole of prerevolutionary Cuba at appointed times throughout the year. While Miami Stadium continued to be the theater for the patroness's annual feast day, Roman developed a spectacular ritual for her transport from the shrine: the Virgin was to arrive aboard a yacht trailed by other boats, enveloped in flowers and lights, and serenaded by choirs. Crowds of between 10,000 and 20,000 have continued to attend the ceremony since then, and when Pope John Paul II omitted a visit to La Ermita during his 1989 trip to Miami, Cuban-American clerics arranged to have the statue moved to Archbishop Edward McCarthy's house, where the pontiff was sleeping.

For parishioners at the Church of the Little Flower, Mother Luisa's neo-traditionalist sisters appeared in 1991 like ghosts from a prerevolutionary Cuban past, wearing the same scapulars, rosaries, and medallions that Cuban Carmelites and Ursulines once wore. "First of all, the habit," one parishioner said of her initial perceptions of the sisters, "the force and the impact of the habit! . . . We have found that what we thought was dead is alive again."[7] Other Catholics reported having dreams of pre-Castro Cuba, like a woman who dreamed she revisited her childhood church in Havana one night, where she was beckoned to the altar by Jesus Christ himself. Attributing the dream to the Carmelites' power, she declared, "They attract! They are very spiritual."[8] Having not set foot in a Catholic church for twenty-six years, the woman returned to church after the dream. "I was trained in Catholic schools, and nuns are *supposed* to be in habit," another explained. How, she wanted to know, could progressivist Catholic sisters drive expensive cars after taking a vow of poverty? "From veils here to veils up here!" the woman exclaimed, moving her hand toward the back of her head. "You have to show who you are the way you dress—you show society who you are."

The sisters' perceived holiness was further indicated in the language parishioners use to describe them. One teacher, when asked if she knew of any living saints, immediately cited Sister Marisa, the school's principal.[9] Another explained that "the Holy Spirit speaks through her," and "what she says is what Jesus would have done [*sic*]."[10] Other comments included: "there is something about them," "their spirituality comes from deep inside," and "to me this is the real thing."[11] Furthermore, three of the thirty staff members interviewed had even prayed to Mother Luisa for intercession during times of crisis. One, with encouragement from the sisters, had sought the foundress's intercession to recover from an illness. Another had been praying to the foundress sporadically to "see what happens," still testing for efficacy, while a third had turned to Mother Luisa to help a close friend with multiple sclerosis.

On the one hand, there is no shortage of either Catholic nationalism or anti-Castro sentiment at the Church of the Little Flower in Coral Gables. Most of the Cuban-born parishioners came to the United States as part of the "first wave" of exiles in the early 1960s, and have kept alive vivid memories of their departure from the island. One woman whose father had owned a lumber mill and a towel manufacturing company in Havana saw the state confiscate the whole of her family's assets after a sister was reported for expressing dissident political opinions. As her father was finalizing the details in securing a Spanish visa, he died of a heart attack, for which the parishioner has held Castro personally responsible ever since.[12] On the other hand, the most pressing concerns of local parishioners today no longer center on the early years of exile. Having labored tirelessly for nearly half a century to rebuild their former socioeconomic status in affluent neighborhoods like Coral Gables, white upper-middle-class Cuban Americans look forward to what is most likely their permanent relocation in America, and certainly the future American home of their descendants.

The Carmelites have become important for the parishioners insofar as they have been, in one teacher's words, "re-educating" the staff, parents, and children in so-called traditional values.[13] In the Church of the Little Flower, this has meant attempting to revitalize the traditional Cuban family, whose increasing fragmentation in recent years reflects the stresses and sacrifices of relocating to Miami. Teachers commonly cited high rates of divorce, overemphasis on material acquisition, the lack of moral values in their community, and the decreasing time parents spent with their children as direct effects of parents' endeavors to recreate Cuban upper-class society in a new land. In short, their analysis of American capitalist culture has faulted the public workplace as draining parents of time and energy that could and should be directed to familial life. Consequently, according to both the school's administration and the staff, Saint Theresa's school has increasingly faced the daunting task of assuming the moral upbringing of the parish's next generation of children, becoming, in one woman's words, a "surrogate parent."[14] "I don't know why they [the parents of Saint Theresa's school] had their children," one woman exclaimed.[15] Saint Theresa's vice principal and disciplinarian estimated that "90 percent of the discipline problems are due to lack of supervision in the home."[16]

The need for the sisters' "re-education" has been felt especially by Cuban women, who are still expected, and choose, to retain their traditional familial roles even while holding jobs in the workplace. A 1985 study by Florida International University professor Magaly Queralt points to the changing family roles of Cuban women in America. This is perhaps the single most important factor explaining the anomie amongst the parishioners of Coral Gables. Queralt found that 48.6 percent of Cuban women—87 percent of whom were living at that time in Miami's Dade County—were in the labor force, while the proportion of those in white-collar jobs had risen to 58.6 percent in 1982, up from 48.6 percent in 1970.[17] Significantly, most Cuban-born respondents had no employment experience prior to exile, but "worked in order to help their families regain a lost social and economic standing. The same honor and respectability that in Cuba prohibited the employment of nonpoor/nonprofessional women made employment an obligation in the United States, for the sake of the economic and social well being of the family."[18] At the same time, Queralt calculated the divorce rate among Cuban-American women at 10.7 percent, the highest in the country at the time, while their birthrate in 1982 was the lowest average for any female group, at 1.84 children per family, below the replacement level.[19] The survey further suggested the entrance of Cuban women into the workplace had exposed them to autonomous and independent lifestyles, leading "some . . . [to] re-examine . . . the quality of their marriages."[20]

Ever since their invention in the early 1980s of the "Cuban-American Success Story," Miamian exiles have introduced the language of class and the rituals of consumption into the fashioning of their newly emerging Latino identity. In 1980, the year that Castro released thousands of Cubans from the port city of Mariel, Cuba, the "first wave" of Cuban exiles suddenly found their previous status as Model Americans threatened. While the refugees of the so-called Mariel Boatlift included a proportionally small number of convicts and psychiatric patients, their portrayal by both Fidel Castro and the *Miami Herald* as "social undesirables" triggered an upsurge of Anglo-Protestant racism and nativism directed against the Cuban community as a whole. As Afro- and lower-class Cubans began to enter Miami, the exiles finally were linked with other Latinos in the United States in being portrayed by Anglos as dangerous and socially subversive. In an attempt to retain something of a cultural bridge to Anglo-Protestant America, upper-class Cuban Americans began to highlight their community's economic and cultural achievements. In effect, they touted themselves as having played the American game of capitalism as well as and possibly better than native-born Americans themselves. The myth of the Cuban-American Success Story was born.

In its suggestions of Protestant American mores of individualism and self-reliance, however, the invocation of Horatio Alger's "Success Story" mischaracterizes the true meaning of class and status for Cuban Americans. The success of early exiles in rebuilding their former class status was greatly facilitated by Cuban familial and collective solidarity not suggested in Alger's myth. The juxtaposition of high average family incomes with average or even below average individual incomes among Cuban Americans points to a pooling of efforts and resources by individuals within a family. "The entire family celebrates success" is how one Cuban-born woman in Coral Gables succinctly linked the two ideals.[21] "I didn't want money or a car or anything like that," another parishioner remarked as she talked about her spouse, "I wanted a Catholic husband."[22] Still another felt that her family's greatest "success" was the trust and respect still shown to her by her grown children.[23] Several studies have further indicated that business among Cuban Americans is typically conducted through established interpersonal networks, oftentimes in localized neighborhoods or "ethnic enclaves." From the perspective of Cuban Americans in Coral Gables, the Protestant work ethic seemed absurd. "Americans are a very disciplined people . . . they work like animals," one woman observed. After toiling throughout the week, she reflected, they spent their weekends mowing the lawn. "They never take a break!"[24]

As an integral part of Cuba's Catholic heritage, parochial schools like Saint Theresa have survived their liquidation by Communists in Cuba to thrive in Miami as important institutional vehicles for the upwardly mobile ascent of the elite. Fidel Castro's own alma mater, the Jesuits' Belen Academy, was relocated months after its closing in Cuba from its former seventy-acre campus to one of Al Capone's former liquor warehouses in Miami's Little Havana. Described as the "Harvard of Cuban high schools," the all-boys school has graduated prominent leaders in the exile community of Miami, including Roberto Goizueta, who served as Coca-Cola's chairman of the board, and Xavier Suarez, who served as mayor of Miami.[25] In a 1987 report for the *Miami Herald*, Reinaldo Ramos reported graduates rediscovering through Belen a cultural heritage they had once rejected. "I'll never forget it," an alumnus was reported as saying. "During the debate [in Orlando to elect the president of the Florida Association of Student Councils], one guy from a school in North Florida got up and simply said, 'How can a private Cuban high school represent a large public American high school?' And he was right. We are different. It's a whole different world up there past Orlando."[26]

While it does not attempt to compare itself to Belen, the Carmelites' school, in the epicenter of one of Miami's most elite and affluent neighborhoods, has similarly since the 1960s come to assume connotations of prestige and status among its Cuban-American patrons. "The parents think it's 'better' to send their children here," one woman explained, adding that her community was "very materialistic."[27] Another generalized, "People want to make money; they don't care about anything else." Dismissing questions about the perceived moral value of Catholic education, she responded matter-of-factly that the parents wanted only good grades, "an A on the report card," for their children. When I asked her to explain why this was so, she lowered her glasses and answered sardonically, "You tell me."[28] In pre-revolutionary Cuban society, she declared, public schools, especially in large cities, were notorious for their lack of funding and low educational standards. Only the "really bad ones didn't go to Catholic schools." "I don't want to lie to you," another parishioner said, "Cuba was a Catholic country, but it [attending parochial school] was a status thing."[29] Another woman echoed: "Sending your children to private schools [in Cuba] was a class thing."[30]

As the first institution along a social and educational track toward success, Saint Theresa cannot help but foster in its students a sense of belonging to a close-knit community with both Catholic and class overtones. Seventy-one of the eighty-seven graduates of the 1994 class continued their education at one of three Catholic high schools.[31] As one woman perceived the situation, her students not only attended Mass together, but also went to the same birthday celebrations, oftentimes married each other, and as adults associated as friends.[32] The strength of such ties fostered trust among students; in the opinion of many teachers, it also carried the danger of stigmatizing children who attended public schools. A first-grade teacher made it a point to tell her students that "public school children are human." She reflected on the contrast between her own experience in Miami's public schools and the education at Saint Theresa; grateful to her public education for making her "aware of different people," she related her shock in hearing about the terror of one parochial student of riding a public school bus.[33] Similarly, another American-born Cuban teacher rhetorically asked how many Chinese, African-American, or lower-class children I had noticed at Saint Theresa—the answer being that there were none.[34]

While there is nothing unusual about the merging of religion and culture in the Miamian parish, the preponderance of class and commercial concerns in the Cuban-American religious imagination does reflect Cuba's unique status in the Spanish New World as both a leading exporter and a purveyor of a port-city culture. Unlike the "indigenized" Catholicism of Mexico or the Arizona borderlands, Cuban observance expressed from its beginnings a blessing not of precolonial notions of sacred beings and places, but of the socioeconomic structures introduced by European colonizers. Mexican Catholic pilgrims to the site of La Virgen de Guadalupe's 1537 appearance in today's Mexico City revisit Tepeyac, the sacrificial center of Tonantzin, mother of the gods for the Aztec people. Catholics of the Arizona borderlands continue traditions merging Mexican Catholic devotions with Yaqui beliefs in more-than-human beings dwelling in the local earth and plains. But Cuban-American Catholics make their yearly pilgrimage to a Virgin who moved from the Bay of Nipe to a hillside in Cobre before she was transported to Miami. In contrast to the landlocked patrons of industrialized Mexico or the borderlands, her element is water and her business is trade. In her iconography Our Lady of Charity is depicted hovering above the shipping lanes surrounding Cuba, and today she sits enshrined by the Biscayne Bay in the American port city of Miami.

The Spanish Catholic conversion of indigenous peoples and conquest of lands do not figure in the birth of colonial Cuban society for the tragic but simple reason that the island's indigenous Taino inhabitants were decimated through disease or absorbed politically and culturally into the creole class in the first decades of colonialism. The transformation of Spanish Catholicism from a European faith to a New World tradition began on the island instead with the church's consecration and blessing of the sugar plantations, the *ingenios,* in the sixteenth century. The dedication of plantations to the saints of Tridentine Catholicism in return for their patronage continued up until the rise of the Cuban "sugarocracy" in the nineteenth century, when Enlightenment rationalism came to replace Catholic devotionalism as the preferred ideology of Cuban elites. A brief account of the earlier colonial ceremony of "christening" a sugar plantation is preserved in the *Letters Written in the Interior of Cuba* by Abiel Abbot, a New England pastor visiting the island in the early 1800s:

> Being in a family, which had received a printed invitation to what is strangely called the christening of a sugar estate, I attended the gentlemen of the family to witness the religious ceremonies according to Catholic usage. This ceremonial takes place when a new sugar estate has been planted, the necessary buildings erected, and the commencing of the grinding is proposed. A padrena and madrena, or godfather and godmother, are engaged for the occasion. . . . The ceremonial on the part of the priest is extremely brief, amounting to this:—"In the name of God, go on and prosper." After the benediction, a team of ten oxen started, and the padrena, applied the first cane to the [grinding] nuts, and their humble laborers, the men in white frocks, the women in negligent robes of the same fabric, continued the labor.[35]

In one of the few scholarly references to this conflation of religion and capitalism in Cuban culture, George Brandon has remarked that the ceremony was a "curious and potent example of the power of symbolism and the symbolism of power. It compressed into a few dense acts of religious ritual the whole complex of European capital, American land, and African labor under the hegemony of Spain and all that it depended on." He added that "after [the christening] the African slaves continued the grinding. The planter and his family, friends, and relatives went away to rejoice and feed themselves. Meanwhile, the slaves continued what the godfather had begun, grinding and grinding."[36]

As the nineteenth century unfolded and saints began to disappear from the masters' newly industrialized estates, they nevertheless resurfaced among African slaves, who fashioned their own New World religion of Santeria in a reworking of traditional West African observances. Through distinctive legends, dances, and customs, Afro-Cuban slaves reinterpreted the Catholic saints as manifestations of their own traditional holy beings, the *orishas*, who helped sanctify the slaves' suffering and labor in the context of modern capitalism. Among the ruling Cuban creole classes, Catholic myth and ritual continued to pervade the marketplace culture as a marker of what Pierre Bourdieu has called "symbolic capital," or inheritance of social status.[37] The patronage of parochial schools, for example, distinguished upper-class from lower-class members of creole society and fostered early bonds among future members of the elite, while the underfunded public educational system was reserved for lower-class creoles and free Afro-Cubans. The incorporation of Catholic saints by Afro-Cubans, for whom the unconcealed practice of traditional religions was prohibited by colonial law, did not detract from the fact that Catholicism in Cuba came early on to symbolize racial and class divisions within society rather than collective solidarity in a shared national past.[38]

The elevation of Our Lady of Charity from local to national saint in 1916 and the subsequent efforts of the church to redress social inequities came too late in Cuba's history to reverse a much older conflation of religion and class. It was not until the 1940s, more than four hundred years after the island's birth as a Spanish colony, that the church began to take an active interest in reforming the country's longstanding injustices of poverty and racism through the Catholic Action groups begun by Archbishop Manuel Arteaga of Havana. While Cuban Catholic leaders originally supported Castro's 1959 overthrow of Fulgencio Batista as consistent with their own apostolate, they quickly found themselves in conflict with the state as the revolution assumed a Communist identity. In response to a visit by the Soviet Union's deputy premier in early 1960, Cuba's prelates unanimously signed a pastoral letter embracing Castro's reforms but accusing revolutionaries of human rights violations—including the harassment of Catholics as they left church services.

Vowing to remain no longer supporters of "a church of silence," local Catholic leaders read the letter in churches throughout Cuba, provoking a swift and virulent response by the state. The church was accused of sedition and even alliance with Batista, and in January of 1961 the now-Communist government began its seizure of church property and nationalization of parochial schools. Following John F. Kennedy's failed attempt to topple Castro's regime in April of the same year, the Cuban leader announced the imminent expatriation of all clergy, which began in September as government troops stormed churches throughout Cuba's six provinces. The showdown between church and state came to its close in high drama, as 131 priests were rounded up and put on a ship headed for Spain in a symbolic expunging of the island's foreign, Catholic presence.[39]

Cuban Catholicism thus came to Miami as a nationalist church formed largely in reaction to Castro's Marxist stigmatization of religion as the "opiate of the masses" and its banishment from the island. After nearly a half century in an Anglo-Protestant culture, however, exiles have risen to the arduous task of forging a new and distinctively Latino identity that will outlive the Castro regime and guide their descendants in the future. For white, upper-middle-class Cuban Americans, this is at once a discourse of ethnicity and of class. The parishioners of the Church of the Little Flower, dwelling somewhere between Spanish Catholic and Anglo-Protestant cultures, tell the story of many Cuban Americans living out the Cuban-American Success Story.

On the third and final day of interviewing in Coral Gables, as I was preparing to leave Saint Theresa, a Cuban-born faculty member stopped me in the hallway and asked whether anyone had yet told me about a Father Whittaker. As nobody had, I asked her for clarification—but all she would tell me was to consult the annals of the *Miami Herald,* where I would find ample record, she said, of a conflict illuminating certain dynamics of Saint Theresa parish that many parishioners were perhaps loath to share. Just as she said, subsequent archival research revealed that shortly before the arrival of the Carmelites in Coral Gables, the widespread perception of Saint Theresa's as a gateway to social advancement had led to an explosive and widely publicized conflict between the parishioners and their priest. The heart of the controversy—which had Coral Gables residents picketing outside the church and drove one woman to the hospital with an irregular heartbeat—centered on Father Kenneth Whittaker's perception that the faith of some parishioners had grown cold. While comparing records of parish attendance and enrollment in the parochial school, Whittaker noticed that a significant percentage of parents whose children went to Saint Theresa's school seldom attended weekly Sunday Mass.[40] Appealing to the letter of church law, the Lutheran convert implemented in his parish a succession of eligibility requirements for enrollment of children in the school. These included mandatory Sunday Mass for all school parents, enrollment of all eligible siblings of a Saint Theresa student in the school, and a suggested minimum donation of ten dollars in the weekly collection plate.

The priest's enforcement of his policies led to the dismissal between 1990 and 1991 of fifty Saint Theresa students whose parents did not comply with the rules, one of whom fainted in her kitchen and was rushed to the hospital with heart complications. Other families saw their children denied Confirmation and First Communion because of their alleged lapse in parish attendance. In one interview with the *Miami Herald,* Whittaker justified his actions as efforts to evangelize the "unchurched." "It is incomprehensible to want to have a Catholic education and not practice [the faith]," he told reporters, citing the angry complaints of parishioners as proving "the need [for the] evangelization of the unchurched."[41] Several months after this statement, the priest amended his original plans to require latecomers to Sunday Mass to sit in the church's balcony and replaced the extant home-school association with his own appointees. Then, as if the anger in the parish had reached cosmic proportions, a deranged postal worker and former student of Saint Theresa's school wrenched open the iron gates of the Church of the Little Flower one night and decapitated five statues of the saints. While there was no apparent causal connection between this desecration and the polity battles raging in the parish, the unfortunate incident seemed to sober embittered parishioners and priest alike for a time. The last article appearing in the *Herald* reported the entire church uniting in solidarity to replace the statues and pray for the vandal's forgiveness.[42]

For their part, the accused Cuban-American parishioners—many of whom had volunteered their services in church organizations and prayed regularly at the Church of the Little Flower outside of Masses—considered Whittaker's actions as deeply un-Catholic.[43] Some women prayed the rosary for him. Others condemned his acts by appealing to divine authority. The hospitalized woman, for example, contested Whittaker's actions by pointing out, "This is only a man . . . [h]e is not God. He doesn't have the right to hurt people this way. He should punish me, not my daughter," she insisted, referring to the prohibition of her child's return to Saint Theresa's school.[44] A Cuban-American father, whose daughter was permitted to deliver the 1990 Saint Theresa salutatorian address only after he apologized for complaining at an earlier parents' meeting, vented his disgust for Whittaker before the whole of Miami in a letter to the *Herald*:

> The *Herald*'s May 24 article "A question of sacrifice" could have been described better as a question of finances vs. spirituality. The comparison of the Church of the Little Flower with Exxon or Citicorp is completely out of place, even though one could find more spirituality in a gas-station attendant or bank teller than in the pastor of Little Flower.
>
> With seven high-level positions in the administration of the Archdiocese of Miami, it is no wonder that Father Kenneth Whittaker cannot find time to care for his parishioners at Little Flower.
>
> Although one needs money to run any organization, traditionally the Catholic Church has measured its success in social services and spiritual accomplishments, not in Sunday Mass collections. The business of the Catholic Church is to save souls, not chase them away.
>
> It is clear by all the events of the past 16 months that there is room in Father Whittaker's church for old-fashioned folks; free-thinking, intelligent, modern Catholics need not apply.[45]

In the final analysis, not even the headless saints in the parish alcove could stop the local war. Father Whittaker, a deeply contemplative and prayerful man whose main "hobby" was reading church history, was replaced by the Spanish-born priest Xavier Morras, who welcomed the Carmelites to Coral Gables.

In one particularly revealing comment to the *Herald*, the archbishop of the time, Edward McCarthy, qualified his otherwise consistent support of Whittaker with a suggestion that the turmoil in Coral Gables may have had its roots in competing ethnic understandings of Catholicism:

> To a point, ethnic traditions may play a role in the trouble at St. Theresa, says Archbishop McCarthy.

Over the past 15 years, Little Flower has been adapting to a changing community. Once, its members were mostly non-Hispanic whites. Today, Hispanics—most of them Cuban-Americans—make up well over half of the church and school memberships.

"The impression I have is that in Cuba, there was a different image of parochial schools," McCarthy says. "Since it was a Catholic country [before Castro's revolution], they did not select a parochial school just for religion, and the schools were not necessarily associated with a parish. Many of them may not realize, in the United States, the close relationship between parish and school."[46]

True to the archbishop's perceptions, the battle between priest and parishioners read in many ways like a textbook chapter out of the history of multiethnic American Catholicism. The decidedly Irish-American definition of normative Catholic observance had led to previous conflicts with ethnic groups whose Catholicism centered on paraliturgical devotions. What American clerics once called "the Italian Problem," for example, stemmed from nineteenth- and early-twentieth-century Italian immigrants' sparse attendance at Sunday Mass and from their patronage of saints in street festivals, which appeared garish to the Americanized clergy. Mexican Catholics, too, with their Indianized traditions and home-centered devotions, have been targeted by the American church for assimilation, or—in the euphemistic language of the post–Vatican II church—"cultural evangelization." Making a new home for themselves in the lush surroundings of George Merrick's former Southern paradise, it would seem that Cuban parishioners of the Little Flower had sanctified their membership in an upper-middle-class neighborhood. No less than the "christening of the sugar mills" in colonial Cuba, attendance at lavish church ceremonies and patronage of the elite school continued to bless the prosperity of the Cuban elite and consecrate their success.

Cuban-American observers better versed than Whittaker in the cultural nuances of class have seen past the manifest affluence of exile culture to discern a deeper struggle in trying to live between two worlds. In a 1985 article for the *Herald*—"The American Dream, Cuban Style"—Patricia Duarte offered a profile of the so-called New Guard, Miami's reconstituted aristocracy, that highlighted the subtle but fundamental changes in Cuban class before and after exile. The many upper-class exiles who were forced to rebuild their fortunes in the United States had changed "the old rules of social status, so that pedigree no longer counts as much as it did in Cuba."[47] In comparison to the "Old Guard," some of whom quietly relocated to Palm Beach in the 1950s, Miami's new aristocrats exhibited a penchant for more conspicuous displays of wealth and status. The president of the Social Activities Committee at the Big Five Club—one of Miami's reconstructed, aristocratic beachfront clubs and frequent site of lavish fundraisers—was cited to illustrate: "I once complimented a lady on her beautiful diamond ring. She told me, 'It's $2000; would you like to buy it?'"[48] Once intended to distinguish and celebrate the heritage of a particular class, lavish galas were continued in Miami with unbearable lightness, cut loose from their original context.

In his own reflections on Latino Miami, Gustavo Perez Firmat has also noted what might be called the Cuban-American "art of consumption," the extension of the Cuban transcultural sensibility into the exchanges of the Anglo-Protestant marketplace:

> [Cuban-American culture] honors consumers over creators; or rather, it treats consumption like a creative act. You will find Cuban America not only in museums, concerts, and bookfairs, but also, and perhaps primarily, in shopping malls, restaurants, and discotheques. Cuban America defines itself by a way of dressing and dancing and driving; it expresses itself not only in novels and plays, but in fashion and food, in jewelry and jacuzzis, in advertising slogans and in popular music.[49]

For Perez Firmat, the old customs of consumption in the new context of Miami appear "as a fascinating mixture of class and crass, *kitsch and cache.*" But at the Church of the Little Flower in Coral Gables, some Cubans are turning to the church to find an even deeper meaning to their struggles. To what extent Father Whittaker remained "gone but not forgotten" in the minds of the parishioners I interviewed was unclear; given the strong emotions evoked by the conflict, I decided not to follow up archival research with further interrogation. But what did become apparent in ethnographic research was the extent to which Saint Theresa parishioners continued to struggle with the competing demands of reconstructing upper-class status in Miami and maintaining the traditional Cuban family. On the one hand, Saint Theresa's symbolic role as a marker of class was reported matter-of-factly, as the continuation of a Cuban cultural tradition. "Success is innate in us," one woman said.[50] "Yes, Coral Gables is an old neighborhood, and there is a certain affluence through association here," another echoed.[51] "Cubans are a very hard-working people and not afraid to work for democracy," yet another added.[52] On the other hand, insofar as their pursuit of the American Dream, Cuban style, takes them away from family-centered traditions, the Cuban and Cuban-American parishioners were critical of the dream. As one woman summarized, "Parents work to give their child a better life, but something gets lost. It's a modern American problem, but it's gotten worse in this neighborhood. This culture and this community are very materialistic.

Catholicism is just part of the culture. They don't have it inside. That's why there is so much divorce. Some Cubans don't think beyond the wedding and the big party."[53] Another teacher declared, "There's a certain value put on flaunting your wealth in Cuban Miami, especially the things that show off—like cars and jewelry. It's very visible in school meetings. . . . I think it's too strong. It's like a competition here."[54]

Arriving like ghosts from the prerevolutionary past, the Carmelites have come to remind Coral Gables parishioners of their familial and religious heritage. Unlike Whittaker, whose emphasis on laws and letters perhaps reflected his Lutheran background, the sisters have let their appearance and devotions do much of the talking for them. While they do not condemn what some parishioners deem to be the excesses of materialism in Coral Gables, the Carmelites model for the parish an alternative community espousing decidedly non-materialistic values. In one woman's assessment, the Carmelites "are so caring. . . . They take you to God and to prayer. They are educating the parents as well as the children. They are transforming society."[55] Or in another teacher's evaluation, "Since the Carmelites, Saint Theresa's has become our surrogate family."[56] One Cuban-born parishioner simply stated, "They give us a sense of why we're here."[57] The "miracle" effected by the Carmelites is not so different from the many physical healings they and their foundress are frequently asked to pray for: they mend the tissue of the body social, torn open by the wrenching journey of exile. As one Cuban woman explained, private devotion to both God and the saints is all well and good, "but for the really big problems, you run to the church."[58] The parishioners of Coral Gables appropriate American neotraditionalism selectively, however, always with an eye to the preservation of their own community.

The reception of neotraditionalism in Miami amplifies themes found in the Carmelites' Los Angeles and Arizona parishes. Miamian Catholics, like the Filipino and Mexican Americans in southern California, articulate an ethnic identity in tension with Anglo-Protestant culture. We read in the Cuban-American narrative similar fears of individualism and materialism threatening to destroy the traditional Cuban family, and attempts to refashion Cuban-American identity after the Carmelites' model of homogenous community. Like the Los Angeles parishioners, lay Catholics in Coral Gables see in the theological consensus and communitarian lifestyle of the sisters a possible template for cultural consensus of gender roles in the Latino family. Despite the very real reconfigurations of the Cuban-American family reflected in Magaly Queralt's research, however, the Cuban-American parish does not speak of itself as under siege by Anglo-Protestant culture. This difference between the Los Angeles and Miamian narratives would seem to reflect the fact that Anglo-Protestant culture can no longer claim hegemonic control of urban identity in the Florida metropolis. The powerful Cuban-American elite has succeeded in crafting a narrative of Latino Miami that delineates the parameters of reflection for the parishioners of Coral Gables. Their orientation to Anglo-Protestant culture may be critical, but it is less defensive than that of Los Angeles Catholics. Hence there is not the same depiction in Coral Gables of the ethnoreligious enclave as an oasis or safe haven in a hostile environment.

Like the Catholics in Arizona, the laity of Coral Gables understands the neotraditionalism of the Carmelites in relation to a Spanish Catholic history and culture. The center of the Miamian narrative is neither the institutional church nor the Anglo-Protestant *civis,* but the Cuban exile community. Consistent with Tweed's designation of Cuban-American culture as translocative, the Catholic identity of Coral Gables recombines memories of Cuba with contemporary perceptions of life in the United States. The sisters guide the parish through its present-day trials as "Success Story" exemplars in Miami. Descendents of a Spanish New World culture, the Cuban Americans of this study continue to blend together elements of disparate cultures with a *mestizaje* sensibility, in a further parallel with the Catholics of the Arizona borderlands. Parishioners incorporate the material trappings of their upper-middle-class lifestyle in Coral Gables into their Catholic identity, just as their ancestors blessed the sugar mills and patronized the church as a marker of upper-class status. Redefining themselves in relation to a host of historical, cultural, and economic markers, Cuban-American Catholics in Coral Gables evoke what for them is traditional Catholicism at critical points in their narrative of ethnoreligious identity. By turns the Carmelites are reminders of prerevolutionary Cuba, advocates of the family, and signs of God's sanctioning of their material success. The Tridentine lifestyle and devotions of the sisters are thus instrumental in the imagining of Cuban-American identity, never displacing the concerns of the exile community as the organizing themes of Catholic identity.

6

Gone but Not Forgotten:
The Carmelites in
Postindustrial Cleveland

C LEVELAND, OHIO, used to feature prominently in gallows humor designed to cope with the malaise of the Midwest's dilapidating Rust Belt. "Why did California get earthquakes, and Ohio get Cleveland?" one popular joke began. "Because California got first choice," it retorted.[1] Until the massive urban renewal projects started in 1979 by Mayor George V. Voinovich, Cleveland epitomized the plight of midwestern former industrial centers in a postindustrial age. In his introduction to the history of "the rise and fall of the industrial Midwest," Jon C. Teaford explains:

> From Cleveland to Milwaukee and Cincinnati to Saint Louis stretch the cities of the heartland. Through much of the nineteenth century they were the wunderkinds of the American family of cities, infant prodigies that astonished travelers from throughout the world with their remarkable precocity. By the beginning of the twentieth century they had grown to maturity and stood tall among the nation's urban centers. Four of them ranked among the ten largest cities in America, and six were on the list of the top twenty. The leader of this midwestern band was a broad-shouldered Chicago, the nation's second largest metropolis and a city famed for its strutting self-confidence and feisty bravado. By the second half of the twentieth century, however, Chicago and the other midwestern metropolises had grown old, and their graying business districts and sagging industries became the focus of news stories and travelers' tales. The term *rust belt* entered the American vocabulary, and Youngstown, Detroit, and Peoria

offered a visible definition of this new concept. By the close of the twentieth century, the cities of America's Midwest appeared to have passed
through the entire urban life cycle.[2]

The city of Cleveland came to be known in midwestern parlance as "The
Mistake by the Lake" for its myriad problems to which Teaford alludes.
Plagued by widespread poverty, a crumbling infrastructure, racial tensions,
pollution, and a steadily falling population and tax base, Cleveland at the
turn of the millennium is a ghost of its former self.

This chapter on the Carmelite order in Cleveland is markedly distinguished from the previous three accounts of Catholic identity in its departure from issues of Filipino and/or Latino identity in the appropriation of
neotraditionalist Catholicism. In a midwestern city whose history and self-
image has been characterized predominantly by the story of European immigration to the United States, neotraditionalism is not seen as either Spanish or normatively Catholic, but respectfully relegated to an irretrievable past.
Like the Euro-American parish of San Marino in Los Angeles, Catholics of
the St. Rose of Lima church find in Mother Luisa's order no cultural or ethnic associations through which they might incorporate neotraditionalism
into the pressing concerns of their everyday life. Unlike the San Marino
parishioners, however, Clevelanders do make a historical connection between the Carmelites and their city. They see in the order a reminder of
Cleveland's ethnoreligious European past that has largely disappeared alongside the broader economic and social transformations in their Rust Belt city.
Hence in Cleveland the sisters are not so much scorned as they are eulogized,
incorporated into a narrative of the European immigrant city of yesteryear.

In searching for a new collective identity, the largely working-class and
multiethnic parish of St. Rose of Lima turns to local sports teams, whose
emblems and mascots bedeck the Carmelite school alongside pictures of
Catholic saints. In a region of America where patriotism has long characterized local identity, the enthusiastic identification with the Cleveland
Browns and Indians plays an analogous role to the idealization of suburbia
in Los Angeles: as a totem of participation in the Anglo-American fold. The
Cleveland and San Marino parishes seek no less than the communities of
Los Angeles, the Arizona borderlands, and Miami some sense of belonging
in a social collective. But for these two parishes, the sisters are decidedly "old
world," a throw-back to the preconciliar past. The failure, then, of neotraditionalist Catholicism to win favor in both Cleveland and San Marino returns to the theme of the interaction between ethnic and religious identity
for both liberal and conservative Catholics.

The history of Cleveland recounts the story of both Euro- and African-

American immigration to the Midwest in the wake of nineteenth-century industrialization. Until the building of the Erie and Ohio Canals between 1825 and 1833, Cleveland had remained an isolated settlement on the mouth of the Cuyahoga River draining into Lake Erie in the far western recesses of Connecticut's "Western Reserve," a tract of land the United States government granted in 1795 for settlement by its loyal Revolutionary soldiers. The new series of waterways linking it to East Coast commercial centers came quickly to transform the outpost into a bustling midwestern port city where farmers of the American interior and manufacturers of New York exchanged their goods. By 1840, Cleveland had grown to be the largest city in northeast Ohio.[3] With the following decade's expansion of the Cuyahoga Steam Furnace Company, which manufactured engines for Great Lakes steamships and America's new locomotives, the city was transformed once again from a port city to a major industrial center. New discoveries of petroleum in Pennsylvania and iron ore along the Great Lakes added refineries to its urban landscape, while investors targeted Cleveland as a national railway center in the 1850s, a hub connecting lines from New York, Chicago, St. Louis, and Pittsburgh.

Factory jobs attracted the first wave of European migration to Cleveland as well as the city's first financial institutions. Economic and demographic growth continued between the Civil War and the First World War, with a second wave of Southern and Eastern European immigrants flooding Cleveland in the 1880s. By the end of the nineteenth century, immigrants or first-generation Americans descended from families in Italy, Greece, Hungary, Slovenia, Serbia, Croatia, Czechoslovakia, Poland, and Russia constituted nearly three-quarters of the population.[4] While European migration tapered off with the new quotas on immigration during World War I and in 1924, Cleveland continued to attract new laborers: Southern blacks who came to work in the wartime factories. Notwithstanding its own share of urban problems common to nineteenth-century American cities, including nativist and racial prejudice, class inequities, overcrowding, and pollution, Cleveland had come to stand as a beacon of economic and social advancement for Europeans and Americans alike by the end of the 1920s.

With the stock market crash of 1929, Cleveland's economic vitality and former image came to a sudden and unexpected halt. As factories closed and unemployment levels surged, the city entered a decline from which it has never recovered. A temporary economic resurgence during World War II only added to the city's problems in the long run. Southern blacks, together with whites from the Appalachian Mountains, were again recruited to work in factories, only to be faced with a shortage of housing and forced to live in subdivided single-family homes. The wartime manufacturing opportu-

nities eventually came to an end, and the city returned to high unemployment levels, and now Clevelanders were additionally plagued with overcrowding and substandard living conditions. The choice of many returning
servicemen to live in the more comfortable and affluent suburbs only has-
tened the racial and class stratification between Cleveland's center and periphery that had begun with "white flight" to the suburbs in the 1930s. By
the war's end, the inner city was predominantly black and lower-class white,
surrounded on the east and the west by descendants of former European
immigrants.

Cleveland's social history over the next four decades reads like a litany
of doom. The construction of interstate highways throughout the 1950s re-
carved longstanding neighborhood boundaries within the city and displaced former residents. In 1966, violent riots erupted in the African-American Hough District. In 1976, U.S. District Court Judge Frank Battisti's order
enforcing public school busing backfired in its attempts to desegregate the
city, spurring more middle-class black and white Clevelanders to move to
the suburbs. From 1960 to 1980, the population of inner-city Cleveland
dropped from 876,050 to 573,822.[5] Economically, the situation was just as
bleak. Like other cities of the Rust Belt, Cleveland saw its remaining manufacturing industries leave the area to reap higher profits from lower wages
elsewhere. Between 1958 and 1977, the city lost over 130,000 jobs.[6] The municipal tax base steadily dried up. In 1978, Cleveland declared bankruptcy,
defaulting on its $14 million loan from local banks. In the meantime, the
waters of the Cuyahoga River and Lake Erie, infused with the toxic residues
of former industries, periodically burned.

In 1979, Mayor George V. Voinovich was elected for his vision of a new
Cleveland that appealed to both the city's voters and the business community. Voinovich proposed and successfully implemented a series of urban
renewal projects designed to catalyze tourism, lure business, bolster the tax
base, and change the city's public image. Starting in the early 1980s, former
municipal buildings were "gentrified" and warehouses converted into apartment buildings, shops, and offices. Cleveland built an aquarium, a science
museum, the Blossom Music Center, and the Rock and Roll Hall of Fame,
and cleansed the waters of Lake Erie and the Cuyahoga River. To a large extent, the renewals were successful. Ohio Bell, Eaton Corporation, and British
Petroleum America (formerly Standard Oil) came to establish headquarters
in the business district, and the municipal tax base was replenished. Tourists
began to venture cautiously back into the city. Unfortunately, however, even
the most thoroughgoing projects could do little to restore a labor-intensive
and high-paying economy or change the destitute urban landscape outside
the downtown's commercial fortress. In 1989, the Council for Economic Op-

portunities in Greater Cleveland reported that three-fourths of the local county's poor lived within the city, while racial tensions and an ailing public school system continued to characterize the urban landscape for inner-city residents.[7]

The Carmelite sisters of Los Angeles have settled in the extreme northwest corner of the Rust Belt city at Saint Rose of Lima Church. Until the early 1980s, the largely Irish-American parish drew affluent Catholics from the Edgewater district, or "Gold Coast," along Lake Erie and middle-class home owners in the Cudell district closer to the church. Since that time, however, the white flight—or "fright and flight" as one parishioner chose to call it—which has long characterized Cleveland demographics finally spread to the circumference of the city.[8] Starting in the mid 1970s, younger families began moving west to the suburbs, while many of the older middle-class parishioners retired in the multistory retirement home across the street from the church. Today, the streets just south of the parish have become working-class white and Latino, mostly Puerto Rican, with a few Vietnamese and African-American families. Catholics to the north are middle-class, Euro-American renters. The subdivision of Cudell's former single-family homes into inexpensive apartments has helped maintain a transient parish, no longer a place to buy a starter home. From 1975 to 1996, membership at Saint Rose fell from 2,200 to 1,850 families.[9]

By the mid 1990s, both longstanding and recent members of Saint Rose were describing their parish as "a neighborhood trying to be a neighborhood" or a neighborhood "just trying to hang on to some community."[10] "This area used to be West Side Irish," one woman—whose ancestors came from County Cork, Ireland—explained. "It used to be much more of a *neighborhood*. They are still trying to hang on to it."[11] Another parishioner who was raised "right down the street," on West 69th in a shrinking Italian-American neighborhood, similarly observed, "My parish, Mount Carmel, was very Italian. But here it's more liberal and relaxed—there are no parish boundaries—there are people from a lot of parishes here."[12]

The urban poverty endemic to much of inner-city Cleveland has also crept into Cudell. One Carmelite, a native of Los Angeles, characterized her parishioners as "worried" and "just trying to hang on."[13] Broken homes, substance abuse by parents, and child abuse head the list of problems faced daily by the sisters and their lay staff. "In the Glory Days, the school had a very good reputation," she said, "but today it has become a refuge for most folks—who don't have anywhere else to turn." She paused for a minute and added: "Boy, L.A. is the place that's supposed to be messed up, but I've got news for you: Cleveland is pretty bad off."[14] She underscored her point with a few stories from her first year teaching: the kidnapping and rape of a boy from a recreation center a few blocks away from the church; the repeated abuse of a fifth-grade student at Saint Rose by his uncle; the frequent retention of parents in drug and alcohol treatment centers.[15]

In light of the social fragmentation and poverty at Saint Rose, it might seem that Mother Luisa's Carmelites would present to Clevelanders the kind of "oasis" recounted by Catholic parishes in Los Angeles, but they do not. In light of the European Catholic heritage of Cleveland that dates back to the nineteenth century, it might seem that neotraditionalist Catholicism would merge with the cultural identity of Irish- or Italian-American parishioners, but it does not. As the history of the order both within the church and in the other three American communities makes clear, the Carmelites' oppositional relationship to the modern world takes root only in those communities at a certain distance, for either theological or ethnohistorical reasons, from Anglo-Protestant America. Like the affluent Los Angelenos of San Marino, the parishioners of Cleveland—in spite of all their hardships—still retain a deep allegiance to their city. No amount of civic fragmentation or economic depression can justify for these Catholics a final break from their midwestern urban heritage, which is what membership in the neotraditionalist tradition would require.

Since the 1960s, however, Clevelanders are much less certain of their identity than they used to be. Demonstrations at the 1968 Democratic convention in Chicago and the shooting of four college students by national guardsmen at Ohio's Kent State University symbolized the end of an era throughout the Midwest, which had defined itself since the early twentieth century as epitomizing all that was "most American." Before its own Hough District race riots, Cleveland's identity was closely tied to the realization of the American Dream by its European immigrants. Today, the old immigrant neighborhoods have largely disappeared, and the old America is gone. While Clevelanders' allegiance to both nation and city continues to be expressed through a near religious support of the local sports teams—whose banners, mascots, and records hang throughout the parochial school—they are searching for a new collective purpose. In addition to rejecting neotraditional Catholicism as an ideal for the future, Rust Belt Catholics perceive it as part of a cherished, but ultimately irretrievable, urban past.

Mother Luisa's American sisters assumed they were coming to Cleveland to help Father James Viall reform his parish. When Viall first arrived at Saint Rose in 1975, he was outraged to find the Sisters of Saint Joseph using Planned Parenthood literature in their sex education classes. Never known for his fear of confrontation, the priest summarily confiscated the literature and burned it; this was signal enough for the sisters to leave. A tall, powerful man then in his mid-forties, Viall had already served as the origi-

nal president of the Consortium Perfectae Caritatis, the organization of neotraditionalist sisters today headed by the Carmelites' mother superior as the
Council of Major Superiors of Women Religious. Finding a replacement
was not too difficult. Consortium Dominicans from Nashville, Tennessee,
quickly came to staff the school, until Bishop James Hickey of Washington,
D.C., siphoned them off for his own institutions. After an interim stay by
an Iowa order of Franciscans, Mother Luisa's Carmelites came to Viall's aid
in 1991, and they have remained ever since.[16]

Retired from his higher-profile ecclesiastical career, Viall introduced his
vision of Catholic leadership to the local church. In his opinion, the liberal
transformation of American Catholicism following Vatican II reflected ecclesiastical leaders' failure of nerve to uphold the true faith. If neotraditionalist Catholic leaders would lead the American church more boldly, he
believed, the church would see both its membership and the number of
priestly vocations increase.[17] Asking that they remain anonymous, Viall
shared stories of colleagues whose theological positions wavered to accommodate political changes in church leadership. "Don't become a priest if
you're too ambitious," he concluded, "it's too dangerous." True to his own
principles, the priest has kept liturgical innovations in his own parish to a
bare minimum—even altar girls are forbidden—because "people don't
want surprises when they go to church."[18] Parents whose children attend the
parochial school are required to sign yearly contracts pledging to attend parent meetings and periodic lectures by neotraditionalist guest speakers at the
local parish.[19]

After five years of working alongside their ecclesiastical ally, however,
the Carmelites have noticed a discernible difference between their schools
in California and the one in Ohio: the strong ethnic identifications particularly among Cleveland's Euro-American parishioners, which the sisters attribute to the legacy of "East Coast" culture. The school's principal explained,
"People here want a solid faith for their children, and there's a heritage in
Cleveland of Catholic schools. They grew up on the East Coast. It's not that
it's necessarily more traditional [theologically] here—I think they're really
starving to get back to their roots."[20] Another sister, a native of Huntington
Park, California, contrasted California and Ohio Catholicism more sharply.
"My ethnicity is not that important to me," she said, "but the people back
east here are different. They're friendly and hospitable, for sure. But this
church seems more divided. There seems to be more polarization here: either extremely conservative—I mean, like back to 1955—or extremely liberal. Sometimes I wonder if it's not part of the ethnic tension."[21]

In light of the recent demographic changes of Saint Rose's church, the
ethnic affiliations noted by the sisters mark a decidedly nostalgic orienta-

tion by both priest and staff members to their city. Viall's strong theological convictions were ultimately rooted in an idealization of an older Cleveland landscape that no longer reflects his own city. "Cleveland is a very Catholic city. We have the Irish and the Italians and the Germans and the Polish here," he explained, neglecting to add that these immigrants had been assimilated into Anglo-Protestant culture more than half a century earlier.[22] Himself a descendant of Rhode Island Puritans, the historic dissidents of New England's theocracy, Viall described the post–Vatican II liberal reforms: "Protestantism is a four-hundred-and-fifty-year-old heresy that would have died out if it weren't for the Council," he lamented.[23] An elderly Sister of Saint Joseph, who was retained as Saint Rose's school librarian for her neo-traditionalist views, echoed the priest's sentiments. After the Vatican II reforms, she said, "you just as well might be a Protestant—there's nothing distinctive about you anymore."[24] The sister then went on to reminisce about her childhood village just east of Ohio, an ethnic enclave of German and Irish Catholics in the early twentieth century.[25]

While less hopeful than the priest for an inner-city Catholic cultural revival, other staff members nevertheless employed demographic distinctions between the "east and west sides" rooted in nineteenth-century geography to describe their city. Vicariously identifying themselves as "west siders," local Catholics characterized Cleveland-east-of-the-Cuyahoga River, the historic home of local corporate barons and New England settlers, as retaining an air of snobbery and high culture. In contrast, the west side was described as the home of working-class European immigrants. "This side of town you were encouraged to retain ethnic traditions, You needed a passport to get to the east side," one woman explained.[26] Parishioners further expressed their identification with the old neighborhoods in their opinions about desegregation and busing in the Cleveland public schools. "Judge [Frank J.] Battisti ruled for busing," an Italian-American parishioner smoldered, referring to a 1976 ruling by the United States District Court. "It was nice to go to school in your own neighborhood."[27] "Busing broke up the neighborhoods, and this is the alternative to public school. But you can see the effects of it here: there's a lot of apathy, a lot of neglect across the board with parents. A lot of children are having children [i.e., teenage pregnancies]. No one's taking responsibility anymore."[28] Another explained, "There's been a lot of change in Cleveland, definitely—especially in education. I think Cleveland's been struggling with its identity. There's too much transitoriness. I think the battle for community is being lost."[29]

The mythic dimensions of urban geography in Cleveland were clearly revealed in the aftermath of the busing order. Originally prompted by a lawsuit by the National Association for the Advancement of Colored People,

Judge Frank J. Battisti's 1976 ruling was intended as a logical way to distribute educational resources fairly and equitably across segregated neighborhoods. Its reception by Clevelanders, however, was anything but reasoned. Just four years after the ruling, enrollment in Cleveland public schools had dropped to two-thirds of its former level, as both blacks and whites relocated en masse to outlying suburbs. In 1985, Dr. Frederick "Doc" Holiday, the city's first black superintendent of schools, who had been appointed by courts to oversee the changes, ended his bitter three-year-long struggle against Cleveland's entrenched racism by shooting himself in the chest on the steps of a public school.[30] The succinct explanation by a Saint Rose parishioner that busing had "mixed the east and west sides," seemed a poignant enough conclusion: busing had upset sociohistoric delineations inscribed on the neighborhood streets.[31]

Idealizations of the ethnic neighborhood have come increasingly to characterize local, popular, and even scholarly portrayals of Cleveland. The nineteenth-century immigrant neighborhood allegedly embodied all that was good and true in the city's collective character. Something of its larger-than-life status is captured in an essay by Edward M. Miggins, a prominent Cleveland historian.

> Certainly the concern for one's neighbor was the highest achievement in Cleveland's ethnic and minority communities that stood between the spires and stacks. America's individualism and materialism were restrained or tempered by the values of nationality or family life and religious traditions celebrating peace, justice, and loving fellowship. Jobs below the "stacks" made people leave their social enclaves, but they realized the importance of the connection of economic activity or steady work to their familial and neighborhood life. Our age celebrates the divorce of the two in the worship of acquisitive individualism or materialism, mobility, and destruction or replacement of the old with the new. America can find an alternative moral and social vision by understanding and recapturing the creativity and courage of its immigrant and migrant people who built churches, fraternal organizations, and schools in their urban neighborhoods as a communal strength against the economic and social turmoil of their day.[32]

On the one hand, both interviews with local parishioners and the aftermath of busing make clear that local Clevelanders share with Miggins this idealization of their nineteenth-century past. On the other hand, the cool support for both Father Viall and the Carmelites at Saint Rose of Lima suggests the fragility and finally the obsolescence of nostalgia for reconstituting social bonds in a fragmented, postindustrial city. Staff members describe their students as apathetic and listless, while local parishioners are conspicuously absent from the school's staff. Excepting one Jewish woman, the teachers are the Euro-American descendants of the immigrants, most of whom commute from the outlying suburbs.

Neotraditionalist Catholicism is perceived quite clearly by staff members as a legacy of the "Old Cleveland." Under the administration of Consortium sisters like the Carmelites, the school has become a link to the ethnic past, and suburban Catholics have sent their children back to the parish of their ancestors.[33] Closer to the inner city, however, the discrepancy between past and present simply cannot be ignored. In addition to its recent ethnic transformation, Cudell and adjacent Lakewood have purportedly become one of Cleveland's most visibly gay neighborhoods. "Haven't you noticed all the rainbow flags around here?" one parishioner asked bemusedly. "This is the 'Gay Ghetto.' I often wonder how the children here make sense of what the sisters [and priest] teach them. They get one thing in school; then they go home and see something completely different on the streets and on TV. I really wonder how they deal with it."[34] There is a costume shop across the street from Saint Rose; the traditionally clad sisters have been mistaken on more than one occasion, she said, for costumed drag queens on their way to a party.[35]

Both priest and sisters are accordingly relegated to an idealized but irretrievable past—signified alternatively as "tradition," "the old ways," or childhood memories:

> The traditions here are consistent. That's what the people like. This is the way it is: you either like it or leave it. Father Viall doesn't bend.[36]

> The old ways were best" is what is said here. It sets this place apart.[37]

> Religion here is the true religion. And this is what I grew up with.[38]

> The Carmelites are very Old Catholic—no, I shouldn't put it that way— very traditional. Maybe sometimes it gets too tunnel-visioned here, with all the talk of women in their places: I have a problem with that, their views about women in the priesthood. But they're strong women with strong convictions. They take charge of things. Holy women, I guess you could say.[39]

> The Carmelites are like an endangered species. They should charge people to pay admission. This is a very Catholic town, but they don't usually have real nuns.[40]

To some extent, the disappearance of European Catholic neighborhoods like Cudell implicates the church as a victim of its own success. The relocation of Euro-Americans to the suburbs reflects not only a reactionary "white flight" from the problems of the inner city, but also the final chapter in their assimilation into American society, which was endorsed and facilitated by the "traditional" church for at least two decades. Now that most of them are gone, some Catholics question retrospectively the wisdom of the old policies.

From its founding as an independent diocese in 1847, Cleveland worked diligently to eliminate the cultural, linguistic, and social distinctions between immigrant communities and Anglo-Protestant American culture. In his overview of midwestern Catholicism, historian Stephen J. Shaw explains:

> The history of the Catholic parish in the Midwest is to a large extent (though not exclusively) the history of the ethnic parish. . . . It is my thesis that these parishes served as "way stations" of ethnicity and Americanization. The parish was the focus of immigrants' daily life and the principal institution that carried on their native traditions, but it was also the indispensable force that pushed its members into mainstream American life. The language of priests and teachers, the parish bulletins, the extensive network of elementary and high school education, all served to affirm the past, but, at the same time, helped the immigrant accept the society in which he had settled. Bishops such as . . . [Richard] Gilmour of Cleveland [from 1872 to 1891] accepted the ethnic parish as the necessity of the day. It was within the ethnic parish that immigrants struggled to keep what they had and learn from the new. The dioceses of the Midwest pushed them to be both American and Catholic, and the parish was the way-station.[41]

Before the days of Gilmour's "ethnic parish" to which Shaw alludes, Cleveland's first bishop, Louis Amadeus Rappe, fought in vain to suppress the retention of distinctive European Catholic traditions by the city's first German and Irish immigrants. After decades of receiving complaints from his constituency, the American church finally succeeded in persuading Rappe to resign his post in 1870.[42] Gilmour's strategy represented something of a compromise between the American church institution and the laity. While immigrants were allowed to perpetuate their religious traditions within designated ethnic parishes, the Cleveland diocese continued to work for the cultural assimilation that Rappe had championed.

The church's desire to assimilate "ethnic Catholics" reflected a more widespread perception in the 1800s of Catholics as dangerous "papists," allies of a church allegedly opposed to all that was good and true in American democracy: freedom, individualism, and critical thinking.[43] The former parishioners of Saint Rose's church, the Irish immigrants, were accordingly stigmatized as dubiously intelligent, potentially violent, and undeniably alcoholic. Partly in loyalty to their past, partly in resistance to assimilation, the Irish clung to their own religious traditions, which included strong support for the institutional church. Irish immigrants came from a history marked by religiocultural Catholic resistance to British colonization, and the parish was particularly revered. In America, they quickly came to dominate church leadership, gracing Cleveland with new church buildings and spearheading the growth of its parochial schools. For other European immigrants, the ethnic church facilitated the Americanization of their observances more noticeably. In 1884, the American church met as a national body in Baltimore to standardize both worship and education, effecting religious and cultural uniformity among European Catholics from diverse backgrounds.

Fresh waves of immigration from southern and eastern Europe ensured the continuance of Cleveland's distinctive neighborhoods and religious traditions well into the 1930s. With America's entrance into the Second World War, however, the final assimilation of Euro-American Catholics into Anglo-Protestant culture began. Not only did a common national cause unite Protestants and Catholics in shared sacrifice, but the booming postwar economy and decidedly patriotic culture helped erode both religious and ethnic distinctions among white Americans. With support from the G.I. Bill, the descendants of immigrants returned home to realize educational and socioeconomic success in a country they could now unreservedly call their own. In the meantime, against the backdrop of a new Cold War against atheistic Communists, the American Catholic church emerged to support, with muted qualifications, the supremacy and righteousness of the American nation. For more than two decades, Euro-American Clevelanders moved "up and out" of the inner city with the blessing of both their church and their country.

Unfortunately, however, the coming-of-age of Cleveland's Euro-American descendants was cut short by the tumultuous events of the 1960s. An interrelated series of national developments and traumatic events, including the civil rights movement, the assassination of Catholic president John F. Kennedy, the Vietnam War, and the rise of a new hippie counterculture, came to shatter the patriotic nationalism of the Cold War years. The shock waves were felt strongly throughout America's Heartland. In Cleveland itself, rioting broke out for four days in July 1966 throughout the African-American Hough District, drawing in the National Guard and taking the lives of four residents. In 1968, Students for a Democratic Society protested at the Democratic convention in Chicago, and in October of the following year, violent demonstrations orchestrated by the radical left-wing Weathermen erupted in Chicago's streets. In May of 1970, the country watched in horror as National Guardsmen shot and killed four college students during an antiwar protest at Ohio's Kent State University, thirty-five miles south of Cleveland.

In his study of the meaning of the Middle West in American culture, James R. Shortridge has discussed the close association between the regional identity of the Midwest and the national identity of America. From its inception in the first decade of the 1900s until the 1950s, the myth of the Middle West was primarily a story of American pastoralism, the harmonizing of culture and nature. As discussed by Leo Marx in his classic work *The Machine in the Garden,* pastoralism dates back at least as far as Virgil's *Eclogues,* in which the poet extols the virtues of his imaginary life in Arcadia, a garden situated midway between corrupt Roman civilization and the untamed wilderness. As the first Europeans were settling in the Americas, Shakespeare imagined the New World as the Arcadian paradise in his play *The Tempest,* an idea that was seized by such influential intellectuals of the American colonies as Thomas Jefferson, who bequeathed to the country its own pastoral image of the patriotic farmer planting gardens amidst the savage Indian wilderness.[44] The mythology of the Middle West appropriated this older, national identity, recasting the East Coast as a decadent culture and the West Coast as the site for untamed impulses in the American character. As long as the Anglo-Protestant nation was strong, industrial centers like Cleveland were simply absorbed into the narrative: farms and factories alike worked to support the cause of Jeffersonian democracy, while institutions like the Catholic church worked diligently to ensure the Americanization of urban immigrants.[45]

The national unrest of the 1960s thus left a particularly strong impact on midwestern culture. In states like Ohio where a long history of industrialism had already undermined a pastoral self-image, its effects were most corrosive. As early as the 1950s, Shortridge suggests, the pastoral myth had already started to recede into a legendary past for inhabitants of the region's cities:

> [A] new perspective on the region emerged [in the 1950s and early 1960s]. This was nostalgia. Slowly and uncertainly during the 1950s a vague sense of loss seems to have developed among many city dwellers. One can infer this from a careful reading of the popular literature. Instead of generating wholesale condemnation by writers, small towns and traditional farms, indeed the entire Middle-Western culture, began to be labeled quaint. Support for this viewpoint quickened in the mid 1960s, and by the early 1970s it was perhaps the dominant image that outsiders held about the region. From this perspective, the Middle West had become a museum of sorts. No up-and-coming citizen wanted to live there, but it had importance as a repository for traditional values. The Middle West was a nice place to visit occasionally and to reflect on one's heritage. It was America's collective "hometown," a place with good air, picturesque farm buildings, and unpretentious "simple" people.[46]

Based on the results of his own national survey, Shortridge suggests that Ohio and Michigan, the region's most heavily industrialized states, dropped off the "cognitive map" of the Midwest after the 1960s altogether. "The old pretext of seeing only the rural side of Ohio and Michigan," he writes, "became increasingly awkward after the late 1960s, as racial conflict and industrial collapse in Detroit, Cleveland, and elsewhere became major national news stories."[47] Subsequently, the region moved west and south, toward Kansas and Nebraska, in the collective imagination of both Americans and midwesterners.

Shortridge's study suggests that the mixture of nostalgia and apathy evoked by neotraditionalist Catholicism in Cleveland mirrors the demise of Middle Western mythology throughout the state more generally. After the 1960s, Ohio pastoralism survived only as a cherished memory, catalyzing the present-day search for a new symbolic center. For a short time, Ohio was resignified by the National Collegiate Athletic Association as part of a new region, "the Mideast," but has settled uneasily as a far west satellite of the East Coast: its designation by native West Coast Carmelites.[48] In Cleveland itself, the ethnic neighborhood has been substituted as the urban equivalent of the agrarian "home town," the mythologized locus of pastoral values. It, too, is gone but not forgotten. In the meantime, the city has searched for a new label of its own, wavering between the "North Coast" and the slightly more popular "Great Lakes City."

Despite these profound cultural transformations and more longstanding socioeconomic trials, however, Clevelanders, in a further reflection of their midwestern heritage of patriotism, have never lost hope for either their city or their nation. Today, Clevelanders' support of their local sports teams, symbols of local community, is near legendary in the nation's sports culture. Commenting on their steadfast support of the Indians baseball team through decades of embarrassing losses, one commentator observed,

> Remarkably, Clevelanders have exhibited little angst about this horrible run of baseball. At worst, they are indifferent about it, as they were in 1985, when only 65,181 people showed up at cavernous, 74,208-seat Cleveland Stadium during the season; or in '56, when 356 people dropped by for a September game. "I remember the place was so empty and so quiet," broadcaster Herb Score, the former Indian ace, says of that game, "that from the pitching mound I could here [sic] the clacking of the typewriters up in the press box." At best, fans are warmly sentimental and fatalistic about all the losing, as evidenced by the subtitle of a recently published book, *The Curse of Rocky Colavito*, which traces the Tribe's struggles to the 1960 trade of the slugging outfielder: *A Loving Look at a Thirty-Year Slump.*[49]

An even more dramatic display of fan loyalty erupted in 1995, the year Art Modell announced the imminent relocation of the city's football team, the Browns. The day after the decision was announced, livid fans tossed huge chunks of ice onto the playing field during a Browns–Oilers game, and hung a huge "Rot-in-Hell, Modell" banner from the bleachers. Other Clevelanders gathered outside the team's locker room demanding to see the owner, who had already retreated to his Florida home in anticipation of their ire. Even the mayor, fearing financial losses to his city, spewed to a reporter, "I will tell you, my friend, there will be no peace until the NFL [National Football League] owners meet on January 17 [to sanction or challenge Modell's move]. And there may not be peace afterward, if we don't keep the Browns."[50]

Despite the protests, the Browns ended up relocating, for a time, to Baltimore. But the fervor for local athletics has not disappeared from Saint Rose parish. If they are cool about the Carmelites and ambivalent about ethnicity, parishioners stand by the Indians and the Browns with a passion rivaled only by their hatred of busing. "The working class community identifies with sports—the Indians are really big here—in this neighborhood especially, the sports are really big," one woman explained.[51] Judging from the ubiquity of baseball paraphernalia throughout their school, the Carmelites have embraced the craze more than their suburban staff members, in a gesture of solidarity with the multiethnic, working-class parish. Beside pictures of Mary and Jesus and framed prayers to the saints, the stickers, flags, and pennants of the Cleveland Indian—the team mascot—were interspersed throughout the school during the baseball season. Above the northern exit in the main hallway hung a six-foot-long computer-printed banner reading, "God Help our Tribe in their new season." Transparent stickers of the Cleveland Indian's cartoon head were stuck to the windows of doors, and a large bar graph of the students' favorite sports was posted on a wall.

Historian of religions Catherine L. Albanese has drawn attention to the mythic and ritual dimension of organized sports as a form of "American cultural religion," the expression of predominantly Protestant values in and through the stories and pastimes of popular media culture:

> Sports . . . have provided a ritual-like setting for millions of Americans. By setting up boundaries and defining the space of the game, sports have helped Americans fit a grid to their own experience in order to define it and give it structure. Hence, it is not surprising that our public games have given people a code of conduct for everyday living. If the ball field is a miniature rehearsal for the game of life, it tells us that life is a struggle between contesting forces in which there is a winning and a losing side. The message too, is that success depends on teamwork in which members of the winning side conquer the opposing team by pulling together. And in this contest to the end, competition becomes a value in itself and generates a set of accompanying virtues that identify a good team player. Loy-

alty, fair play, and being a "good sport" in losing are all examples of these virtues. So, too, are self-denial and hard work to achieve victory.[52]

If Catholicism can no longer claim to represent Cleveland's neighborhood or cultural heritage as it once could for much of the inner city's working-class population, organized sports can provide provisional grounds for civic identity, a point that has not been lost on the savvy Carmelites. In a final interview with the principal, the sister displayed a large Cleveland Indians flag donated to the school by a local resident, unfurling the cloth gracefully amidst the waving folds of her own habit. A genuine fan of the team whose office window displayed a Cleveland Indian, the sister understood perfectly well the sociological dimensions of their game. The Indians, she elaborated, were a winning team who won the American League Pennant in 1994 through hard work and team spirit, enduring years of loss with patience and fortitude. Since they epitomized the Catholic principles the order espoused, she would make sure their flag hung outside the school.[53]

In this region of the country, however, the odds are greatly stacked against a Carmelite victory. Elaborating further on the mythic dimension of baseball, Albanese has explained, "[T]he division into two teams who battle each other in the game resembles the dualistic biblical account of a final millennial battle. As in the story of that ultimate war, it is clear in the game that there is a good team (our side) and a bad team (the opposing side). . . . Each team, in its own understanding, is on the side of right, and so each team must exhibit innocence."[54] In Cleveland, the Carmelites and their parishioners play for different teams, despite a common interest in baseball. For the sisters, America is fallen. For Clevelanders, America is down but not defeated. In their support of local sports teams, Clevelanders participate in a ritual extolling the mores of Anglo-Protestant America. Each side can ultimately claim that God is on their side, but the sisters and the priests are vastly outnumbered. Were it not for their perceived obsolescence, the neotraditional Carmelites might very well meet with the same heated resistance in Cleveland that they do in San Marino, the only other parish where their neotraditionalist Catholicism is clearly at odds with local civic identity.

In the meantime, the Catholic church in Cleveland continues to be, as it has been since the nineteenth century, a central arena where citizens raise the questions of who they are as an urban collective. In the midwestern home parish of the Consortium's original leader, the history of the Carmelites returns to the fragmentation of national American identity during and after the 1960s. If the Heartland is truly reflective of the Anglo-Protestant cultural majority, then Euro-American Catholicism at the turn of the millennium would seem to have lost its center. At Saint Rose of Lima, Euro-American

Catholics idealize their ancestors with nostalgia and longing, while new-comers to Cleveland cheer their city from the sidelines, absent from the staff of their own local school. Whether America itself is gone or just forgotten is a question that Clevelanders have relinquished to the unpredictable currents of history.

As for the fate of Father Viall's plans to reform his parish in light of neotraditionalist teachings, the Cleveland parish's cool reception of the Carmelites directs our reflections back to the unifying theme of this study: the mutual interdependence of religious and cultural identity. If the narratives from Filipino-, Mexican-, and Cuban-American parishes record a mutually reinforcing relationship between Spanish Catholic culture and American neotraditionalism, the status of the Carmelites in the multiethnic parish of Saint Rose reflects a mutually undermining relationship between the ideals of consensus and pluralism as models for community. Simply stated, there is too glaring a discrepancy between Viall's conservatism and the lived reality of the Cleveland parish. As in the other narratives included in this study, however, this discrepancy is not reflected in the Cleveland interviews as a theological dispute. Instead, Clevelanders assess the relevance of neotraditionalism in reference to a social ideal that can effectively evoke solidarity amongst their parish. No less than Filipino and Latino parishioners, they see in the theological consensus demanded by neotraditionalist sisters a proposed model for social organization. Lacking the cultural homogeneity of the other parishes, however, Clevelanders simply cannot associate the sisters' communitarian ideals with the diversity of their own community.

Turning to the pluralistic ideal of *e pluribus unum* long enshrined in Anglo-Protestant culture, Clevelanders find in sports teams a more suitable metaphor for their culturally and ideologically heterogeneous parish. Baseball and football ask of the spectators nothing more than their temporary identification with a team, and—in the case of baseball—a moment of reverential silence while the "Star Spangled Banner" is sung. These are decidedly less rigorous conditions for participation in a community than assent to eternal truths separating the chosen from the damned. Like the San Marino parish, which turns to Anglo-Protestant cultural ideals for their celebration of the individual, St. Rose of Lima relegates neotraditionalism to the unretrievable past: the heyday of ethnically homogenous European immigrant communities. While they search for a new urban identity, they continue to salute the American nation through their avid allegiance to sports teams. When parishioners assign neotraditionalist Catholicism to a previous historical era, they are signifying their excision of its ideals from their present community.

Conclusion

I N 1995 MARY JO WEAVER and R. Scott Appleby published *Being Right: Conservative Catholics in America,* a collection of scholarly essays intended to construct a conceptual map of conservative Catholicism in the postconciliar church. In her introduction, Weaver cited the omission of a chapter on the Council of Major Superiors of Women Religious as a conspicuous lacuna, explaining that sisters from the council who had been approached for interviews had viewed the project with suspicion and declined their help. "A number of them had read or heard about Donna Steichen's caricature of my work in her book *Ungodly Rage,* and believed that I was a neopagan, goddess-inspired abortion activist. As one sister said in a letter to me, 'I was told that you were dangerous. . . . In an earlier age you would have been excommunicated. . . . We have nothing in common.'"[1] A study of the conservative sisters, whom Weaver categorized as "hard-nosed," was accordingly missing from the subsequent book. I would like to conclude by drawing some general conclusions about conservative Catholicism based on the preceding history of the Carmelite sisters—who have played a historic role in shaping the Council of Major Superiors of Women Religious—and offer them retroactively to Weaver's and Appleby's seminal study mapping postconciliar conservative Catholicism.

While the overview of conservative women religious in these pages is limited to the study of a single order, it nevertheless raises several issues germane to the study of the American church more generally. First, the status of the Carmelite sisters as the leading order of the Council of Major Superiors of Women Religious suggests that their theology and ecclesiology is representative of the group as a whole, thus helping to shed light on a faction of the church that has hitherto eluded scholarly study. Second, the inclusion of ethnographic chapters on Los Angeles, the Arizona borderlands, and Miami spotlights aspects of Latino religiosity in the discussion of conservative Catholicism. These chapters shift the focus of scholarship on Catholic conservatism away from an exclusive preoccupation with ecclesial polity and a Euro-American church. Finally, the plurality of religiocultural identities reflected in this study raises important historiographical issues of how best to conceptualize the postconciliar church without implicitly advancing the theological and/or cultural biases of neotraditionalist, Latino, or liberal Catholics.

It should be highlighted at the outset that the study of the Carmelite sisters is focused primarily on religious symbols and not on the doctrinal teachings of the neotraditionalist order. At the risk of oversimplifying the array of theological, historical, and cultural perspectives reflected in the foregoing pages, it might be said that this book has been primarily the study of the religious habit. From the interviews of older sisters, who summarized the stormy Vatican II years in memories of retaining their Mexican habits; to feminist critiques of the cloister as a symbol of women's marginalization; to the reflections of lay parishioners, who unanimously focused on the sisters' demeanor as the starting point for all further reflections on the neotraditionalist order, the dress of the Carmelites emerges as a unifying theme throughout the study. This is an important qualification in beginning to situate the order within the postconciliar church, since studies on conservative Catholicism frequently begin by considering its doctrinal and political positions. Discussions of women in the church, abortion, and homosexuality—to cite three examples of divisive issues commonly marking the "culture war" between liberal and conservative Catholics—virtually do not figure in the reflections of both sisters and laity on their conservative identity.

This observation is of course not meant to mischaracterize the Carmelites as detached from issues of religious and religiopolitical orthodoxy. What is striking, however, is that doctrinal orthodoxy does not emerge from interviews with either sisters or laity as the guiding theme of their Catholic narratives. For the sisters, assent to literalist interpretations of Vatican teachings is perhaps presupposed in their stated vow of obedience to the church magisterium and so excluded as self-explanatory in their elaboration of Carmelite monasticism. For parishioners, pronouncements of doctrine are simply not central in the construction of Catholic identity, leaving it for a future study to uncover the theological nuances of the conservative laity. In either case, however, the orthodox dimension of conservative identity is overshadowed or at least supplemented by a strong emphasis on what Andrew Greeley has referred to as the "sacramental imagination" of Roman Catholics.

> Catholics live in an enchanted world, a world of statues and holy water, stained glass and votive candles, saints and religious medals, rosary beads and holy pictures. But these Catholic paraphernalia are mere hints of deeper and more pervasive religious sensibility which inclines Catholics to see the Holy lurking in creation. . . .
>
> This special Catholic imagination can appropriately be called sacramental. It sees created reality as a "sacrament," that is, a revelation of the presence of God. The workings of this imagination are most obvious in the Church's seven sacraments, but the seven are both a result and a reinforcement of a much broader Catholic view of reality.[2]

The Carmelites and their laity from all parishes are riveted by the habits, the crucifixes, and the rosaries of Mother Luisa's Mexican heritage, markers of conservative identity that are at once visual and symbolic. The symbolic dimension of essentialist monasticism facilitates the flight of the religious imagination both vertically toward supernatural realms and horizontally toward the social world.

The Carmelites and their lay supporters share a belief in a supernatural realm that can manifest through the intercession of God and the saints in the affairs of everyday life. For both sisters and parishioners, it is the order's traditional appearance that most powerfully triggers their associations with a realm beyond the pale of the visible world and behind the veil of death: the habits, rather than official doctrine, do the talking for them. Hence we have stories of bullet-proof rosaries, visionary dreams, and miraculous healings seeming to vindicate the sisters' claim that the magisterium and its theological positions they defend are more-than-human, beyond the meddling of liberal theologians. The symbolic imagination of both Carmelites and parishioners also extends horizontally to include a host of other details not normally included in the purviews of Catholic "essentials." Here again we can point to a shared belief among sisters and laity: that the sacred world of Catholicism should be kept separate from mundane society. In addition to pointing "upward" toward heaven, the habit marks the Carmelite order as set apart from the ordinary world.

The sisters' choice to separate themselves from secular society implicitly encompasses nondoctrinal reflections on the contemporary world. As the first chapter discussed, the Carmelite sisters and the neotraditionalist orders they represent in the Council of Major Superiors of Women Religious sharply disagree with liberal women religious that Anglo-Protestant culture should be the normative model for the postconciliar church. This study suggests that questions of gender and power are themselves subsumed in a more fundamental split over the mythic status of America. Some feminist critics of cloistered women have insisted that essentialist monasticism renders women "invisible." But Carmelite sisters retort by noting how traditional religious are increasingly invisible in the postconciliar American church. In order to reconcile these apparently contradictory claims, the metaphors of visibility and invisibility must be understood in reference to their unspoken sociological assumptions.

If we presuppose that an egalitarian, democratized social ideal represents the normative model for the postconciliar church, then it is true that essentialist monasticism marginalizes women to the sidelines of power. But if we accept, with the neotraditionalists, the preconciliar, hierarchical church as the normative model, then doffing the habit is tantamount to withdrawing from the *ecclesia* altogether. Such a debate would seem to reflect strictly ecclesiological issues of church organization were it not for the fact that liberal and conservative Catholics alike support their positions with distinctive theologies of Anglo-Protestant culture. In the terminology of Catherine L. Albanese, liberal sisters have "expanded" their ecclesiological models largely to embrace Anglo-Protestant mores of pluralism, voluntarism, and individualism, while the neotraditionalists have "contracted" away from the host culture and in the process demythologized Anglo-Protestant ideals as "self-evident."

The relationship of the Carmelites to Anglo-Protestant culture is best described as one of critical tension. While their rejection of the democratic *polis* as a model for religious community is clear, and intensified through their identification with Mother Luisa as a martyr persecuted by modernity, the sisters nevertheless interact with the laity in the hopes of shaping America in conformity to their own ideals. In his essay "The Neoconservative Difference," George Weigel clarified the critical relationship between American society and conservative Catholics such as the Carmelites:

> Neoconservative Catholicism in America has never sought to construct an undifferentiated apologia for the American experiment in ordered liberty. Rather, we have sought a critical engagement with the experiment, historically as well as in terms of contemporary controversies. But unlike some of our colleagues to port and starboard, we have tended not to think of the American experiment as fundamentally ill-founded. We reject the progressives' critique of the American Founding in both its vulgar-Marxist and race/gender-deconstructionist forms; but we also reject the notion that the Founding was the triumph of a radical Lockean individualism and volun-

tarism, of which today's Republic of the Autonomous Self is but the logical consequence. . . .

What America lacks today . . . is a religiously grounded public philosophy capable of informing and disciplining the public moral argument
that is the lifeblood of democracy.[3]

An account related by a Filipino parishioner in Los Angeles offers a poignant
image of the Carmelites' tenuous co-existence with public Protestant culture. After a ballet performance at the Crystal Cathedral in Garden Grove,
California, the sisters shook hands with a former Ms. America contestant,
who told them how wonderful it was for her to see traditional Catholic
monastics once again.[4] Reminiscent of Ronald Reagan's 1980 presidential
campaign slogan, "Let's Make America Great Again," this image reminds
us that the sisters have not given up altogether on "informing and disciplining the public moral argument." Like Pope John Paul II, however, the
sisters do not underestimate the difficulty of this task, frequently invoking
apocalyptic imagery to paint a rather dire picture of contemporary American society. Believing in the ultimate triumph of God over the forces of evil,
the sisters are optimistic about the long-term outcome of divine history,
but their portrayal of life in American society in the interim is one of a righteous battle.

Mary Jo Weaver has suggested that conservative Catholics generally al-
lege that "the challenge of accountability . . . rests with those who have
changed [since Vatican II], whose hold on their Catholic identity is not as
firm as conservatives think it should be."[5] For the conservative Catholics in
this study, the challenge of accountability rests with those who implicitly el-
evate Anglo-Protestant culture over the preconciliar model of the church as
a mythic social ideal. When the American Carmelites remember Mother Luisa
dodging bullets, they are alluding to their own experiences of struggle—not
only in the postconciliar church but as members of contemporary society.
The sisters who circulate from one parish to the next throughout the United
States have little incentive to abandon their own or the papacy's apocalyptic vision of the modern world. The interviews collected from this study
record a variety of sobering if not depressing scenarios of contemporary
America, marked by gang violence, economic depression, political exile, and
postindustrial malaise. The Carmelites' interactions with parishioners thus
seem to vindicate their own and Pope John Paul II's condemnation of contemporary society.

A neotraditionalist order such as the Carmelites provides its members
with a clear social alternative to the Anglo-Protestant culture it disparages.
The Carmelite order is in many ways the antithesis of what Weigel has car-
icatured as the Republic of the Autonomous Self. From the perspective of

the cloister, the individualistic ethos of Anglo-Protestant society leads not to a liberating experience of freedom, but rather to aimlessness and isolation. In addition to offering clearly defined theological doctrines, the sisters provide both each other and contemporary Catholics the experience of a communitarian society. They ask women to subordinate a measure of their individual freedom in return for inclusion in a society that will tend to their every need: physical, emotional, and spiritual. From the liberal perspective, this is an unacceptable price to pay for group inclusion. But Catholics who today are attracted to Mother Luisa's order are explicitly elevating this social ideal over a democratic one. Through the myths and rituals of Tridentine Catholicism, this countercultural community is given a shape and a genealogy. Consistent with Emile Durkheim's classic analysis of religion, the symbols of the neotraditionalist order serve to galvanize a community even as they represent supernatural realities. "That is why we can rest assured in advance that the practices of the cult, whatever they may be, are something more than movements without importance and gestures without efficacy," Durkheim wrote. "By the mere fact that their apparent function is to strengthen the bonds attaching the believer to his god, they at the same time really strengthen the bonds attaching the individual to the society of which he is a member."[6] Unlike Durkheim and like-minded sociologists of religion, my intention here is not to reduce religion to a reified notion of "society." As we have noted, the Tridentine symbols of the Carmelites simultaneously elicit both social and theological reflections from sisters and laity alike. But by the Carmelites' and lay parishioners' own admission, the social dimension of neotraditionalism plays a central role in their religious self-understanding.

As we have seen, however, the Carmelites' countercultural status amplifies themes found in such American genres as noir film and literature. Dire warnings of America's destiny from the West Coast continue a longstanding tradition in American arts and letters. As discussed extensively by scholar Leo Marx, a continuous thread of despair over the state of the country runs through many of the classic novels of the nineteenth century. While Ralph Waldo Emerson tentatively embraced industrial society as heralding a new day for the American republic, Henry David Thoreau was lamenting his compatriots' "lives of quiet desperation" in *Walden*. Following him was Herman Melville—allegorizing the conquest of nature as a maniacal and self-destructive pursuit in *Moby Dick*—and Mark Twain, whose Huckleberry Finn sought to escape a patently absurd and socially oppressive world by taking to the Mississippi with his friend Jim. In all of these works, American society is moving toward some terrible end as a result of what Marx calls the intrusion of "the machine in the garden"—the encroachment of modernity in a country that once defined itself as an agrarian culture.[7] Echoed in such twentieth-century classics as F. Scott Fitzgerald's *The Great Gatsby,* dystopian themes of America's fall are every bit as American as the liberal sisters' celebration of democracy.

It is arguably only those who identify themselves most as American citizens who would care enough about their country to bemoan its alleged fall. Postconciliar splits in the Catholic church between liberal and neotraditionalist factions are intensified by disagreements over the political fate and future of the nation, as James Hunter has outlined in his *Culture Wars.* The terms "liberal" and "conservative" as commonly used are thus more than simply theological distinctions. They are simultaneously religious and political markers reflecting the various degrees of identification Catholics feel with Anglo-Protestant culture and distinctive political analyses diagnosing the nation's strengths and weaknesses. Up until the Second World War, it was commonly immigrants from southern and eastern Europe who, experiencing American culture from its social margins, preserved Catholic traditions at odds with Anglo-Protestant culture. The fact that a neotraditionalist order today appeals to educated women from ostensibly "Americanized" backgrounds suggests, however, that the assimilation of these immigrants' descendants into Anglo-Protestant society does not automatically ensure the democratization or Protestantization of the church. As noted in the introduction, early postconciliar observers of the church presupposed such a sociological model, which must now be abandoned in light of more recent cultural and ecclesiological developments.

The present study of Mother Luisa's Carmelites reflects a church that is no longer exclusively European-American. Conservative Catholics include in their fold members of Spanish Catholic, New World cultures, who appropriate Tridentine symbols as part of their normative socioreligious pasts. An analogous relationship of critical tension with Anglo-Protestant society unites the Filipino and Latino Catholics of this study with the sisters. These parishioners see modeled in the cloistered community an ethos of communitarianism that for them is threatened by the individualistic ethos and materialism of Anglo-American society. Recall here that in Los Angeles and Miami, concerns of familial fragmentation loom large in the interviews. In Los Angeles, gangs emerge as both a real and a symbolic marker of the dangers of individualism. In the parishioners' own analysis, adolescents are drawn to gangs because there is no more family to which to turn, while the Carmelite schools themselves become likened to gang-controlled "turf" protecting parishioners from Anglo-Protestant society. In Miami, the strains and pressures of exile are felt most acutely in the fragmentation of the family, and the Carmelites are seen as "re-educating" Cuban descendants in their own traditional communitarian mores. The sisters' theological and ecclesiological teachings on assent to received tradition, obedience to authority, and careful delineations between "insiders" and "outsiders" reinforce parishioners' traditional cultural emphasis on familial solidarity, an important aspect of ethnic cohesiveness more generally. This association between the cloister and the ethnic collective is strengthened by the fact that Mother Luisa's order originated in a Spanish Catholic country and culture; with this association in mind, the parishioners perceive the cloister as something of a mirror of their own group.

To the extent that descendants of Filipino, Mexican, and Cuban immigrants are inevitably exposed to the influences of Anglo-Protestant culture through such vehicles as the media, the maintenance of ethnic identity through assent to neotraditionalist teachings represents not only a continuation of their past traditions, but a self-conscious choice to defend and construct cultural boundaries in the United States. Where Anglo-Protestant culture dominates the local culture, we find images of ethnoreligious identity that are as reactionary as the neotraditionalist Catholicism of the order: the "oases" and "Carmelite turf" of Los Angeles besieged by violence and moral corrosion, and the surrogate family of the Miami parish attempting to *re*-educate itself in traditional mores. In the one parish where Mexican culture holds sway in defining local identity, issues of boundary maintenance are less pronounced; the parish of Douglas/Agua Prieta takes for granted both its Mexican and its Catholic identity, accepting the Carmelites simply as a continuation of borderlands Catholicism. What this observation suggests is that the Catholic "tradition" of Latino communities is to some extent as invented as the sisters' neotraditionalism. While it remains outside the scope of this study, it is enough here to note that Catholicism has undergone important transformations in countries like the Philippines, Mexico, and Cuba since Vatican II. The parishioners' claim that they are simply continuing tradition obscures the changes in their respective homelands.

The particular demographic and historical influences that shape Filipino and Latino communities in the United States lessen the extent of their acculturation into Anglo-Protestant culture. These groups represent both "borderland" and "diasporic" cultures. In the case of Mexican and Cuban Catholics, geographical proximity between their communities in the United States and their respective homelands ensures both a steady influx of new immigrants and a constant cultural exchange between the United States and countries of origin. In the case of Filipino Catholics, demographic pathways of migration to the United States—shaped primarily by economic disparities between the two countries—ensure their continued arrival in cities such as Los Angeles into the foreseeable future. It is this transnational status of Filipino and Latino communities—the perpetual interaction between American-born Catholics and immigrants from their homelands—that prevents their facile comparison with previous generations of European immigrants to the United States. If immigrants from southern and eastern Europe could be expected, given enough time and education, to "assimilate" into Anglo-Protestant culture, members of these transnational cultures are fashioning ethnic identities in tension with Anglo-Protestant culture that are "here to stay" in a transnational global community.

In spite of its ideological commitment to pluralism, the liberal church—insofar as it uncritically espouses mores of individualism over communal solidarity and rids Catholic spaces of Tridentine symbols—distances itself from a Latino constituency that already comprises one third of the church, as well as transnational communities like the Filipino parishes of this study that retain the Catholic devotions of their homelands in the United States. It is not without some irony that the Carmelite sisters, who disparage notions of "enculturated Catholicism," have come so effectively to accommodate Latino and Filipino Catholics in the United States church. The observation of one parishioner in Douglas/Agua-Prieta that it "doesn't matter where the Carmelites come from as soon as they put on that habit" accurately notes that the Tridentine observances of the order expedite its reception by descendants from Spanish Catholic countries. The sisters may reject academic theories of enculturated Catholicism, but their retention of the Mexican foundress's lifestyle and devotions has unwittingly allied them with Catholics estranged from a Protestantized liberal church for cultural reasons.

The findings of this study are supported by the scholarship of Alan Figueroa Deck, who has argued that "conservative" Catholicism gains appeal within Latino cultures primarily for its retention of Tridentine symbols. In his contributing essay to Weaver's and Appleby's collection, "'A Pox on Both Your Houses': A View of Catholic Conservative-Liberal Polarities from the Hispanic Margin," Deck elaborated on the centrality of the "sacramental imagination" in Latino Catholic culture:

> First, as is often true of oral cultures, the role played by the imagination is primary. A reflexive, cognitive, individualized awareness of the "objective," historical, social, political, economic, and cultural underpinnings of their religion are generally lacking. Second, cultural and religious meaning is communicated not by the articulate print medium, by discrete, easily retrievable, objective sources (books, catechisms), but by polyvalent symbols and traditional rituals whose meanings are not readily accessible to ratio-

nal analysis. The departmentalization and fragmentation characteristic of modern cultures has yet to occur or has only partially occurred in the Hispanic world. The symbols are therefore organic.[8]

Deck was careful to point out, however, that the appeal of "conservative" rituals does not necessarily indicate theological consensus between the conservative church and its Latino constituency. Rather, "[The symbols] strike a chord deep in the identity and collective memories of a people. . . . The symbols and rituals are the heritage of a community, a collectivity. They are not the domain of experts endowed with scientific know-how and disconnected from the mythos of the people, their root metaphors and stories."[9] This latter observation is clearly supported by the narratives of Catholic identity recorded in the Latino and Filipino parishes of this study. Simply stated, the center of these narratives is not the institutional church but the culture, history, and contemporary social concerns of the parishioners.

Deck's argument that the terms "liberal" and "conservative" lose their meaning when applied to Latinos returns to the point that doctrinal polarities in the American church reflect a discourse about the future of Anglo-Protestant America that is to some extent culture-bound. Insofar as their primary concerns relate to the preservation of Spanish Catholic cultures, the lay Catholics of this study cannot be classified within a schema defined by Anglo-Protestant concerns about the fate of the nation. In Deck's words:

> It makes no sense to transfer conservative/liberal antagonisms onto third world peoples, to suggest that eventually they will get to where the moderns are. Polycentrism is a reality of today's world. The neuralgic point is modernity, the confrontation with modernity. Third world peoples in general tend not to perceive and interpret the world in the same way that modern Westerners do. They have been less influenced by literacy. They are less individualistic, less enamored of univocal concepts of truth and universal rationality, less fascinated with the knowing subject in isolation from others. The programmatic ideal of modern Western civilization—its conceptualist, ahistorical methodologies, its faith in technique and universal pragmatic reason—is increasingly called into question. Hispanics are surely influenced by these trends, but many, even those thoroughly immersed in North American culture, are not capitulating to them.[10]

In this study, we have not one but two conservative Catholic factions, seemingly united by their common embrace of Tridentine devotionalism and critique of Anglo-Protestant culture. Filipino and Latino communities appropriate neotraditionalism selectively as a strategy for maintaining and strengthening the boundaries of their cultures. The Carmelites employ the same symbols to create a countercultural community intended to guide the church and Anglo-Protestant society to an alleged moral high ground. This distinction suggests not so much a theological divide between the sisters and the laity as a strategic appropriation of Tridentine symbols in light of differing sociopolitical objectives.

It is fair to say that every expression of Catholicism represented in the present study in some way embellishes the doctrinal pronouncements of the church with narratives of cultural identity. The Carmelites and their liberal Catholic detractors both spin tales of Anglo-Protestant America: the one dystopian, the other reminiscent of American Revolutionary rhetoric. Spanish Catholic cultures narrate their own stories relative to their own histories, cultures, and social concerns. Those local parishes that reject Mother Luisa's order—the San Marino and Cleveland parishes—fall back on symbolic models of community found in the repository of what Catherine Albanese has categorized as the "cultural religion" of American Protestantism: suburbia and organized sports.[11] In the first case, upper-class parishioners live out the Anglo-Protestant dream of Los Angeles in swank neighborhoods, instilling values of "success" and academic competition in their children. In the second case, the ethnically heterogeneous parish in Cleveland finds the social ideal of *e pluribus unum* modeled for them in local sports teams. The question thus evoked by this study is not which community or parish represents "ethnic Catholicism," but rather whose communal or cultural identity is being expressed in a given faction of the postconciliar church, and for which political reasons.

As Alan Figueroa Deck reminds us, "polycentrism is a reality of today's world"—and of the postconciliar American church as well. No single narrative of the foregoing study can claim privileged status as most indicative of postconciliar Catholicism. I have already alluded in the introduction to the hazards of characterizing this study as a foray into "popular religion." Such a designation, to clarify, implicitly prioritizes the doctrinal aspect of the Carmelite order as the most central component of its identity, and relegates the religiosity of Filipino, Mexican, and Cuban Catholics—together with the biography of the foundress itself—as "peripheral" Catholic concerns. It is instructive to note that if we instead prioritize San Marino or Cleveland as the "central" narratives of the study, we find ourselves repeating historiographical suppositions of the early postconciliar years in a designation of neotraditionalism as indicative of a church of times past or of a church of "spurious supernaturalism." Then again, if we summarize the history of the Carmelite order from the perspective of the Filipino and Mexican parishes of the Los Angeles parishes, or the Cuban-American parish of Miami, we conclude that neotraditionalism is primarily a defensive and reactionary bulwark against a dominant Anglo-American culture. But if we portray Carmelite monasticism from the perspective of the Ari-

zona borderlands—a region of the United States beyond the pale of Anglo-American culture and religious institutions—we conclude that neotraditionalism is in fact normative, with little against which to defend itself. What, then, is an accurate and useful historiographical framework by
which to explain the present study?

Based on the study of Mother Luisa's order and on preliminary studies
of the postconciliar "conservative" church, I suggest that we can imagine
American Catholicism as a theater of dynamic interactions between at least
three distinctive ethnoreligious or religiocultural poles. The first is the liberal Catholic church itself, which reflects a fusion between Roman Catholic
religious and Anglo-American cultural ideologies. The second is a neotraditionalist church, an "invented tradition" that offers its members communal
solidarity through literalistically interpreted theological tenets and a standard
repertoire of rituals inherited from the Roman Catholic tradition. The third
is the "borderland," or transnational, church of communities descended
from Spanish Catholic, New World countries, fashioning an ethnoreligious
identity betwixt and between the United States and their homelands. A plurality of American Catholic identities emerges from cultural and theological interactions between any two of these three poles. In the present study,
I have recorded conflicts between liberal and neotraditionalist groups over
the normativity of Anglo-American culture as a model for the church. We
also have narratives of Catholic identity born from the interaction of neotraditionalist Catholicism and borderland communities, whose differences
are masked by the ambiguous symbolism of Tridentine rituals and liturgies.
A third interaction not recorded in this study would be between the liberal
Catholic church and the borderland communities, reflected in the historical emergence of such groups as PADRES (Padres Asociados por los Dere-
chos Religiosos, Educativos, y Sociales—Priests Associated for Religious, Educational, and Social Rights) and Las Hermanas ("The Sisters"—advocates
for Latina leadership in the church and society).[12] Even as they celebrate notions of cultural pluralism and enculturated Catholicism, groups like these
reflect a democratization of non-Euro-American Catholicism, a refashioning of cultural identity more tolerant of egalitarian and democratic ideals
than the ethnoreligious identities reflected in this study.

Conceptualized spatially, the three distinctive American churches are
located in the United States, Rome, and the transnational borderland spaces
of respective communities. They are thus reflective of three distinct religiocultural homelands, which happen to converge within the political territory
of the United States. But the postconciliar church would seem to be more
of a global church than a national one, and its constituents more the prod-
uct of a truly polycentric world than an assemblage of "ethnic enclaves" or-

biting around an Anglo-Protestant center. I would suggest with Deck that the designations of "conservative" and "liberal" be subjected to more careful scrutiny relative to the cultural backgrounds and/or political objectives of a given Catholic community, if not abandoned altogether. Since the 1960s, the cultural fabric of the United States has changed and Anglo-Protestant mythology has been critically examined from several perspectives, necessitating new models and new categories by which to conceptualize the postconciliar church. The story of the Carmelite Sisters of the Most Sacred Heart of Los Angeles since the Second Vatican Council is the story both of that shifting church and transformed country and of the efforts by some Catholics to shield themselves against such change.

NOTES

INTRODUCTION

1. John F. Kennedy, "Inaugural Address," in Jay David, ed., *The Kennedy Reader* (New York: Howard W. Sams Publishers, 1967), 8.

2. James Davidson Hunter, *Culture Wars* (New York: BasicBooks, 1991), 44.

3. Harold Bloom, *The American Religion* (New York: Touchstone Books, 1992).

4. Harvey Cox, *The Secular City* (New York: Macmillan Company, 1965), 4.

5. Andrew M. Greeley, *Religion in the Year 2000* (New York: Sheed and Ward, 1969), 165.

6. Lawrence H. Fuchs, *John F. Kennedy and American Catholicism,* 3d ed. (New York: Meredith Press, 1967), 230.

7. George Weigel, "The Neoconservative Difference," in Mary Jo Weaver and R. Scott Appleby, eds., *Being Right: Conservative Catholics in America* (Bloomington: Indiana University Press, 1995), 141.

8. Catherine L. Albanese has traced the impact of Puritan belief and observance on societal mores, national ideology, and mass-media culture in what she refers to as public Protestantism, civil religion, and cultural Protestantism, respectively. Together, these three, interrelated mythic complexes constitute what she calls the "one religion" of Anglo-Protestant culture. See "Part Two: The Oneness of Religion in America" in Albanese, *America: Religions and Religion,* 3rd ed. (New York: Wadsworth Publishing Company, 1999), 395–501.

9. Ibid, 281–82.

10. See Chapter 3, "Historical Roots of the Culture War," in Hunter, 67–106.

11. See Jay P. Dolan, *The Immigrant Church* (Baltimore: Johns Hopkins University Press, 1975).

12. See "Epilogue," in James Truslow Adams, *The Epic of America* (Boston: Little, Brown, and Company, 1931), 401–17.

13. Peter Hebblethwaite, "The Roman Pope Is Still a Pole," *National Catholic Reporter,* October 16, 1981, p. 10.

14. Peter Hebblethwaite, "John Paul in Poland: Among His Own, Pope Spoke His Heart," *National Catholic Reporter,* June 15, 1979, p. 22.

15. Peter Hebblethwaite, "Pope Foresees Growing Battle between Good and Evil," *National Catholic Reporter,* January 9, 1981, p. 16.

16. Ibid.

17. For an excellent overview of developments in Roman Catholicism after the Second Vatican Council, see Adrian Hastings, ed., *Modern Catholicism: Vatican II and After* (New York: Oxford University Press, 1991).

18. James Baldwin, "The Fire Next Time," in *James Baldwin, Collected Essays* (New York: Library of America, 1998), 304.

19. Eric Hobsbawm and Terence Ranger, eds., *The Invention of Tradition* (New York: Cambridge University Press, 1983), 2.

20. The term "Spanish Catholicism" is used in this study simply to highlight the significant cultural and religious similarity between Mexican, Cuban, and Filipino cultures: their shared history as former colonies of sixteenth-century Spain. The designation of any one of these cultures as "Spanish Catholic" is not meant to accentuate the European over the non-European components of their respective identities.

21. "Monasticism," *The New Catholic Encyclopedia.*

22. "Carmelites," *The New Catholic Encyclopedia.*

23. The sociogeographical metaphor of "borderlands," generally attributed to the writings of Gloria Anzaldúa, conceptualizes Latino identity as a continuous recombination of symbolic elements from Latin American, Anglo-Protestant, and North American indigenous cultures. See Gloria Anzaldua, *Borderlands/Las Fronteras: The New Mestiza* (San Francisco: Spinsters/Aunt Lute Press, 1987).

24. Gustavo Perez Firmat, *Life on the Hyphen: The Cuban-American Way* (Austin: University of Texas Press, 1994), 17.

25. E. San Juan, Jr., *From Exile to Diaspora: Versions of the Filipino Experience in the United States* (Boulder: Westview Press, 1998), 7.

26. "Since 1970, the number of Hispanics in the U.S. has more than doubled, and according to the 1990 census 22.4 million Hispanics now live in the U.S. A conservative estimate that represents 9 percent of the U.S. population [sic], it makes them the second largest minority group in the nation; African Americans represent the largest minority group with a population of approximately 30 million in 1990." Jay P. Dolan, "Conclusion," in Jay P. Dolan and Allan Figueroa Deck, *Hispanic Catholic Culture in the U.S.* (Notre Dame, Ind.: University of Notre Dame Press, 1994), 440–41. Deck has estimated that Latinos already or will soon constitute almost half of the American Catholic population. See Deck, *The Second Wave* (New York: Paulist Press, 1990), 12.

27. Thomas Tweed, *Our Lady of the Exile* (New York: Oxford University Press, 1997), 139. Tweed defines translocative religions as "moving symbolically between the homeland and the new land," in contradistinction to "locative" religions "associated with a homeland where the group resides" and "supralocative," with "diminished ties to both the homeland and the adopted land."

28. Richard Rodriguez, *Days of Obligation: An Argument with My Mexican Father* (New York: Penguin Books, 1992), xvi.

1. THE EMERGENCE OF A NEOTRADITIONALIST ORDER

1. David C. Bailey, *Viva Cristo Rey!* (Austin: University of Texas Press, 1974), 142–43.

2. Camilio Maccise, *The Life and Work of Reverend Mother Maria Luisa Josefa of the Most Blessed Sacrament, Foundress of the Congregation of the Carmelite Sisters of the Most Sacred Heart Of Guadalajara, and of the Institute of the Carmelite Sisters of the Most Sacred Heart of Los Angeles* (unpublished, 1989), 81.

3. Helenita Colbert, *To Love Me in Truth: Mother Luisa Maria Josefa of the Blessed*

Sacrament, Servant of God. (Alhambra, Calif.: Carmelite Sisters of the Most Sacred Heart of Los Angeles, 1987), 82–83.

4. Ibid., 87.

5. Ibid., 53.

6. "Decree on the Appropriate Renewal of the Religious Life (*Perfectae Caritatis*)," in Walter M. Abott, ed., *The Documents of Vatican II* (New York: Herder and Herder, Associated Press, 1966), 468.

7. "Dogmatic Constitution on the Church (*Lumen Gentium*),"and "Pastoral Constitution on the Church in the Modern World (*Gaudium et Spes*)," in *Documents of Vatican II*, 14–101 and 183–98.

8. *"Lumen Gentium,"* 20–22.

9. George A. Kelly, *The Battle for the American Church* (Garden City, N.Y.: Doubleday and Co., 1979), 257–60.

10. Gene Burns, *The Frontiers of Catholicism: The Politics of Ideology in a Liberal World* (Berkeley and Los Angeles: University of California Press, 1992), 150.

11. Ibid., 151.

12. "Statements by the Sisters of the Immaculate Heart of Mary, Los Angeles," in Sarah Bentley Doely, ed., *Women's Liberation and the Church* (New York: Association Press, 1970), 70–71.

13. Burns, 75.

14. Doely, 71.

15. Interview S10.

16. Peter Hebblethwaite, "Pope Unveils His Papacy: 'Restoration' Era Begins," *National Catholic Reporter,* October 19, 1979, p. 18.

17. Ibid.

18. Ibid.

19. Ibid., p. 1.

20. Peter Hebblethwaite, "Encyclical Nails Objective Right and Wrong," *National Catholic Reporter,* October 8, 1993, pp. 8–9.

21. The exact ratio of conservative to liberal women religious in the United States remains undocumented. The total number of American sisters remains at approximately 100,000 (Burns, 132). The number of those affiliated with the traditionalist Council of Major Superiors of Women Religious has been estimated to be approximately 10,000 by Mother Vincent Marie Finnegan, council president. Burns notes (p. 152, n. 109) that "it is difficult to state how large the [traditionalist] consortium has been over the years. . . . [B]ecause it tried to maintain a public image of a communications group, rather than a formal organization in competition with the [liberal] LCWR, it had a loose organizational structure in which the definition of 'membership' was not always clear." The 1994 "Vocations Directory" of the traditionalist council states only that it "has 140 members [i.e., religious communities] representing 95 Congregations and Provinces" (Table of Contents).

22. See Sacred Congregation for Religious, "Essential Elements of the Religious Life" (Vatican City: Libreria Editrice, 1983).

23. Council of Major Superiors of Women Religious, "Statutes of the Council of Major Superiors of Women Religious," article 2, section 2a., in "Proceedings of the First National Assembly of the Council of Major Superiors of Women Religious in the United States of America. Techny, Illinois, October 23–25, 1992," 44.

24. Maccise, 1.

25. Interview S3.

26. See ch. 6, "Radicalization on the Periphery of Power," in Burns.

27. See ch. 3, "Catholics in the English Colonies," and ch. 4, "A New Beginning," in Jay P. Dolan, *The American Catholic Experience* (New York: Doubleday and Co., 1985).

28. Doely, 17–20.

29. Carmelite Sisters of the Most Sacred Heart of Los Angeles, *Carmelite Sisters of the Most Sacred Heart of Los Angeles,* (promotional brochure) (Alhambra, Calif.), 2.

30. Ibid.

31. Ibid., 3.

32. Carmelite Sisters of the Most Sacred Heart of Los Angeles, *Carmelite Vocation,* (promotional brochure) (Alhambra, Calif.).

33. The order of the Carmelites dates back to the early thirteenth century, when a group of penitent lay hermits founded an order in the western face of Mount Carmel in today's Israel. Dedicating themselves to the Virgin Mary, for whom they built and oratory on Mount Carmel, the early Carmelite community came to be known as the Brothers of Our Lady Mount Carmel. Legends claiming the biblical prophet Elijah as the order's founder began to circulate among later generations of European Carmelites.

34. Ibid.

35. Ibid.

36. Ibid.

37. Interview S1.

38. Interview S2.

39. Interview S3.

40. Interview S4.

41. Interview S5.

42. Interview S4.

43. Interview S6.

44. Interview S7.

45. Interview S4.

46. Margaret Brennan, "Enclosure: Institutionalizing the Invisibility of Women in Ecclesiastical Communities," in Elisabeth Schüssler Fiorenza and Mary Collings, eds., *Women—Invisible in Theology and Church* (Edinburgh: T. and T. Clark, 1987), 40.

47. Elisabeth Schüssler Fiorenza, "Breaking the Silence—Becoming Visible" in Schüssler Fiorenza and Collins, 4.

48. Peter Hebblethwaite, "The Roman Pope Is Still a Pole," *National Catholic Reporter,* October 16, 1981, p. 12.

2. MOTHER LUISA'S CANONIZATION
AND THE SANCTIFICATION OF NEOTRADITIONALISM

1. Camilio Maccise, O.C.D., *The Life and Work of Reverend Mother Luisa Josefa of the Most Blessed Sacrament, Foundress of the Congregation of the Carmelite Sisters of the Sacred Heart of Guadalajara, and of the Institute of the Carmelite Sisters of the Most Sacred Heart of Los Angeles* (unpublished, 1989), 118.

2. Ibid., 157.

3. Ibid.

4.Ibid., 172.

5. See ch. 10, "The Church in America," in C. H. Haring, *Spanish Empire in America* (New York: Oxford University Press, 1952).

6. David C. Bailey, *Viva Cristo Rey!* (Austin: University of Texas Press, 1974), 14.

7. Maccise, 12.

8. Helenita Colbert, *The Flower of Guadalajara* (Alhambra, Calif.: Carmelite Sisters of the Most Sacred Heart of Los Angeles, 1987), 4.

9. Maccise, 15.

10. Ibid., 17.

11. Ibid., 19.

12. Ibid., 23.

13. Ibid.

14. Building upon the studies of rites of passage by Arnold Van Gennep, Turner has argued that religious rituals mark the passage from one social state into another. The process has three distinctive phases: separation from the former state, a liminal state in which the former status is symbolically dissolved and instructions for the next state are imparted, and reaggregation into the new state. In his analysis, the liminal state is particularly dangerous and powerful since during this time the initiate exists outside any particular social order in a realm of symbolic formlessness and potential chaos. The social bonds that will unite members in the next social state are forged during this time, as they band together in an egalitarian community as initiates. To their societies they symbolize the ever-present threat of social disintegration and are thus perceived as threatening and powerful. Turner attributes much of the spiritual powers of saints and monastics in the Roman Catholic tradition to their "institutionalized liminality" or permanent state of existing on the boundaries of society. See Turner, *The Ritual Process* (Chicago: Aldine Publishing Co., 1969), 127–28.

15. Maccise, 26.

16. Ibid., 26–27.

17. Ibid.

18. Ibid., 34.

19. Haring, 181–82.

20.Maccise, 73.

21. Ibid., 70.

22. Maccise, 30.

23. Ibid., 61.

24. Ibid., 121.

25. Bailey, 42.

26. Maccise, 45.

27. Ibid., 74–75.

28. Ibid., 87.

29. Bailey, 139.

30. Maccise, 65–66.

31. Victor Turner, *Image and Pilgrimage in Christian Culture* (New York: Columbia University Press, 1978), 38.

32. Peter Hebblethwaite, "Pope Discusses Millennium with Cardinals," *National Catholic Reporter*, July 1, 1994, p. 17.

33. Kenneth Woodward, *Making Saints* (New York: Simon and Schuster, 1990), 120.
34. Hebblethwaite, "Pope Discusses Millennium with Cardinals," 17.
35. Peter Hebblethwaite, *In the Vatican* (Bethesda, Md.: Alder and Alder, 1986), 108.
36. Woodward, 377.
37. Ibid.

3. THE URBAN CLOISTER

1. See John Leddy Phelan, *The Hispanization of the Philippines: Spanish Aims and Filipino Responses, 1565–1700* (Madison: University of Wisconsin Press, 1959).
2. Interview C7.
3. Interview C10.
4. Interview C3.
5. Interviews C1, C3.
6. Interview C1.
7. Interview C9, C10.
8. Interview C4.
9. Interview C 3.
10. Interview C1.
11. Interviews C6, C8, C9, C10.
12. Interviews LB1, LB2, LB3, LB9.
13. Interview LB2.
14. Interview LB9.
15. Interview LB1.
16. Interview LB9.
17. Interview MS1.
18. Interview LB3.
19. Interview LB2.
20. Interviews LB2, LB4.
21. Interviews LB3.
22. See Linda A. Revilla, "Filipino American Identity: Transcending the Crisis," in Maria P. P. Root, ed., *Filipino Americans: Transformation and Identity* (Thousand Oaks, Calif.: Sage Publications, 1997), 95–111.
23. Phelan, 80.
24. Interview LP6.
25. Interview LP3.
26. Interview K1.
27. Interview MS1.
28. Interview LP1.
29. Interview LP1.
30. Interviews LP2, LP4, LP5.
31. Interviews LP2, LP3.
32. Interview LP2.
33. Interview LP6.
34. Interview MS2.
35. Interview LP6.
36. Interview LP1.

37. Raymond Chandler, *The Simple Art of Murder* (New York: Random House, 1988), 17–18. I am grateful to David T. Barker, M.Div., of Atlanta, Georgia, for sharing this reference with me.

38. Mike Davis, *Ecology of Fear: Los Angeles and the Imagination of Disaster* (New York: Metropolitan Books, 1998), 276.

39. Ibid.

40. Jesse Katz, "Stray Bullet Shatters Couple's Dream to Leave Gang Area," *Los Angeles Times,* March 20, 1992, p. A1.

41. Ibid., p. A21.

42. Ibid.

43. Anthropologist Mary Douglas in her now classic essay *Purity and Danger* has underscored the observation that designations of danger are typically ascribed to those persons, places, or things that have eluded classification in a particular society's ordering of the world. "So many ideas about power are based on an idea of society as a series of forms contrasted with surrounding non-form," she writes. "There is power in the forms and other power in the inarticulate area, margins, confused lines, and beyond the external boundaries. If pollution is a particular class of danger [because it denotes unclassified objects], to see where it belongs in the universe of dangers we need an inventory of all the possible sources of power. . . . The effects are the same the world over: drought is drought, hunger is hunger; epidemic, child labor, infirmity—most of the experiences are held in common. But each culture knows a distinctive set of laws governing the way these disasters fall" (Mary Douglas, *Purity and Danger* [New York: Praeger, 1966], 98).

44. Interview SM2.

45. Interview SM2.

46. Interview SM6.

47. Interview SM1.

48. Interview SM3.

49. Interview SM5.

50. Interview SM7.

51. Interview SM1.

52. Interview SM4.

53. Ibid.

54. Following the 1848 annexation of northern Mexico by the United States, privately held lands in Los Angeles were ceded by Mexican owners to Anglo-American investors. Public lands once owned by the *ayuntamiento,* or municipal council; the common lands, or *ejidos;* and the municipal lands, or *proprios*—including the "downtown" Los Angeles *pueblo*—were also sold to developers. The new elite was at liberty to transform its newly acquired property into subdivisions or "proto-townships," complete with privately funded roads and waterways. In time, the building of Los Angeles's infrastructure fell largely to private investors, who alone had enough money to pay the bills. The early transformation of Los Angeles to an Anglo-Protestant city rested on a triumphant and nearly total privatization of the *civis* that would come to influence a distinctive conception of urban community in the decades to come. By the end of the nineteenth century, middle- and working-class white Midwesterners began to stream in growing numbers to southern California. Older ideals of "the good life"— rooted in Jeffersonian images of independent farming—had begun to crumble in the Midwest under the pressures of industrialization. The Euro-American bourgeoisie was

restlessly searching for new pursuits of happiness, a need that was happily met by Los Angeles planners. Starting in 1890, the city's investors began to market Los Angeles as a city where the Anglo-American ideals of individualism could be realized to the fullest extent in private home ownership in a sunny, dry climate. The suburbanization of Los Angeles had been born. Subdividers transformed vast tracts of land into settlements even before newcomers arrived, typically choosing a gridiron pattern of perpendicularly crossing streets. Robert Fogelson writes in his classic overview of the suburbanization of Los Angeles, *The Fragmented Metropolis* (Cambridge: Harvard University Press, 1969), "The single-family house offered privacy, reinforced the family unit, included outdoor space, and conferred status and absolute ownership" (67).

4. UNDERGROUND CARMELITES

1. Interview DAP14.
2. Interview DAP1.
3. Interview DAP9.
4. Interview DAP3.
5. Interviews DAP1, DAP3.
6. "$150,000 Loretto Academy Completed," *Douglas Daily International,* August 2, 1924, p. A1.
7. Interview DAP2.
8. Ervin Bond, *History of Douglas, Arizona* (Douglas, Ariz.: Ervin Bond, 1976), 1–8.
9. Ibid., 30.
10. Interview DAP12.
11. Interview DAP14.
12. Interview DAP5.
13. Arizona Department of Commerce, *Community Profile: Douglas* (1995).
14. Frank Mangin, "National Catholic Schools Week Spotlights Lestonnac, Loretto," *Douglas Sunday Dispatch,* January 28, 1996, p. 1.
15. Interview DAP1.
16. Ibid.
17. Interview DAP14.
18. Interview DAP4.
19. Interview DAP13.
20. Interview DAP3.
21. Interview DAP13.
22. Ibid.
23. Ibid.
24. Ibid.
25. See Introduction, "Milagros and the Cult of Saint Francis," in Eileen Oktavec, *Answered Prayers: Miracles and Milagros along the Border* (Tucson: University of Arizona Press, 1995), 3–21.
26. Ibid.
27. James Griffith, *A Shared Space: Folklife in the Arizona-Sonora Borderlands* (Logan: Utah State University Press, 1995), 35–53.
28. *University of Arizona Bulletin* 19, no. 4 (October 1948): 24.
29. Ibid., 33–34.

30. Ibid., 17.

31. Ibid., 30.

32. Ibid., 32.

33. Interview DAP10.

34. As Frederick Jackson Turner's classic work makes clear, the wars and capitalist ventures waged in the nineteenth-century landscapes west of the Mississippi played an instrumental part in forging the mythic identity of Anglo-America. If the eastern seaboard was the historic site of Puritan and Revolutionary dramas and the South a theater of both African-American struggles and white attempts to recreate a feudal aristocracy in the New World, the West was the place where America created itself symbolically in opposition to imagined "savages" and an "untamed wilderness." In places like Douglas, the myth of Anglo-American "civilization" reached a mythic and socioeconomic climax. The frontier became a place where Euro-Americans decimated indigenous cultures and forced the vanquished to live on reservations, expanding United States territory west, north, and south to its present political boundaries. In the Southwest, Anglos also waged war with Mexican settlers, annexing half of their country in 1848 after the Mexican-American War. With their Catholic heritage and mixed Spanish, Indian, African, and European blood, Mexicans were classified as a type of savage society and expected to accede under Anglo rule not only to political domination but to cultural assimilation as well. In the history of the West, the meaning of "civilization" became intimately associated with cultural conquest and domination, epitomized in the symbol of the gun-slinging white hero of the Western genre. Women were relegated to the margins of this history, together with the "primitive" Indians and "backward" Mexicans, while the rich natural resources of the western landscape were marked as "virginal" targets for Anglo colonization and control.

35. Interview DAP12.

36. Interview DAP3.

37. Interview DAP6.

38. Interview DAP4.

39. Carlos A. Schwantes, *Bisbee: Urban Outpost on the Frontier* (Tucson: University of Arizona Press, 1992), 116.

40. Interview DAP12.

41. Interview DAP14.

42. Interview DAP11.

43. Ibid.

44. Interview DAP10.

45. Ibid.

46. Ibid.

47. Interview DAP5.

48. Ibid.

49. Interview DAP11.

50. Griffith, 3.

51. Ibid., p. 5.

52. Frank Mangin, "New Pressures for Border Wall," *Douglas Daily Dispatch,* January 1, 1996, p. A1.

53. "Agents Find Drug Tunnel to U.S.," *New York Times,* May 19, 1990, p. 7.

54. In "Some Finding Gold in Passage under Border," *Los Angeles Times,* July 25, 1990, p. A5.

55. Interview DAP11.
56. Interview DAP4.
57. Interview DAP7.
58. Interview DAP11.

5. BETWIXT AND BETWEEN

1. City of Coral Gables, "Map of Coral Gables, Florida" (October 1993).
2. "Tomorrow—Church of the Little Flower Will Be Dedicated in Coral Gables" (advertisement), *Miami Daily News and Herald,* December 7, 1927, p. D18, in Samuel D. LaRoue Jr., ed., *Church of the Little Flower: 65 Years of Worship and Service, 1924–1991* (Coral Gables, Fla.: Church of the Little Flower, 1993), 10.
3. Interview M20.
4. Ibid.
5. James M. Cox, George E. Merrick, and Frank Bohn, "Enterprise, Education, and Economics in Florida," in Frank Bohn, ed., *Man Pushes Forward: A Fountain of Youth* (Coral Gables, Fla.: University of Miami Press, 1926), 22.
6. Ibid., 28.
7. Interview M2.
8. Interview M3.
9. Interview M24.
10. Interview M29.
11. Interviews M6, M24, and M23.
12. Interview M3.
13. Interview M2.
14. Interview M13.
15. Ibid.
16. Interview M29.
17. Cathy Lynn Grossman, "Cuban Women: Changing Their Lifestyle in Exile," *Miami Herald,* March 11, 1986, p. B1.
18. Ibid., p. B2.
19. Ibid.
20. Ibid.
21. Interviews M6, M14, M15, M22.
22. Interview M11.
23. Interview M4.
24. Interview M2.
25. Reinaldo Ramos, "Class of '81 Embraces Cuban Roots," *Miami Herald,* March 1, 1987, p. A20.
26. Ibid.
27. Interview M7.
28. Interview M10.
29. Interview M6.
30. Interview M2.
31. Carmelite Sisters of the Most Sacred Heart of Los Angeles, "Saint Theresa School Newsletter," June 1994, p. 1.
32. Interview M19.

33. Ibid.

34. Interview M20.

35. Abiel Abbot, *Letters Written in the Interior of Cuba, between the Mountains of Arcana, to the East, and of Cusco, to the West, in the Months of February, March, April, and May, 1828* (Boston: Bowles and Dearborn, 1829), 35–36.

36. George Brandon, *Santeria from Africa to the New World* (Bloomington: Indiana University Press, 1993), 49.

37. Following Karl Marx, Pierre Bourdieu analyzes society primarily as a theater of ongoing struggle and competition for power between classes and individuals. Power is symbolically expressed and controlled, in his analysis, through the possession and acquisition of different types of "capital": wealth (economic capital), access to persons of power (social capital), specialized knowledge (cultural capital), and status (symbolic capital). See Pierre Bourdieu, *Distinction: A Social Critique of the Judgment of Taste* (Cambridge, Mass.: Harvard University Press, 1984).

38. In his contributing essay to Jay P. Dolan's and Jaime R. Vidal's *Puerto Rican and Cuban Catholics in the U.S., 1900–1965* (Notre Dame, Ind.: University of Notre Dame Press, 1994), Lisandro Perez has suggested five reasons why the church failed in Cuba to effect the religiously nationalistic identity of Spain's other New World colonies. The first reason was Cuba's geopolitical status: as the leading port city of the Spanish Americas and cultural capital of Cuba, Havana had been, since the seventeenth century, a haven to the various worldviews and customs that blew in and out of its harbors. From the island's colonial beginnings, Catholicism could claim no hegemony in Cuba's decidedly cosmopolitan culture. Second, despite its importance as a New World port, Cuba was relegated to the historical sidelines of the early Spanish Americas. Colonizers invested both capital and ecclesiastical personnel in the infinitely more lucrative Mexican and South American colonies, where mines of gold captured the real interests of Spanish kings. Consequently, Cuba suffered a shortage of priests that lasted until the Revolution. Third, when Cuba finally did yield a handsome profit through its rise as the world's greatest sugarocracy in the nineteenth century, it was Enlightenment rationalism rather than Catholicism that came to shape the historical consciousness of modern Cuba. Indeed, Cuba's wealth had been multiplied not through rituals but through the application of modern management and technology to the island's sugar plantations. Fourth, the already weakened church assured its further demise when it opposed Cuban independence in 1898. Fifth and finally, Protestant sects came, largely from the United States, to contribute to the country's longstanding ideological pluralism through their active proselytizing in the late nineteenth and early twentieth centuries. Despite Perez's characterization of the Catholic church in Cuba as a weak institution, however, the mingling of Catholic and cultural identity was no less strong or significant in the island's history for its development along intrasocietal lines of class and race rather than those of national boundaries. According to Gustavo Perez Firmat in *Life on the Hyphen* (Austin: University of Texas Press, 1994), the historically weak institution in Cuban culture has not been the church but rather the nation itself. Returning to the geopolitical status of the island as a port city culture, Perez Firmat notes the longstanding absence from Cuban arts and letters of the metaphors of stasis, boundaries, and center that have commonly been used to articulate the identity of other modern political communities. Lacking a sense of continuity with an indigenous, ancestral past and splintered internally by the divisions of race and class, Cuba found its most au-

thentic expression, he argues, in what Cuban anthropologist Fernando Ortiz called "transculturation." Outlined in the 1947 *Cuban Counterpoint: Tobacco and Sugar,* transculturation describes a process through which foreign cultural elements enter Cuba, are stripped of traditional features, and are combined with other forms. As the title of the anthropological classic might suggest, the material locus of transcultural identity has not been an idealized homeland but rather the commodities produced and consumed in Cuba. While neither Perez Firmat nor Ortiz discusses the place of religion in Cuban society, both nevertheless suggest a fruitful analysis of both Catholicism and Santeria as transculturated religious forms in a marketplace culture. Like the traditions imported to the New World in other Spanish colonies, both the Roman Catholic and African lineages were stripped of their previous associations to place, while both Catholic and African traditions flourished in the sugar economy. While masters received absolution from their sins and promises of eternal salvation, their slaves were reborn as children of the *orishas.* Sugar was sacramentalized, and rum and tobacco incorporated into traditional African rituals.

39. Perez, 191.
40. Anthony Faiola, "A Question of Sacrifice," *Miami Herald,* May 24, 1991, p. E1.
41. Adon Taft and Liz Balmaseda, "Turmoil at Little Flower," *Miami Herald,* July 27, 1990, p. E3
42. Anthony Faiola, "Parish Seeks Solace amid Defiled Statues," *Miami Herald,* May 31, 1991, p. B1.
43. "Whittaker Just Wants to Put the Past to Sleep," *Miami Herald,* May 24, 1991, p. E3.
44. Taft and Balmaseda, p. E3.
45. "Readers' Forum," *Miami Herald,* June 13,1991, p. E4.
46. Faiola, "A Question of Sacrifice," p. E3.
47. Patricia Duarte, "The American Dream Cuban Style," *Miami Herald,* April 2, 1985, p. D3.
48. Ibid.
49. Gustavo Perez Firmat, *Life on the Hyphen* (Austin: University of Texas Press, 1994), 13–14.
50. Interview M14.
51.Interview M12.
52. Interview M15.
53. Interview M7.
54. Interview M10.
55. Interview M2.
56. Interview M13.
57. Interview M2.
58. Interview M6.

6. GONE BUT NOT FORGOTTEN

1. Jane Ward, "All Cities Suffer When Cleveland Loses the Browns," *American City and County* (January 1996): 4.
2. Jon C. Teaford, *Cities of the Heartland: the Rise and Fall of the Industrial Midwest* (Bloomington: Indiana University Press, 1993), vii.

3. Carol Poh Miller and Robert A. Wheeler, "Cleveland: The Making and Remaking of an American City, 1796–1993," in W. Dennis Keating, Norman Krumholz, and David C. Perry, eds., *Cleveland: A Metropolitan Reader* (Kent, Ohio: Kent State University Press, 1996), 34.

4. Ibid., 39.

5. Ibid., 46.

6. Ibid., 44.

7. Ibid., 46.

8. Interview CL2.

9. Interview CL6.

10. Interview CL1.

11. Interview CL8.

12. Interview CL7.

13. Interview CL1.

14. Ibid.

15. Ibid.

16. Interview CL6.

17. Ibid.

18. Ibid.

19. Interview CL14

20. Interview CL11.

21. Interview CL1.

22. Interview CL 6.

23. Ibid.

24. Interview CL5.

25. Ibid.

26. Interview CL2.

27. Interview CL7.

28. Interview CL8.

29. Interview CL3.

30. Carol Poh Miller and Robert Wheeler, eds., *Cleveland: A Concise History, 1796–1990* (Bloomington: Indiana University Press, 1990), 189.

31. Interview CL14.

32. Edward M. Miggins, "Between Spires and Stacks: The People and Neighborhoods of Cleveland," in Keating, Krumholz, and Perry, 199.

33. Interview CL8.

34. Interview CL4.

35. Ibid.

36. Interview CL7.

37. Interview CL4.

38. Interview CL13.

39. Interview CL8.

40. Interview CL4.

41. Stephen J. Shaw, "The Cities and the Plains, a Home for God's People: A History of the Catholic Parish in the Midwest," in Jay P. Dolan, ed., *The American Catholic Parish* (New York: Paulist Press, 1988), 306.

42. *Encyclopedia of Cleveland History,* "Roman Catholics."

43. See Catherine L. Albanese's discussion of the "Roman Catholic Plot" in her con-

clusion to *America: Religions and Religion,* 3d ed. (New York: Wadsworth Publishing Co., 1999), 505–10. It should be noted here that Cleveland was a particularly active missionizing field for Protestant missionaries, and home of Congregational minister Josiah Strong. In his 1885 work, *Our Country,* Strong defended the racial supremacy of Anglo-Saxons and the religious superiority of Protestantism. Southern and Eastern European Catholics were prime targets of Anglo-Protestant nativist fears and activist efforts to assimilate them into the dominant American culture.

44. See ch. 2, "Shakespeare's American Fable" and ch. 3, "The Garden," in Leo Marx, *The Machine in the Garden* (New York: Oxford University Press, 1964).

45. James R. Shortridge, *The Middle West: Its Meaning in American Culture* (Lawrence: University Press of Kansas, 1989), 27–68.

46. Ibid., 67.

47. Ibid., 68.

48. Ibid., 95–96.

49. Tom Verducci, "Grand Opening," *Sports Illustrated* 80, no. 14 (April 11, 1994): 43.

50. Ibid., 59.

51. Interview CL2.

52. See ch. 14, "Cultural Religion: Millennial Explorations of Dominance and Innocence," in Albanese, 476.

53. Interview CL11.

54. Albanese, 476.

CONCLUSION

1. Mary Jo Weaver, "Introduction: Who Are the Conservative Catholics?" in Mary Jo Weaver and R. Scott Appleby, eds., *Being Right: Conservative Catholics in America* (Bloomington: Indiana University Press, 1995), 8.

2. Andrew Greeley, *The Catholic Imagination* (Berkeley: University of California Press, 2000), 1–2.

3. George Weigel, "The Neoconservative Difference," in Weaver and Appleby, *Being Right,* 154–55.

4. Interview C3.

5. Weaver, 8.

6. Emile Durkheim, *The Elementary Forms of the Religious Life,* trans. Joseph Ward Swain (New York: Macmillan Publishing, 1965), 258.

7. See ch. 5, "Two Kingdoms of Force," in Leo Marx, *The Machine in the Garden* (New York: Oxford University Press, 1964), 145–226.

8. Alan Figueroa Deck, "'A Pox on Both Your Houses': A View of Catholic Conservative-Liberal Polarities from the Hispanic Margin," in Weaver and Appleby, *Being Right,* 97.

9. Ibid.

10. Ibid., 101.

11. In her study *America: Religions and Religion,* Catherine Albanese distinguishes cultural religion as a variant of what she calls the "one religion" of Anglo-Protestant culture, or "the ordinary religion of American culture, which comes through the media, the public-school system, government communications, and commer-

cial networks" in the United States (13). Transmitted primarily through entertainment media and commercial networks, cultural religion delineates the social creeds and values of Anglo-Protestantism and prescribes behaviors or presents models through which individuals might enact these mores. See chapter 14, "Cultural Religion: Millennial Explorations of Dominance and Innocence," in Albanese, *America: Religions and Religion,* 3d ed. (New York: Wadsworth Publishing Co., 1999), 463–501.

12. See Timothy M. Matovina, "Representation and the Reconstruction of Power: the Rise of PADRES and Las Hermanas," in Mary Jo Weaver, ed., *What's Left? Liberal American Catholics* (Bloomington: Indiana University Press, 1999).

BIBLIOGRAPHY

Primary Sources

Abbott, Walter M., S.J., ed. *The Documents of Vatican II*. New York: Association Press, 1966.
Carmelite Sisters of the Most Sacred Heart of Los Angeles, California. "Saint Theresa School Re-registration Packet (1995–1996 School Year)." Photocopy distributed to families of Saint Theresa School, Coral Gables, Florida.
———. "St. Theresa School Newsletter." June, 1994.
———. "Carmelite Vocation." Promotional Brochure.
———. "Carmelite Sisters of the Most Sacred Heart of Los Angeles." Promotional Brochure.
———. "Notes with Rev. Simeon de la Sagrada Familia, O.C.D. regarding the Status of the Process of Canonization of Mother Luisita." August 17–18, 1988.
———. "Minutes of the General Council Meeting." March 8, 1992.
Catechism of the Catholic Church. Chicago: Loyola University Press, 1994.
Colbert, Helenita. *The Flower of Guadalajara*. Alhambra: Carmelite Sisters of the Third Order, 1951.
———. *To Love Me In Truth: Mother Luisa Josefa of the Blessed Sacrament, Servant of God*. Alhambra, Calif.: Carmelite Sisters of the Most Sacred Heart of Los Angeles, 1987.
Maccise, Camilo, O.C.D. "Life and Work of Reverend Mother Maria Luisa Josefa of the Most Blessed Sacrament, Foundress of the Congregation of the Carmelite Sisters of the Sacred Heart of Guadalajara, and of the Institute of the Carmelite Sisters of the Most Sacred Heart of Los Angeles." Unpublished manuscript. March 13, 1989.
Veritatis Splendor. Vatican City: Libreria Editrice Vaticana, 1993.

Secondary Sources

Abbot, Abiel. *Letters Written in the Interior of Cuba, between the Mountains of Arcana, to the East, and of Cusco, to the West, in the Months of February, March, April, and May, 1828*. Boston: Bowles and Dearborn, 1829.
Adams, James Truslow. *The Epic of America*. Boston: Little, Brown, and Co., 1931.
"Agents Find Drug Tunnel to the U.S." *New York Times*, May 19, 1990, 7.
Albanese, Catherine L. *America: Religions and Religion*. 3rd ed. New York: Wadsworth Publishing Co., 1999.
———. *Sons of the Fathers: The Civil Religion of the American Revolution*. Philadelphia: Temple University Press, 1976.

Alegria, Fernando and Jorge Ruffinelli. *Paradise Lost or Gained? The Literature of Hispanic Exile.* Houston: Arte Publico Press, 1990.

Anaya, Rudolpho and Francisco Lomeli. *Aztlan: Essays on the Chicano Homeland.* Albuquerque: University of New Mexico Press, 1989.

Anderson, Benedict. *Imagined Communities: Reflections on the Origins and Spread of Nationalism.* New York: Verso, 1983.

Anzaldua, Gloria. *Borderlands/La Frontera: The New Mestiza.* San Francisco: Spinsters/Aunt Lute, 1987.

Appleby, Joyce, Lynn Hunt, and Margaret Jacob. *Telling the Truth about History.* New York: W.W. Norton and Co., 1994.

Arizona Department of Commerce. "Community Profile." Douglas, Ariz., 1995.

Armstrong, Foster, Richard Klein, and Cara Armstrong. *A Guide to Cleveland's Sacred Landmarks.* Kent, Ohio: Kent State University Press, 1992.

Bailey, David C. *Viva Cristo Rey! The Cristero Rebellion and the Church-State Conflict in Mexico.* Austin: University of Texas Press, 1974.

Balmaseda, Liz. "Latin Schools Offer Education in Culture." *Miami Herald,* April 18, 1982, D18.

Barrera, Mario. *Race and Class in the Southwest: A Theory of Racial Inequality.* Notre Dame, Ind.: University of Notre Dame Press, 1979.

Beckwith, Sarah. *Christ's Body: Identity, Culture, and Society in the Late Medieval Writings.* New York: Routledge, 1993.

Bernal, Guillermo. "Cuban Families." In Monica McGoldrick, John K. Pearce, and Joseph Giordano, eds., *Ethnicity and Family Therapy.* New York: Guilford Press, 1987.

Bethell, Leslie, ed. *Cuba: A Short History.* New York: Cambridge University Press, 1993.

Betto, Frei. *Fidel and Religion.* New York: Simon and Schuster, 1987.

Bhabha, Homi K., ed. *Nation and Narration.* New York: Routledge, 1990.

Bingham, Richard D., and Randall W. Eberts. *Economic Restructuring of the American Midwest.* Boston: Kluwer, 1990.

Bloom, Harold. *The American Religion: The Emergence of the Post-Christian Nation.* New York: Touchstone Books, 1992.

Bohn, Frank. *Man Pushes Forward: A Fountain of Youth.* Coral Gables: University of Miami Press, 1926.

Bond, Ervin. *History of Douglas, Arizona.* Douglas, Ariz.: Ervin Bond, 1976.

———. *Cochise County, Arizona, Past and Present.* Douglas, Ariz.: Erwin Bond, 1984.

Bonutti, Karl. *Selected Ethnic Communities in Cleveland: A Socio-economic Study.* Cleveland: Cleveland State University, 1974.

Boswell, Thomas D. *The Cubanization and Hispanicization of Metropolitan Miami.* Miami: Cuban American National Council, 1994.

Boswell, Thomas D., and James R. Curtis. *The Cuban-American Experience: Culture, Images and Perspectives.* Totowa, N.J.: Rowman and Allanheld, 1984.

Bourdieu, Pierre. *Distinction: A Social Critique of the Judgment of Taste.* Cambridge, Mass.: Harvard University Press, 1984.

Bradley, Hugh. *Havana.* New York: Doubleday, Doran and Co., 1941.

Brandon, George. *Santeria from Africa to the New World: The Dead Sell Memories.* Bloomington: Indiana University Press, 1993.

Braudel, Fernand. *The Mediterranean and the Mediterranean World in the Age of Philip II.* New York: Harper and Row, 1972.

———. *Relics and Social Status in the Age of Gregory of Tours.* Reading: University of Reading, 1977.

———. *Society and the Holy in Late Antiquity.* Berkeley: University of California Press, 1982.

Briggs, Kenneth. *Holy Siege: The Year That Shook Catholic America.* New York: Harper Collins Publishers, 1992.

Brown, Peter. *The Cult of Saints: Its Rise and Function in Latin Christianity.* Chicago: University of Chicago Press, 1981.

Brownstein-Santiago, Cheryl. "Ceremony, Mass to Celebrate Patron Saint of Cuba." *Miami Herald,* September 4, 1984, A5.

Burkett, Elinor. "Priest and Parish Are Back in Battle." *Miami Herald,* March 22 1991, E1.

Burns, Gene. *The Frontiers of Catholicism: The Politics of Ideology in a Liberal World.* Berkeley: University of California Press, 1992.

Camarillo, Albert. *Chicanos in a Changing Society.* Cambridge, Mass.: Harvard University Press, 1979.

Capen, Richard G. "Cuba Has Nailed Religion to the Cross." *Miami Herald,* February 10, 1985, D3.

Carrillo-Beron, Carmen. *Traditional Family Ideology in Relation to Locus of Control: A Comparison of Chicano and Anglo Women.* San Francisco: R. and E. Research Associates, 1974.

Castro, Fidel. *Fidel Castro: Major Speeches.* London: Stage 1, 1968.

Chambers, Iain. *Migrancy, Culture, Identity.* New York: Routledge, 1994.

Chartier, Roger. *On the Edge of the Cliff: History, Language, and Practices.* Baltimore: Johns Hopkins University Press, 1997.

Chidester, David. "The Church of Baseball, the Fetish of Coca-Cola, and the Potlatch of Rock n' Roll: Theoretical Models for the Study of Religion in American Popular Culture." *Journal of the American Academy of Religion* 59, no. 4 (Fall 1996): 743–767.

Christian, William A. *Local Religion in Sixteenth-Century Spain.* Princeton, N.J.: Princeton University Press, 1981.

―――. *Apparitions in Late Medieval and Renaissance Spain.* Princeton, N.J.: Princeton University Press, 1981.

―――. *Person and God in a Spanish Valley.* New York: Seminar Press, 1972.

City of Coral Gables. "Map Brochure of Coral Gables." October 1993.

Clapp, James A. *The City: A Dictionary of Quotable Thought on Cities and Urban Life.* New Brunswick, N.J.: Center for Urban Policy Research, 1984.

Cunningham, Lawrence S. *The Catholic Experience.* New York: Crossroad, 1986.

David, Jay. *The Kennedy Reader.* New York: Bobbs-Merrill, 1967.

Davidson, N. S. *The Counter-Reformation.* New York: Basil Blackwell, 1987.

Davis, Mike. *City of Quartz: Excavating the Future in Los Angeles.* New York: Vintage Books, 1992.

―――. *Ecology of Fear: Los Angeles and the Imagination of Disaster.* New York: Metropolitan Books, 1998.

Deck, Allan Figueroa. *The Second Wave.* New York: Paulist Press, 1990.

Del Castillo, Richard Griswold. *The Los Angeles Barrio, 1850–1890.* Berkeley: University of California Press, 1979.

Dickens, A.G. *The Counter-Reformation.* Harcourt, Brace and World, 1969.

Dinnocenzo, Michael, and Josef P. Sirefman. *Immigration and Ethnicity.* Westport, Conn.: Greenwood Press, 1992.

Discalced Carmelites of Boston and Santa Clara. *Carmel: Its History, Spirit, and Saints.* New York: P. J. Kennedy and Sons, 1927.

Doely, Sarah Bentley, ed. *Women's Liberation and the Church.* New York: Association Press, 1970.

Dolan, Jay P. *The American Catholic Experience.* New York: Doubleday and Co., 1985.

―――. *The American Catholic Parish.* New York: Paulist Press, 1988.

―――. *The Immigrant Church.* Baltimore: Johns Hopkins University Press, 1975.

Dolan, Jay P., and Allan Figueroa Deck, eds. *Hispanic Catholic Culture in the U.S.: Issues and Concerns.* Notre Dame, Ind.: University of Notre Dame Press, 1994.

Dolan, Jay P., and Jaime R. Vidal, eds. *Puerto Rican and Cuban Catholics in the U.S., 1900–1965.* Notre Dame, Ind.: University of Notre Dame Press, 1994.

Dolgin, Janet L., David S. Kemnitzer, and David M. Schneider, eds. *Symbolic Anthropology.* New York: Columbia University Press, 1978.

Douglas, Mary. *Purity and Danger.* New York: Praeger, 1966.

Duarte, Patricia. "The American Dream, Cuban Style." *Miami Herald,* April 2, 1985, D1.

Durkheim, Emile. *The Elementary Forms of the Religious Life.* New York: Free Press, 1915.

Ebaugh, Helen Rose Fuchs. *Women in the Vanishing Cloister.* New Brunswick, N.J.: Rutgers University Press, 1993.

Edgell, Stephen. *Class.* New York: Routledge, 1994.

Ellis, John Tracy. *American Catholicism.* Chicago History of American Civilization. Rev. ed. Chicago: University of Chicago Press, 1969.

Faiola, Anthony. "A Question of Sacrifice." *Miami Herald,* May 24, 1991, E1.

———. "Parish Seeks Solace Amid Defiled Statues." *Miami Herald,* May 31, 1991, B1.

Fogelson, Robert. *The Fragmented Metropolis.* Cambridge, Mass.: Harvard University Press, 1969.

Folk Tales from the Pantagonia Area, Santa Cruz County, Arizona. Tucson: University of Arizona Press, 1949.

Fuchs, Lawrence H. *John F. Kennedy and American Catholicism.* New York: Meredith Press, 1967.

Garcia, Maria C. "Quest for the Best: the Private School Explosion." *Miami Herald,* April 18, 1982, D15.

———. "Family's Powerful Embrace." *Miami Herald,* September 11, 1984, B1.

Garcia, Mario. *Mexican Americans.* New Haven, Conn.: Yale University Press, 1993.

Geary, Patrick. *Furta Sacra: Thefts of Relics in the Central Middle Ages.* Princeton, N.J.: Princeton University Press, 1978.

Geertz, Clifford. *The Interpretation of Cultures.* New York: Basic Books, 1973.

Giddens, Anthony. *The Consequences of Modernity.* Stanford, Calif.: Stanford University Press, 1990.

Greeley, Andrew M. *The Catholic Imagination.* Berkeley: University of California Press, 2000.

———. *Religion in the Year 2000.* New York: Sheed and Ward, 1969.

Griffith, James. *A Shared Space: Folklife in the Arizona-Sonora Borderlands.* Logan: Utah State University Press, 1995.

Grossman, Cathy Lynn. "Cuban Women: Changing Their Lifestyle in Exile." *Miami Herald,* March 11, 1986, B1.

Guide to Examination of Conscience. Miami: Shrine of Our Lady of Charity, n.d.

Gutierrez, Barbara, "Miami Cubans Blast American Bishops' Trip to Cuba." *Miami Herald,* January 26, 1985, B2.

Halesby, Sandor, and John Kirk, eds. *Cuba in Transition.* Boulder, Colo.: Westview Press, 1992.

Handlin, Oscar. *The Uprooted.* Boston: Atlantic Monthly Press Book, 1973.

Haring, C.H. *The Spanish Empire in America.* New York: First Harbinger Books, 1963.

Hastings, Adrian, ed. *Modern Catholicism: Vatican II and After.* New York: Oxford University Press, 1991.

Hebblethwaite, Peter. *In the Vatican.* Bethseda, Md.: Alder and Alder, 1986.

———."Encyclical Nails Objective Right and Wrong." *National Catholic Reporter,* October 8, 1993, 8–9.

———. "John Paul in Poland: 'Among His Own, Pope Spoke His Heart.'" *National Catholic Reporter*, June 15, 1979, 22.

———. "Pope Discusses Millennium with Cardinals." *National Catholic Reporter*, July 1, 1994, 17.

———. "Pope Foresees Growing Battle between Good and Evil." *National Catholic Reporter*, January 9, 1981, 16.

———. "Pope Unveils His Papacy: 'Restoration' Era Begins." *National Catholic Reporter*. October 19, 1979, 1.

———. "The Roman Pope Is Still a Pole." *National Catholic Reporter*, October 16, 1981, 12.

———. "World Youth Day Tied to 'Culture of Pilgrimage.'" *National Catholic Reporter*, July 2, 1993, 12.

Herberg, Will. *Protestant-Catholic-Jew*. Rev. ed. Garden City, N.Y.: Anchor Books, 1960.

Herrera-Sobeck, Maria. *Northward Bound: The Mexican Immigrant Experience in Ballad and Song*. Bloomington: Indiana University Press, 1993.

History of the Archdiocese of Miami, 1958–1978. Miami: Archdiocese of Miami, Florida, n.d.

Hobsbawm, Eric J. *Nations and Nationalism since 1780*. Cambridge: Cambridge University Press, 1990.

Hobsbawm, Eric J., and Terence Ranger, eds. *The Invention of Tradition*. New York and Cambridge: Cambridge University Press, 1983.

Hunter, James Davidson. *Culture Wars: The Struggle to Define America*. New York: Basicbooks, 1991.

John of the Cross. *The Dark Night of the Soul*. Trans. Kurt F. Reinhardt. New York: Frederick Ungar, 1957.

Johnson, Paul. *Pope John Paul II and the Catholic Restoration*. London: Weidenfeld and Nicolson, 1982.

Johnson, Paul M. "Awake by the Lake." *Sport* 86, no. 11 (November 1995): 86–91.

Katz, Jesse. "Stray Bullet Shatters Couple's Dream to Leave Gang Area." *Los Angeles Times*, March 20, 1992, A1.

Keating, W. Dennis, Norman Krumholz, and David C. Perry, eds. *Cleveland: A Metropolitan Reader*. Kent, Ohio: Kent State University Press, 1996.

Kelly, J. N. D. *Early Christian Creeds*. New York: David McKay Co., 1960.

Kertzer, David L. *Ritual, Politics, and Power*. New Haven, Conn.: Yale University Press, 1988.

King, Peter. "Down and Out in Cleveland." *Sports Illustrated* 83, no. 21 (November 13, 1995), 28–33.

Lapham, Lewis H. *Money and Class in America*. New York: Weidenfeld and Nicholson, 1988.

Lee, Martin A. *The Beast Reawakens*. New York: Little, Brown, and Co., 1997.

Limerick, Patricia. *The Legacy of Conquest: The Unbroken Past of the American West*. New York: W. W. Norton and Co., 1987.

Lincoln, Bruce. *Discourse and the Construction of Society*. New York: Oxford University Press, 1989.

———. *Myth, Cosmos, and Society*. Cambridge, Mass.: Harvard University Press, 1986.

LaRoue, Samuel D., Jr. *Church of the Little Flower: 65 Years of Worship and Service, 1924–1991*. Coral Gables: Church of the Little Flower, 1993.

Long, Charles H. *Significations: Signs, Symbols, and Images in the Interpretation of Religion*. Philadelphia: Fortress Press, 1986.

Longford, Lord. *Pope John Paul II*. London: Michael Joseph, 1982.

Lopez-Miro, Sergio. "Where the 'Cuban-' Ends and 'American'' Begins." *Miami Herald*, February 1, 1990, A19.

Maidique, Modesto A. "Cuban Family + American Institutions = New Miami." *Miami Herald,* November 29, 1987, C1.

Malkin, Elisabeth. "Mexico: A New Rumble of Revolt." *Business Week,* April 24, 1995, 54.

Mangin, Frank, "National Catholic Schools Week Spotlights Lestonnac, Loretto." *Douglas Sunday Dispatch,* January 28, 1996, 1.

———. "New Pressures for Border Wall." *Douglas Daily Dispatch,* January 26, 1996, A1.

Marty, Martin E., and R. Scott Appleby, eds. *Religion, Ethnicity, and Self-Identity: Nations in Turmoil.* Hanover, N.H.: University Press of New England, 1997.

Marx, Leo. *The Machine in the Garden.* New York: Oxford University Press, 1964.

Mauss, Marcel. *The Gift.* New York: W.W. Norton and Co., 1967.

Miller, Carol Poh, and Robert Wheeler. *Cleveland: A Concise History, 1796–1990.* Bloomington: Indiana University Press, 1990.

Mintz, Sidney. "The Caribbean as a Socio-Cultural Area." *Cahiers d'Histoire Mondiale* 9, no. 4 (1966): 912–37.

———. "The Caribbean Region." *Daedalus* 103, no. 2 (1974): 45–71.

Monroy, Douglas. *Thrown among Strangers.* Berkeley: University of California Press, 1990.

Montenegro-Gonzalez, Hayd. *Interpersonal Relations between Faith Healer and Client.* Ann Arbor: University Microfilms International, 1986.

Ojeda, Mario. *Mexico: The Northern Border as a National Concern.* El Paso: Center for Inter-American and Border Studies, 1983.

Oktavec, Eileen. *Answered Prayers: Miracles and Milagros along the Border.* Tucson: University of Arizona Press, 1995.

Orsi, Robert Anthony. *The Madonna of 115th Street.* New Haven, Conn.: Yale University Press, 1985.

Ortiz, Dominguez. *The Golden Age of Spain, 1516–1659.* New York: Basic Books, 1971.

Ortiz, Fernando. *Cuban Counterpoint: Tobacco and Sugar.* Trans. Harriet de Onis. Durham, N.C.: Duke University Press, 1995.

Otto, Rudolf. *The Idea of the Holy.* New York: Oxford University Press, 1970.

Payne, Stanley. *Spanish Catholicism.* Madison: University of Wisconsin Press, 1984.

Pérez, Lisandro. "Revisiting the Cuban Americans' 'Success Story.'" *Miami Herald,* March 27, 1988, C5.

Perez, Louis A., Jr. *Cuba between Reform and Revolution.* New York, Oxford: Oxford University Press, 1988.

Perez Firmat, Gustavo. *Life on the Hyphen.* Austin: University of Texas Press, 1994.

———. *The Cuban Condition.* Cambridge: Cambridge University Press, 1989.

Phelan, John Leddy. *The Hispanization of the Philippines: Spanish Aims and Filipino Responses, 1565–1700.* Madison: University of Wisconsin Press, 1959.

Pido, Antonio J. A. *The Pilipinos in America: Macro/Micro Dimensions of Immigration and Migration.* New York: Center for Migration Studies, 1986.

Portes, Alejandro, and Alex Stepick. *City on the Edge: The Transformation of Miami.* Berkeley: University of California Press, 1993.

Proceedings: First National Assembly of the Council of Major Superiors of Women Religious in the United States of America. Washington, D.C.: Council of Major Superiors of Women Religious in the United States of America, 1992.

Ramet, Pedro, ed. *Catholicism and Politics in Communist Societies.* Durham, N.C.: Duke University Press, 1990.

Ramos, Reinaldo. "Class of '81 Embraces Cuban Roots." *Miami Herald,* March 1, 1987, A1.

Rios-Bustamante, Antonio, and Pedro Castillo. *An Illustrated History of Mexican Los*

Angeles, 1781–1985. Los Angeles: University of California, Los Angeles Chicano Studies Research Center, 1986.

Rodriguez, Richard. *Days of Obligation: An Argument with My Mexican Father.* New York: Penguin Books, 1992.

Roman, Augustin A. "The Popular Piety of the Cuban People," Master's Thesis, Barry University, 1976.

Romo, Ricardo. *East Los Angeles: The Making of a Barrio.* Austin: University of Texas Press, 1983.

Rosenthal, Bernard, and Paul E. Szarmach, eds. *Medievalism in American Culture.* Binghamton, N.Y.: Medieval and Renaissance Texts and Studies, 1989.

Rouse, Roger. "Mexican Migration and the Social Space of Postmodernism." *Diaspora* 1, no. 1 (Spring 1991): 16.

Ruether, Rosemary Radford. "Mary in U.S. Catholic Culture." *National Catholic Reporter,* February 10, 1995, 15.

Rushin, Steve. "The Heart of a City." *Sports Illustrated* 83, no. 24 (December 4, 1995): 58–67.

Sacred Congregation for Religious. "The Essential Elements of the Religious Life." Vatican City: Libreria Editrice, 1983.

San Juan, E. *From Exile to Diaspora: Versions of the Filipino Experience in the United States.* Boulder, Colo.: Westview Press, 1998.

Schüssler Fiorenza, Elisabeth, and Mary Collins, eds. *Women—Invisible in Theology and Church.* Edinburgh: T. and T. Clark, 1987.

Schwantes, Carlos A., ed. *Bisbee: Urban Outpost on the Frontier.* Tucson: University of Arizona Press, 1992.

Sennett, Richard. *The Uses of Disorder.* New York: Alfred A. Knopf, 1970.

Shafer, Ingrid H., ed. *The Incarnate Imagination: Essays in Theology, the Arts and Social Sciences in Honor of Andrew Greeley.* Bowling Green: Bowling Green State University Popular Press, 1989.

Shortridge, James R. *The Middle West: Its Meaning in American Culture.* Lawrence: University Press of Kansas, 1989.

Slater, Candace. *City Steeple, City Streets.* Berkeley: University of California Press, 1990.

Smith, Jonathan Z. *Imagining Religion.* Chicago: University of Chicago Press, 1982.

———. *Map Is Not Territory.* Leiden: Brill, 1978.

———. *To Take Place.* Chicago: University of Chicago Press, 1987.

"Some Finding Gold in Passage under Border." *Los Angeles Times,* July 25, 1990, A5.

Taft, Adon. "Mariel's 'Godless' Refugees." *Miami Herald,* March 1, 1985, B1.

Taft, Adon, and Liz Balmaseda. "Turmoil at Little Flower." *Miami Herald,* July 27, 1990, E1.

Teaford, Jon C. *Cities of the Heartland: The Rise and Fall of the Industrial Midwest.* Bloomington: Indiana University Press, 1993.

Teresa of Avila. *The Interior Castle.* Trans. Kieran Kavanaugh, O.C.D., and Otilio Rodriguez, O.C.D. New York: Paulist Press, 1991.

Thérèse of Lisieux. *The Little Flower of Jesus.* Trans. Thomas N. Taylor. New York: P. J. Kennedy and Sons, 1926.

Thomas, Nicholas. *Entangled Objects: Exchange, Material Culture, and Colonialism in the South Pacific.* Cambridge, Mass.: Harvard University Press, 1991.

Tuan, Yi-fu. *Space and Place: the Perspective of Experience.* Minneapolis: University of Minnesota Press, 1977.

Turner, Kay Frances. *Mexican-American Women's Home Altars: The Art of Relationship.* Ann Arbor: University Microfilms International, 1984.

Turner, Victor W. *Blazing the Trail: Way Marks in the Exploration of Symbols.* Tucson: University of Arizona Press, 1992.

———. *Dramas, Fields, and Metaphors; Symbolic Action in Human Society.* Ithaca, N.Y.: Cornell University Press, 1974.

———. *Image and Pilgrimage in Christian Culture.* New York: Columbia University Press, 1978.

———. *The Ritual Process.* Chicago: Aldine, 1969.

Tweed, Thomas. *Our Lady of Exile: Diasporic Religion at a Cuban Catholic Shrine in Miami.* New York: Oxford University Press, 1997.

Van Tassel, David D., and John J. Grabowski, eds. *The Encyclopedia of Cleveland History.* Bloomington: Indiana University Press, 1996.

Verducci, Tom. "Grand Opening." *Sports Illustrated* 80, no. 14 (April 11, 1994): 42–45.

Wach, Joachim. *Sociology of Religion.* Chicago: University of Chicago Press, 1944.

Wallace, Martin. *Recent Theories of Narrative.* Ithaca, N.Y.: Cornell University Press, 1986.

Ward, Jane. "All Cities Suffer When Cleveland Loses the Browns." *American City and County,* January 1996, 4.

Weaver, Mary Jo, ed. *What's Left?: Liberal American Catholics.* Bloomington: Indiana University Press, 1999.

Weaver, Mary Jo, and R. Scott Appleby. *Being Right: Conservative Catholics in America.* Bloomington: Indiana University Press, 1995.

Weiss, Richard. *The American Myth of Success.* New York: Basic Books, 1969.

Whelan, Ned. *Cleveland: Shaping the Vision; a Contemporary Portrait.* Chatsworth, Calif.: Windsor Publications, 1989.

White, Hayden. *Metahistory: The Historical Imagination in Nineteenth-Century Europe.* Baltimore: Johns Hopkins University Press, 1973.

Williams, George Huntston. *The Mind of John Paul II.* New York: Seabury Press, 1981.

Williams, Peter. *Popular Religion in America.* Englewood Cliffs, N.J.: Prentice-Hall, 1980.

Wilson, Stephen, ed. *Saints and Their Cults.* Cambridge: Cambridge University Press, 1984.

Woodward, Kenneth L. *Making Saints: How the Catholic Church Determines Who Becomes a Saint, Who Doesn't, and Why.* New York: Touchstone Books, 1990.

Young, Katherine. *Bodylore.* Knoxville: University of Tennessee Press, 1994.

INDEX

DARRYL CATERINE is a specialist in the history of religions in the Americas. He earned his degrees in religious studies from Harvard University and the University of California at Santa Barbara. His current scholarly interests focus on the interactions between religion and culture in both the United States and Latin America. Caterine presently teaches in the Department of Religion at Dartmouth College.